The Wall around the West

The Well-ma ... ti ... ...

The Wall around the West

*State Borders and Immigration Controls
in North America and Europe*

Edited by
Peter Andreas and Timothy Snyder

ROWMAN & LITTLEFIELD PUBLISHERS, INC.
Lanham • Boulder • New York • Oxford

ROWMAN & LITTLEFIELD PUBLISHERS, INC.

Published in the United States of America
by Rowman & Littlefield Publishers, Inc.
4720 Boston Way, Lanham, Maryland 20706
http://www.rowmanlittlefield.com

12 Hid's Copse Road
Cumnor Hill, Oxford OX2 9JJ, England

British Library Cataloguing in Publication Information Available

Library of Congress Cataloging-in-Publication Data

The wall around the West : state borders and immigration controls in North America and
Europe / edited by Peter Andreas and Timothy Snyder.
    p.   cm.
    Includes bibliographical references and index.
    ISBN 0-7425-0177-9 (alk. paper) — ISBN 0-7425-0178-7 (pbk. : alk. paper)
    1. North America—Emigration and immigration—Government policy.
    2. Europe—Emigration and immigration—Government policy.   3. Emigration and
immigration—Government policy.   I. Andreas, Peter, 1965–   II. Snyder, Timothy.

JV63501 .W35   2000
325.4—dc21   00-055255

Printed in the United States of America

∞™ The paper used in this publication meets the minimum requirements of
American National Standard for Information Sciences—Permanence of
Paper for Printed Library Materials, ANSI/NISO Z39.48-1992.

Contents

Preface

Borders in North America and Europe are being reasserted through ambitious and innovative state efforts to regulate the transnational movement of people. The purpose of this volume is to examine the practice, politics, and consequences of the construction of this "wall around the West." The trends we describe run counter to the conventional wisdom that borders are increasingly outmoded in an integrating world. As this volume demonstrates, along rich-poor divides globalization can be consistent with the reinforcement of state borders.

This collection of original essays crosses professional and geographic borders, uniting political scientists, historians, sociologists, geographers, and policymakers from both sides of the Atlantic. Although much has been written in recent years on the immigration policies of advanced industrialized countries, this is one of the first attempts to address the transformation of North American and European border controls in historical and comparative perspective.

The chapters of this volume were first presented at a workshop sponsored by the Weatherhead Center for International Affairs and the Harvard Academy for International and Area Studies, Harvard University. We thank Jorge Domínguez, the director of the Weatherhead Center, and Samuel Huntington, the chair of the Harvard Academy, for supporting this collaborative effort. In addition to the authors who presented and then revised their work, we owe special thanks to others who helped make the workshop stimulating and productive: John Coatsworth, Jorge Domínguez, Elizabeth Hastie, Samuel Huntington, Robert Pekkanen, Carlos Rico, and Marcelo Suarez-Orozco. Gary Freeman and James Hollifield provided useful comments as we prepared the volume, and Jennifer Knerr of Rowman & Littlefield skillfully guided it through production.

We are grateful to Jasmina Burdzovic and Milada Vachudová for their tolerance of (and, sometimes, complicity in) our own experiences of crossing borders.

Europe

Middle America

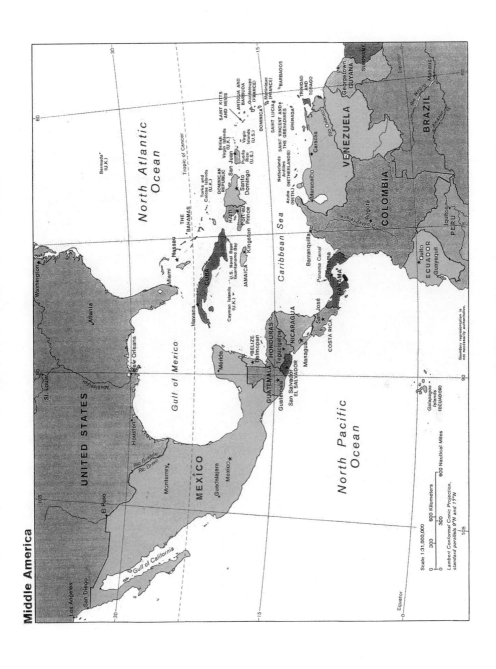

1

Introduction: The Wall after the Wall

Peter Andreas

The construction of walls has had a prominent place in human history. Most famously, in the third century B.C., China began to build the Great Wall. Some five centuries later, Hadrian undertook a similar if less ambitious construction project in northern England. In the medieval era, heavily fortified walls surrounded European cities. In the twentieth century, the best-known barriers were the militarized Maginot Line and the Berlin Wall. Today, the political popularity of walls persists, but the nature of these walls and the threats they are built to repel have changed. The new walls are designed not to keep people in or to keep militaries out, but to deter a perceived invasion of "undesirables"—with unwanted immigrants leading the list of state concerns. Nowhere is this more evident than along the geographic fault lines dividing rich and poor regions: most notably the southern border of the United States and the eastern and southern borders of the European Union (EU). This volume examines the practice, politics, and consequences of building this "wall around the West."[1]

BRINGING BORDERS BACK IN

It has become intellectually fashionable to dismiss borders as increasingly irrelevant to the human experience in the so-called age of "globalization." Mathew Horsman and Andrew Marshall sum up the conventional wisdom: "The significance of national borders for western Europe, as for other developed regions of the world, has been vastly reduced by the three forces of military change, economic development and modern communications technology."[2] Others perceive a progressive "desacralization of territory," and contend that the state's purposes "now become inclusive rather than exclusive or enclosed."[3] Some free market liberals have even popularized the notion of an emergent "borderless world."[4] Territory, we are told, is losing its meaning in the new era of the "virtual state."[5] These cheerful views stress the benign, pacifying effects of economic integration, and assume that this interdependence must lead to the rollback of the state and the erosion of its borders.

The sweeping global transformations of recent decades have certainly reduced the military and economic relevance of borders, especially for advanced industrialized states. Market expansion and access, not territorial conquest and acquisition, is now the name of the game across much of the globe. The celebrated debordering of the state, however, is far more selective than the inflated rhetoric of globalization would suggest. Debordering is being accompanied in many places by a partial rebordering in the form of enhanced policing. Even as many borders have been demilitarized in the traditional realm of national security,[6] as well as economically liberalized to facilitate commercial exchange, they are also now more criminalized to deter those who are perceived as trespassers.[7] Thus, it may be more accurate to say that the importance of territoriality is shifting rather than simply diminishing.[8] This volume is about bringing borders back into the study of international politics. It emphasizes that, far from disappearing, many borders are being reasserted and remade through ambitious and innovative state efforts to regulate the transnational movement of people. The trends highlighted in this volume reaffirm Jagdish Bhagwati's observation that immigration controls are "the most compelling exception to liberalism in the operation of the world economy."[9] Although some prominent free market advocates, such as *The Wall Street Journal*, argue that there should be "open borders for labor," this advice falls on deaf ears. The practical reality is that most of the world's inhabitants face formidable barriers to cross-border movement. And in many places, these barriers are being reinforced. Even though freedom of exit has spread with liberal democratic forms of government, this is a hollow right without freedom of entry. Thus, when it comes to immigration controls, nation–states very much remain "bordered power-containers."[10] Despite the relaxation of barriers to the flow of goods, information, and capital, when it comes to regulating the movement of people, "the national state claims its old splendor in asserting its sovereign right to control its borders."[11]

This volume contributes to our understanding of an increasingly important area of state regulatory activity, and adds fuel to broader debates about the changing nature of state borders and territorial politics at the dawn of the twenty-first century. In the cases examined here, what is changing is not the geographic location of borders but rather their character and role. This has involved both a physical reassertion of border controls and an ideological redefinition of border functions. This is reflected in the heightened prominence of immigration control concerns in the U.S. and EU policy discourse about borders. In both places, territorial politics are increasingly about territorial policing.

VARIETIES OF REBORDERING

In both North America and western Europe, rich integrating states are undertaking ambitious projects to regulate borders despite (and in some cases because of) growing economic ties with poorer neighbors. Nevertheless, the practice and politics of tightening state controls vary significantly between the two cases. Most obviously, the EU is an attractive institution that plans to enlarge, while the United States is a state (and thus cannot be "joined"). Thus, although the U.S. border control effort largely represents a unilateral reassertion of national sovereignty, European border controls reflect a multilateral "pooling of sovereignty." This has taken its most concrete form through the Schengen Agreement, which calls for the elimination of internal EU border checks and at the same time a harmonization and tightening of external border checks. This means that what once were treated exclusively as national borders and national controls have now become part of a new European space of free movement—insulated by a hardened outer wall.

Importantly, the EU border enforcement strategy also involves turning its immediate neighbors into a kind of "buffer zone." Countries such as Poland have been deemed "safe" countries, meaning that asylum seekers who cross through those countries en route to western Europe can be deported. The carrot of future entry into the EU and visa-free access to the West has ensured Polish and Czech cooperation in deterring the flow of illegal immigrants through the territory of those countries.[12] By contrast, the current domestic U.S. political context makes it extraordinarily difficult to even imagine a similar scenario in which Washington offers visa-free entry for Mexicans and future labor market access in exchange for cracking down on migrant smugglers and fortifying Mexico's border with Guatemala. Similarly, as Hungary, the Czech Republic, and Slovakia frankly admit that their border control policies are designed to conform to EU expectations, Mexico carefully avoids projecting any impression of capitulating to U.S. pressure.

In other words, wall building in the EU is embedded within the broader institutional framework and process of European integration. Although the EU project aims to remove national borders within the Schengen zone, in fact the EU wall is considerably thicker than its U.S. counterpart. Not only has the EU's external frontier come to resemble a state border, it in effect extends outward into neighboring countries, and inward into European societies. The presence of the state in everyday life is far more pervasive in much of Europe than in the United States. In many European countries this includes the use of national identity cards and more extensive regulation and monitoring of the workplace. The U.S. wall may be physically higher and more visible—in the form of steel fencing, stadium lights, and high-tech equipment—but is also noticeably thinner than in the EU. United States immigration controls are largely concentrated along the borderline itself, leaving the workplace and the broader society less regulated.[13]

DILEMMAS OF REBORDERING

Yet regardless of the considerable differences between the European and North American wall-building projects, border control strategists in both places face the same awkward and inescapable dilemma: how to make their borders more secure while simultaneously making sure that they remain business friendly. Rather than barriers that halt all movement, today's borders are supposed to function more like filters that separate out the unwanted from the wanted cross-border flows. Domestic political pressure in the United States and western Europe has necessitated that governments at least project the appearance of effective border controls, but economic integration has required that these borders also function as increasingly efficient bridges that facilitate cross-border economic exchange. The wall around the West, in other words, is by design highly permeable. Although the advanced industrialized countries of the West may possess the technical capacity to seal their borders, the enormous economic costs and political consequences make this an unrealistic option (despite the wishes of some conservative isolationists).

The nearly 2,000-mile-long U.S.–Mexico border, for example, is the busiest land crossing in the world. In 1998, 278 million people, 86 million cars, and 4 million trucks and rail cars legally entered the country from Mexico. Cross-border trade has doubled since 1993, making Mexico the second largest trading partner of the United States. However, because of U.S. anxieties about the influx of illegal immigrants and drugs, the border has also become one of the world's most heavily patrolled. The number of U.S. Border Patrol agents assigned to the border has more than doubled since 1993. The Immigration and Naturalization Service (INS, the parent agency of the U.S. Border Patrol) now has more agents who are authorized to carry firearms than any other federal law enforcement force. The deployment of new agents has been matched by more fencing, equipment, and surveillance technologies. Thus, the seeming paradox of U.S.–Mexico integration has been the creation of both a borderless economy and a barricaded border.[14] U.S.–Mexico relations have consequently become both more intimate and more strained at the same time. Even though migrant labor has long been one of Mexico's leading exports, it is noticeably absent from the North American Free Trade Agreement (NAFTA). Despite Mexico's wishes, U.S. officials insisted early on that labor migration was off the table in negotiating the trade accord. Indeed, tariffs on the export of cheap labor have been rising in the form of increased policing—denying and defying the existence of a long-established and deeply entrenched informal cross-border labor market.

Managing the twin policy objectives of *facilitating* cross-border economic exchange and *enforcing* border controls will remain a delicate and inherently frustrating political task. One favorite coping strategy has been to construct an elaborate state-of-the-art electronic filter. For example, EU officials have put in place a shared computer system at border crossings (the Schengen Information System) that links the databases of all Schengen countries with the names of criminal aliens, rejected asylum seekers, and others deemed "undesirable." Along Germany's eastern border, where cross-border commerce and travel have boomed in recent years, border guards have turned to carbon dioxide sensors to help them detect illegal immigrants hiding in truck cargo containers. Paralleling intensified enforcement, new ports of entry have been opened up to facilitate the rapidly rising number of border crossings. As the number of legal crossings has risen, so too has the number of arrests for attempted illegal entry. Border checks have caused long delays and enormous traffic jams—a highly visible and practical daily reminder that the old East–West divide persists in new ways.

Along the southern border of the United States, laser visas and an array of high-tech gadgets are being developed to more carefully scrutinize border crossers.[15] At the same time, new technology has helped to make the border a faster bridge for frequent business travelers. Thus, at some border ports of entry, automated commuter lanes are now available for business commuters who have undergone a background check and pay a special border-crossing fee. And in some major airports, such as Los Angeles, frequent travelers can now insert an identity card and their hand into a scanning machine instead of waiting in long lines.[16] Similarly, in west European airports, there are separate lines for those who are from Schengen countries and for those who are not, with the latter subjected to longer delays and more intensive scrutiny.[17] These state practices not only serve instrumental police functions but reinforce perceived differences between "insiders" and "outsiders."

Regardless of how effective these improved border management strategies actually are in weeding out the undesirable from the desirable flows, there is a powerful political and bureaucratic imperative to at least project an impression of territorial control and to symbolically signal official commitment to maintaining such control.[18] The degree of harmony or conflict in the process of deepening and expanding the economic integration process in both regions will significantly depend on how concerns about unwanted border crossings are politically managed, even if not resolved.

A PREVIEW OF THE VOLUME

This collection of original essays crosses both professional and geographic borders, bringing together a broad range of political scientists, historians, sociologists, geographers, and policymakers from both sides of the Atlantic and both sides of the wall around the West. The three sections of the volume offer an analytically useful and unusual opportunity for cross-national and cross-regional comparisons. The first section of the volume is historical and comparative. Focusing primarily on Europe, Malcolm Anderson takes us on a sweeping tour of the transformation of border controls during the second half of the twentieth century. He then turns to an analysis of the public anxieties unleashed by the dramatically changed functions of frontiers in the 1990s, and discusses the innovative and collaborative border regulatory mechanisms that have been put in place to compensate for the abolition of internal border controls in the EU. Anderson concludes with a discussion of the factors that make European border controls both similar to and distinct from those in North America.

John Torpey's chapter examines the regulation of migration in the North Atlantic world during the twentieth century. Countering widespread claims that states are increasingly powerless to regulate migration, Torpey stresses that from a longer historical perspective we must explain not why so many people move, but why so few do. Global labor migration, it should be pointed out, involves about 120 million people—only 2.3 percent of the world's inhabitants.[19] Although this is not numerically insignificant, it provides an important reminder that most people are not mobile. States play a central role in determining who comes and goes, and what destinations may be available to them. Torpey traces how states and the interstate system developed over time the capacities to regulate migration ("the monopoly over the control of movement"), and shows the effects of these capacities on migratory patterns in Europe and the United States.

The chapter by Virginie Guiraudon and Gallya Lahav demonstrates that states have creatively adapted to changing circumstances in an effort to increase their capacity to control the cross-border movement of people. States are operating under new constraints, particularly the liberal norms upheld by judicial institutions entrenched since the 1970s and the consequences of the end of the Cold War in the 1990s. Working around these constraints, liberal democratic states have sought to control population flows before and after border crossings by enlisting local, private, and transnational actors. Guiraudon and Lahav reconceptualize the immigration control "playing field" along two axes: the public/private sector, and the local/international level. This enables an analysis of policy instruments such as cooperation with sending and transit countries, coordination of policies among EU states, carrier and employers' sanctions, and the drafting of local elected officials and social services. Although policy tools have been transferred across the Atlantic in both directions, the authors point to substantial structural and cultural differences that mediate the types of policies that countries adopt and their effectiveness.

The second section of the volume focuses on case studies from the recent experience along the southern border of the United States. Rather than examining U.S. immigration control policy as a general phenomenon, these chapters illustrate the merits of geographically defined case studies of how state control efforts play out in distinct ways across different sections of the border (specifically, the Florida–Caribbean border, the Texas–Mexico border, and the California–Mexico border). Variations in these border control campaigns reflect the distinct geographies, political and social contexts, and historical legacies of each border area.

Christopher Mitchell's chapter on border controls in South Florida explains how the U.S. government was able to reduce the flow of "boat people" from Cuba and

Haiti. Although Caribbean migration has stimulated South Florida's growth, U.S. policy toward Cubans and Haitians turned increasingly restrictive following the refugee crisis of 1980. To deploy its patrol vessels most effectively, Washington modified its foreign policy and obtained the cooperation of the Cuban and Haitian governments. Domestically, Mitchell shows how the U.S. government also had to chart a course among powerful local, state, and national currents of public opinion. Mitchell concludes the chapter by elucidating the factors that make the South Florida experience distinct from other U.S. immigration control efforts. He notes, for example, that Washington appears unlikely to emphasize "migration diplomacy" with Mexico and Central America, since those nations are less willing than Cuba and Haiti to cooperate in restraining emigration.

Focusing on the California–Mexico border, especially the rapidly growing Tijuana–San Diego border region, Joseph Nevins interrogates the relationship between strengthening boundary enforcement by U.S. authorities and their simultaneous opening of the border to trade and investment. Although these sharply contrasting border trends may seem contradictory and certainly create some practical policy tensions, Nevins argues that they are also complementary, and relate to different functions of the modern territorial state. In this account, the state's effort to create a more secure and orderly border is intimately intertwined with what Nevins calls the "NAFTAization of the border."[20]

Turning to the Texas–Mexico border, David Spener provides a detailed, on-the-ground evaluation of the U.S. crackdown against illegal immigration. He notes that even though the United States certainly possesses the coercive means to control the border, it has so far not directed those means to that end. After explaining the underlying logic of the U.S. border deterrence strategy, Spener points to various contradictions and limitations that undermine the effectiveness of the control effort in practice. This includes, for example, limited detention space, official corruption, the rapid adaptability of migrant smugglers, and most importantly, the nation's continuing thirst for cheap foreign labor. But although the border crackdown has so far failed to significantly deter illegal entry, Spener suggests that it can nevertheless be viewed as a success in terms of further criminalizing and marginalizing a "workforce that is at once economically vital but culturally and politically threatening." In this sense, a policy that fails to achieve its stated instrumental goal—deterrence—can still enjoy broad domestic support.

The section concludes with a chapter by Gustavo Mohar and María Elena-Alcaraz, two Mexican officials deeply involved in the politically difficult job of managing the migration issue in the bilateral relationship. They rightly point out that much has been said in recent years about U.S. efforts to tighten controls along the southwest border, but the policy response on the Mexican side is less well known. Compared to its largely hands-off orientation of the past, the Mexican government has adopted a more activist and engaged approach to immigration issues in recent years, sparked by the U.S. anti-immigration backlash in the 1990s. The chapter explains what

Mexico has done, both unilaterally and bilaterally in cooperation with the United States, to respond to the tightening of U.S. border controls. The authors also point to some important parallels between the situation along the U.S.–Mexico and Mexico–Guatemala borders.

The third section of the volume examines the shifting nature and form of border controls in post–Cold War Europe. The demise of the Soviet bloc and especially the disintegration of Yugoslavia created increased flows of asylum seekers and economic migrants into western Europe. Although the anticipated floods never came, electorates in EU member states demanded restrictions on immigration. The first three chapters of this section analyze the consequences of strengthened west European border controls for neighboring east European countries expecting to enter the EU in coming years, such as Poland, the Czech Republic, and Hungary. The emergence of a European border control regime has had a ripple effect on the border policies of these aspirants to EU membership, and threatens to marginalize states farther to the east such as Ukraine and Russia. Although the enlargement of NATO has attracted greater attention, Ukrainians and Russians are beginning to understand that the enlargement of the EU is far more likely to create a new division of Europe.

Milada Vachudová's chapter examines how dramatic changes in asylum policies transformed the postcommunist states of east central and southeastern Europe into the EU's new migration gatekeepers. As countries such as Poland and Hungary strive to earn full membership in the EU, they must fulfill EU requirements, including stricter border controls as outlined in the Schengen Agreement. But the strict Schengen rules, she argues, are likely to undermine the long-term interest of present and future EU member states in the economic stabilization and democratization of the whole of Europe. For some postcommunist states, burdensome visa requirements to enter the Schengen space already complicate the democratizing project of local pro-Western elites. As the EU has taken on the functions of a state with respect to border controls, Vachudová suggests that its policies are hostage to the domestic politics of a few of its member states.

Roland Freudenstein also analyzes how Schengen's implementation affects relations with the EU's future member states to the east. Specifically, his chapter investigates the position of Germany (a key member state), Poland (a promising candidate for EU membership), and Ukraine (an important state certain to be excluded from the EU's next enlargement). When Poland joins the EU, its external border will shift from the Odra River (which divides Germany and Poland) to the Buh River (which divides Poland and Ukraine). As a political precondition for joining the EU, Poland will have to make its eastern border less permeable. At the same time, relations with the eastern neighbors, especially Ukraine, are of vital political, economic, and cultural importance for Poland. Freudenstein stresses that an accompanying political strategy will therefore have to be worked out by Poland and the EU, to minimize the destabilizing effects of tightening border controls along what he calls "the Río Buh."

Leszek Jesien, a Polish official who has been closely involved in the process of negotiating Poland's entry into the EU, discusses these problems from the point of view of an important candidate for EU membership. While noting the need to abolish some borders (namely the Polish–German border and the borders between Poland and other candidate countries), the chapter sketches a number of short- and long-term scenarios for the shape of the EU's eastern border. These various scenarios summarize current efforts of the Polish state to strengthen its control capacity at the key borders that will eventually be EU external borders. Jesien concludes that, in the political context of the accession negotiations, candidate countries must undertake certain foreign and domestic policies on their own borders if they are to generate sufficient political trust on the part of EU negotiators, EU member states, and EU publics.

The previous three chapters focus largely on a European political problem (the relationship between EU enlargement and Schengen), but the chapter by Rey Koslowski examines the actual practice of EU border controls and illegal border crossings. Specifically, he traces the interplay between migrant smuggling and EU attempts to police such smuggling. EU members have adopted increasingly restrictive border control, visa, and asylum policies that demonstrate enhanced control of "unwanted" migration through new cooperative institutional mechanisms. In response, the marketization of illegal migration by organized traffickers has increased the capacities of the unwanted to migrate. Human smuggling into the EU, particularly of Kurds and Albanians, presents a significant challenge to EU member state cooperative efforts to erect an effective common external border. Increasing state power over migration has been effectively demonstrated through more restrictive EU asylum policies, which have decreased the number of asylum seekers. But as Koslowski emphasizes, many of those who would have applied for asylum are now crossing borders using the clandestine transportation services provided by professional smugglers. Recent increases in human smuggling and related document fraud have occurred in conjunction with the EU's increasingly restrictive common policy. In this sense, law enforcement and law evasion along the EU's external borders have expanded together. Even though state capacity to control borders has grown, so too has the capacity of those seeking to bypass such controls. The emergence and growth of increasingly sophisticated, organized, and profitable migrant smuggling groups has been one of the more perverse but predictable side effects of tighter immigration controls.

Timothy Snyder concludes the volume with a synthetic essay that reevaluates the major debates concerning the state, regional integration, and globalization in light of the findings of the volume contributors. He stresses that border controls remain a core state function, even if pursued in innovative ways; that attempts to enforce such controls continue to consolidate states as territorial and as membership organizations; and that the category of state power should be recast rather than cast out in discussions of the cross-border movement of people in the twenty-first century.

The management of state borders in North America and Europe provides a useful lens through which to evaluate the transformed nature of territorial politics in a new economic and security environment. The developments examined in this volume indicate that accounts of the withering away of state borders, be they mournful or celebratory, are premature. The border regulatory apparatus of the state is being transformed, not transcended. Even as some traditional border functions have eroded, others have been enhanced, and new ones added. This volume seeks to sharpen our focus on intensified state efforts to regulate the cross-border movement of people, and thus to illustrate one of the more striking ways in which the territorial state is being recrafted in a rapidly changing world.

NOTES

1. It is important to note that this volume is not primarily focused on the causes and consequences of immigration, a topic that is well covered in the expansive immigration literature. Rather, the focus here is on state efforts to control such immigration. Cross-border population flows are necessarily part of the analysis, but only to the extent that this informs our understanding of state controls. Canada is neglected in the coverage of North America, primarily because the volume focuses on the borders between rich and poor countries.

2. Mathew Horsman and Andrew Marshall, *After the Nation-State* (London: Harper-Collins, 1994), 44.

3. David Jacobson, *Rights across Borders* (Baltimore: Johns Hopkins University Press, 1996), 41.

4. Kenichi Ohmae, *The Borderless World: Power and Strategy in the Interlinked Economy* (New York: Harper Business, 1990).

5. Richard Rosecrance, *The Rise of the Virtual State* (New York: Basic Books, 1999).

6. The declining military function of borders has been noted by scholars for a number of decades. See, for example, Jean Gottman, *The Significance of Territory* (Charlottesville: University Press of Virginia, 1973). This is not meant to suggest that military concerns are no longer important. Wars of various kinds, especially internal wars, obviously persist and are widespread. Moreover, as the crisis in Kosovo has demonstrated, what has been treated as a policing concern (deterring unwanted mass migration) and a military concern (deterring the Serb military) can be intertwined.

7. The heightened focus on border policing does not mean that the traditional border tasks of military protection and revenue collection have entirely disappeared. In contrast to the past, however, these core military and economic regulatory border concerns have sharply declined, especially in the industrialized West.

8. Sack defines territoriality as "the attempt by an individual or group to affect, influence, or control people, phenomena, and relationships, by delimiting and asserting control over a geographic area." Robert David Sack, *Human Territoriality: Its Theory and History* (New York: Cambridge University Press, 1986), 19.

9. Jagdish N. Bhagwati, "Incentives and Disincentives: International Migration," *Weltwirtschaftliches Archiv* 120, no. 4 (1994): 680.

10. Anthony Giddens, *The Nation-State and Violence* (Oxford: Polity, 1995), 120.

11. Saskia Sassen, *Losing Control? Sovereignty in an Age of Globalization* (New York: Columbia University Press, 1996), 59.

12. For example, in an effort to impress and appease the EU, in December 1998 the Czech government announced plans to send troops to fortify its border defenses against illegal immigration. The number of immigrants detained at the Czech border doubled in 1998. The sharp rise in detentions and the staging of military exercises by the Czech military to test the Army's participation in border enforcement prompted the French paper *Le Monde* to suggest that a new Iron Curtain was being built—except in this case, of course, without the landmines. The Czech government also plans to impose visa requirements for many former Soviet republics, as well as Romania and Bulgaria. *CTK National News Wire*, January 11, 1999.

13. Although U.S. enforcement efforts are concentrated along the southern border, it should be noted that the INS has also been expanding its offices abroad to focus on organized migrant smuggling.

14. For a more detailed discussion, see Peter Andreas, *Border Games: Policing the U.S.–Mexico Divide* (Ithaca, N.Y.: Cornell University Press, 2000).

15. This has included adapting Cold War leftovers for border control tasks. For example, magnetic footfall detectors originally used in Vietnam are scattered along the border to detect illegal entries, and night-vision equipment used in the Gulf War is now used for border policing. A Border Research and Technology Center was established in 1995 with the specific mission of adapting intelligence and military technology to the problems of border law enforcement. See Sandra Dibble, "Star Wars Arrives at the Border: High Tech Developed by the Military, CIA May Aid Enforcement," *San Diego Union-Tribune*, March 18, 1995.

16. Verne G. Kopytoff, "A Silicone Wall Rises on the Border," *The New York Times*, January 14, 1999.

17. My wife, who is a native of Bosnia, discovered this a few years ago. Flying from Zagreb to New York via Munich and Frankfurt using her Bosnian passport, she was greeted at the German airport gates by two German police officers. After carefully checking her papers, they escorted her to her connecting flights.

18. As Anderson has observed in the case of Europe, "a certain myth of control must gain wide currency to maintain the legitimacy of the EU." Malcolm Anderson, *Frontiers* (Cambridge, UK: Polity, 1996), 187.

19. Peter Stalker, *Workers without Frontiers* (Boulder, CO: Lynne Rienner, 2000), 1.

20. This extends Karl Polanyi's insight that "the introduction of free markets, far from doing away with the need for control, regulation, and intervention, enormously increased their range." Karl Polanyi, *The Great Transformation: The Political and Economic Origins of Our Time* (Boston: Beacon Press, 1944), 140.

Part One
Historical and Comparative Perspectives

2

The Transformation of Border Controls: A European Precedent?

Malcolm Anderson

The changes in border controls across Europe since the end of World War II are both radical and without genuine precedent. Perceptions of borders are changing worldwide as a result of "globalization," but the control of borders has changed more rapidly. These changes are associated with turbulent and rapid political developments in the various phases of the Cold War to the collapse of communism, and from the hesitant beginnings of regional economic integration to the inauguration of a "European Union" (EU). The transformation of border controls in the EU may give some indications about possible scenarios for the North American Free Trade Agreement (NAFTA) and MERCOSUR, if they are transformed into genuine common markets. There are, however, specific factors in the development of the EU that are not, and may never be, present elsewhere.

This chapter gives, first, a sketch of the nature of changes in Europe in the last half century; second, an account of the anxieties triggered by the changed functions of frontiers in the present decade; third, a description of the arrangements currently in place to compensate for the abolition of internal EU border controls; and fourth, and in conclusion, a brief presentation of some of the more far-reaching propositions and arguments concerning border controls.

Although the approach in this chapter is historical rather than theoretical, a particular perspective on border controls underlies it, namely that border controls are embedded in "frontier regimes." Frontier regimes consist of agreements about borders with neighboring states, whether bilateral or multilateral; the practices that have grown up around them; the administration and management of border controls; related systems of police and customs cooperation; and institutions and arrangements for transfrontier cooperation. Implicit in these regimes are the various conceptions of functions that are fulfilled or that, it is thought, should be fulfilled by borders. Also central to the regimes are territorial ideologies—perceptions of the meaning and significance of frontiers held by policy-making elites,[1] by the population of frontier regions, and, more generally, by the inhabitants of a country. The components of frontier regimes are not explored and some, such as transfrontier cooperation,[2] are not even mentioned. The concept of a frontier regime rejects the common assumption that frontiers and border controls are epiphenomena that change as the core characteristics of states, economies (including regional economic integration), and international relations shift. These general factors are more important in determining the course of events, but changes in frontier regimes can have an autonomous influence.

Changes in border controls are frequently treated in public debate as technical administrative matters or as instruments of immigration and crime control. They are neglected in the scholarly literature. But some changes are, at the very least, symptomatic of profound changes in the international system and in the authority of states. To relegate them to a minor branch of public administration, of intellectual interest to immigration lawyers only, is to misunderstand their profound symbolic and political importance. They raise fundamental questions ranging from the reasons why crucial control functions were concentrated on linear borders, the relations of technologies to systems of control, and whether control of persons can effectively be maintained when other kinds of control (on capital movements, on financial and consultancy services, on goods, and on information) are dismantled. These large questions lurk behind the apparently mundane administrative issues of personal identity documents, visa policies, information exchange systems, and regulations concerning immigration, asylum, and access to citizenship.[3] At the political level, different styles of rhetoric used when discussing border controls reflect, sometimes obscurely, different positions on these fundamental questions.

THE HISTORICAL TRANSFORMATION OF BORDER CONTROLS

There is always a tendency to exaggerate the originality and importance of our own times. Nonetheless, by historic standards, there has been a remarkable shift between the closed borders in Europe of the 1940s to the relatively open borders at the end of the twentieth century. Roger Dion wrote, with some justification, in the immediate aftermath of World War II:

> the war of 1939–1945 conferred on political frontiers an efficacy equalling or surpassing that of natural phenomena. A frontier as artificial as the Franco–Belgian separates economic regimes so different that we question a traveller coming from Belgium with as much curiosity as ten years ago one coming from Australia, and the line separating a democratic country from a totalitarian one can be in 1940 more difficult to cross than a formidable mountain barrier. Whether or not corresponding with natural frontiers, the linear frontiers of Europe have become terrible realities.[4]

The economic and political barriers represented by borders were indeed formidable. In western Europe, this was evident by the procedures in place at border crossings; persons and their belongings were scrutinized individually and very closely at border posts. Borders were patrolled by law enforcement agencies; they were clearly marked by obstacles, very often fences; and there was a strong military presence in frontier regions. Passports and visas were necessary for temporary visitors to other countries; residence permits and work permits were required for longer periods of residence; and police agencies imposed reporting systems on aliens and visited work sites where they were employed. The infringement of any regulation usually resulted in immediate deportation without any right of appeal. The executive authority of the state reigned supreme, reflecting a particular view of state sovereignty in which only citizens had rights. Search and seizure powers were absolute, and there was a virtual absence of judicial review of executive actions. Some countries subjected aliens entering or on their territory to more bureaucratic harassment than others because their administrative and cultural traditions varied. In most countries, with some such as Franco's Spain going to extreme lengths, border controls were used to exclude political undesirables.

Running through central Europe, from the Baltic to the Mediterranean (or Black Sea) were the most closed borders in recent European peacetime history. This "Iron Curtain" shared characteristics with other closed borders, both in symbolic representation and in practical forms of control. The symbolism, exemplified by the propaganda of both the Free World and the Communist bloc, represented a line between good and evil, truth and error, justice and oppression, democracy and dictatorship. In practical terms, the frontier was fortified, lined with watchtowers, patrolled by dogs (usually the rottweilers favored by the Nazis) and guards with orders to shoot to kill, and, over part of its length, lethal automatic firing devices. The controls exercised on people by the communist states were draconian. Until the 1980s travel to western countries was restricted to organized groups and official visits. Travel within the Soviet bloc was sometimes easier for tourists, but stringent controls remained in place at all the borders. The rights of the individual in the communist countries were subordinated to a supposed higher good. One result was that they controlled exit of their own citizens (extremely rare in western Europe). They required exit visas; emigration was not normally allowed; and exile was occasionally used as an instrument of policy as, for example, in the celebrated case of Alexander Solzhenitzyn. Some communist countries ransomed their own nationals and allowed foreign governments to purchase the right of exit for, in particular, Jews and ethnic Germans.

However, the degree of closure to the West, even during the most hard-line Stalinist period, did not rival that found by Freiherr von Richthofen on the China–Korea border in 1868.[5] The completeness of this deliberately created "desert" frontier, which nobody should cross under pain of death, was not possible in twentieth-century Europe, even under Stalinism. From the 1950s, the border on the thirty-eighth parallel between North and South Korea has been more closed than the Iron Curtain in Europe was at any time. East Germans managed to reach the West even after the 1961 building of the Berlin Wall, which was intended to close the last way of escape. There were, of course, variations over time and between countries of the Soviet bloc. The Polish sea frontier to Scandinavia was always relatively open, since the Polish government wished to retain contact with the Polish diaspora for domestic political as well as economic reasons. From the moment of Krushchev's proclamation of the doctrine of peaceful coexistence, control of foreigners in Poland was never as tight as in the German Democratic Republic.[6]

None of the specific control measures in place in Europe, both West and East, was without venerable historical precedent. In the heyday of the Byzantine Empire from the seventh to the twelfth centuries, a network of border control posts was in place where cross-border visitors had to present passports and apply for visas. In the interior of the Empire other posts existed to which the foreigner had to report; on exit from the Empire, passports and visas had to be presented.[7] Clearly demarcated and militarized frontiers have been known since antiquity. But what happened in the nineteenth century was new, although it was the almost inevitable outcome of the Westphalian state. The broad acceptance of the doctrine of national sovereignty implied a particular kind of frontier and border control. After the appearance of the modern nation–state in its mature form, at the time of the French Revolution, the coincidence of the military and security border with the frontier of tax regimes, ecclesiastical boundaries, limits of provision of public assistance, public health services, licensed professions, and educational and economic regulatory regimes was completed.[8] It became taken for granted that states had not only the right but the legitimate authority to control all activities on their territory and to do this they needed, in principle, absolute control of passage across their borders. The states' "monopolization of the right to authorise movement" became entrenched (Torpey, this volume). However, one freedom that did not disappear until 1914 was the freedom of members of European elites to roam and take up residence wherever struck their fancy, and this freedom was usually not constrained by the requirement to carry a passport.[9]

The extent of the change in western Europe, initiated by the 1957 Treaty of Rome and culminating in measures introduced in this decade, is the fact that, for twelve of the fifteen members of the EU, there are no border controls on persons (and on goods) between them. Any citizens, whether employed, engaged in any legitimate activity, or retired can freely settle in any other member state of the EU. To achieve free movement of labor the contracting parties gave social and economic rights to citizens of the other member states. Barriers to free movement, such as the nonequivalence of professional qualifications, were negotiated away, particularly following the 1985 Single European Act. Freedom of movement was finally achieved by the 1991 Treaty of Maastricht, which gave rights of residence to nonactive citizens as well as certain political rights to all EU citizens resident in other member states; and by the 1996 implementation of the Schengen accords, which abolished systematic controls on persons at the "internal" borders between Schengen member states. In eastern Europe radical changes in the practices of border controls occurred with dramatic suddenness. The oppressive character of these controls was swept away by the events of 1989. The flight of East Germans, facilitated by the opening of the border by the Hungarians allowing them passage to the West, was followed by the physical dismantling of the Berlin Wall. When the German Democratic Republic could no longer control its borders, it collapsed. The disintegration of the Soviet bloc and communist regimes resulted in the appearance of about 8,000 miles of new international borders in central and eastern Europe, mostly drawn along the lines of old internal administrative boundaries. It also introduced a brief moment of euphoria when freedom of movement for all in Europe seemed a possibility. This euphoria quickly disappeared as western governments became alarmed by the possibility of a mass movement of people, following the precedent of the exodus of East Germans, from East to West. "Joining the West" was the clear aspiration of the peoples and governments of east central Europe because all (including the three Baltic countries that seceded from the former U.S.S.R.) posed their candidature to join the EU and most aspired to membership in NATO.

CONTEMPORARY BORDER ANXIETIES

The changes in European borders in the last half century are less unilinear and more complex than slogans concerning "a Europe without frontiers" or simplistic formulae about globalization, the end of history, or, indeed, the "clash of civilizations" suggest. Although no longer terrible realities because no longer militarized and so obviously repressive, frontiers remain crucially important political, administrative, legal, and cultural/linguistic lines of division. They retain basic control functions in central and eastern Europe and at the EU external border, although within the EU these functions are either being lost or modified (see Jesien, this volume). The dismantling of border controls within the EU and the increased permeability of borders apparent throughout the highly developed world have led to anxieties, even fears, which are exploited in electoral competitions and the bureaucratic competition for resources.[10] Frontiers are unlikely to be challenged by military action in Europe (although the Kosovo case has shown that, in exceptional circumstances, this is possible) but nonetheless the inviolability of frontiers remains an essential part of contemporary notions of security.

Anxieties and fears about security in Europe are difficult to analyze with any precision. They are linked to the great economic and technological transformations of the late twentieth century. Feelings of powerlessness and vulnerability produced by international mergers, international financial movements, and new technologies, and of cultural insecurity triggered by the vast diffusion of popular cultural products and the dominance of the English language are hard to assess, except insofar as they have an effect on government policy such as the negotiation of the "cultural exception" in the Uruguay round of world trade negotiations. Control of territory is still regarded as important in mitigating some of the effects of these developments, but the borders of states are now perceived as much more permeable. Desires are frequently expressed that governments, by using border controls, should do more to protect the interests of their citizens, even when it is palpably impossible for them to do so.

Anxiety, mainly confined to administrative and political elites, is based on the absence of consensus, intellectual or political, about the direction and speed of European integration. Borders within the EU remain, with marginal exceptions, the limits of criminal and civil law jurisdictions, executive police powers, public administration, educational systems, tax regimes (excepting tariffs), social security systems, and many nongovernmental organizations. If present trends continue, breaches in these limits will be increasingly made: there will be progressive integration of public institutions across borders (with systems of coordination characteristic of federal systems), a more rapid integration of social organizations, and an increase in the numbers of cross-border mergers. But there is great uncertainty about whether present trends will continue. The latest building block of European integration, the Treaty of Amsterdam, is subject to three differing interpretations: a minimalist; a maximalist; and the view that it is a transitional agreement on the road to a federal European constitution.

A different kind of anxiety relates directly to the practicalities of border controls. Security and, in particular, the boundary between internal and external security, has been undergoing a conceptual shift. The reasons for this shift are threefold. First, probably the most important, is the disappearance of a direct military threat to the EU of a kind previously represented by the U.S.S.R. Second, a widespread conviction is that a basic justification for the coercive power of the state is the ability to defend the security of its citizens—some threat to their security must therefore exist. Third, new areas of policy have emerged in the late twentieth century as the problems facing advanced industrial societies change. The effect of these factors is that a new kind of security discourse is emerging.[11] Threats to the security of EU member states are now perceived more as criminal than conventional military threats—mafias, drugs, illegal immigrants, traffic in human beings, trade in illegal goods (arms, child pornography, body parts, nuclear materials)—threats to public order by violent elements coming from neighboring countries (football hooligans, disorderly holiday makers, political demonstrators) or as a result of the spilling over of conflicts such as those in Algeria, Turkey, and the former Yugoslavia through refugee crises and terrorist action. In addition, the concept of security has been extended to "societal security"—threats to human rights, to the environment, to cultures.[12]

THE SCHENGEN BORDER SYSTEM

The intention of the Schengen system was to address some of the concerns in the last category of anxiety by "compensating" for the security "deficit" allegedly caused by the abolition of border controls through a series of new cooperative security measures. It also represented a move by some member states toward faster integration than for the EU as a whole—an ambition that received formal authorization in the Maastricht and Amsterdam treaties. Two general points are evident from this increased cooperation between certain member states. First, multispeed integration is a costly, time-consuming exercise that leads to considerable legal uncertainty.[13] Second, the implementation of a new system of multilateral cooperation in the administration of border controls introduced a radically new element in frontier regimes (as defined at the beginning of this chapter). It has a direct or indirect influence on all the existing bilateral and multilateral agreements for the management of frontiers, including forms of police and judicial cooperation.

This system had discreet beginnings in the negotiations leading up to the 1985 Schengen Agreement and the 1990 Schengen Application Convention, supplemented by (now voluminous) rules and practices (taken together, they are now described, in the jargon of the EU, as the Schengen *acquis*).[14] The Schengen Agreement brought together the Benelux Common Travel Area with the proposed open frontier agreement between France and Germany to abolish all border controls on goods and persons between them.[15] The Application Convention set up a series of arrangements, including a strengthening and standardization of controls at the external border, and of police and judicial cooperation between the member states. The system is managed by an Executive Committee, which is now the EU Justice and Home Affairs Council of Ministers, a Central Control Group, and a board for verifying that data protection rules are properly implemented.

All EU member states had entered the system by the time it was implemented in 1996 with the exception of the United Kingdom and the Republic of Ireland (who were given an opt-out in the Amsterdam negotiations). The Irish would be prepared to enter, if it did not mean sacrificing the UK–Ireland free movement area; and the UK government announced, on March 12, 1999, that it would accept all of the *acquis* except the abolition of border controls. Denmark has a different kind of opt-out: it is a member of Schengen but retains the sovereign right to decide whether to accept decisions agreed upon within the Schengen framework. The Scandinavian nonmembers of the EU, Norway and Iceland, have association agreements with Schengen in order to preserve the long-standing Nordic free movement area. All new entrants to the EU must accept the Schengen system in its entirety and, despite its opt-out, the UK government strongly supports this condition.

The main outlines of the Schengen system are the creation of a free movement area without border controls, accompanied by measures to increase security at the external frontier, to combat illegal immigration, to enhance police cooperation, and to improve judicial cooperation. The most significant elements are:

- Strict control of the external frontier according to common rules, contained in the confidential Schengen manual for the external frontier.[16]
- Establishment of a coordinating committee, along with technical inspections of the external borders of all member states (and candidate members) to ensure that they meet the agreed standards.
- The exchange of information on prohibited immigrants, wanted persons, and stolen vehicles through the Schengen Information System (SIS), a computerized central database (now with in excess of 8 million entries) in Strasborg, which supplies information to and receives information from national databases. Data protection is the responsibility of an independent control board.
- A task force that analyzes intelligence about the role of organized gangs in smuggling illegal immigrants into the EU.
- The establishment of national offices of SIRENE (*Supplément d'Information Requis à l'Entrée Nationale*) to deal with difficulties and emergencies.
- Enhanced police cooperation between the participating states, particularly in the frontier regions.
- Measures that facilitate judicial cooperation.
- Movement toward a common visa, asylum, and immigration policy.

The period leading up to the entry into force of the Schengen system (1990–1996) was punctuated by many vicissitudes including the unification of Germany, the huge increase in the number of asylum seekers, and the spilling over of Algerian terrorism into France. Prominent themes in the debate on the system are the limitation of immigration (to zero in the view of Charles Pasqua, the French Minister of the Interior in 1993); the attempt to limit the number of asylum seekers; the links made between security, criminality, and immigrants; and the contradictory discourses of an alleged "fortress Europe" (which, according to pro-immigrant groups, created a Europe that excludes foreigners) and an alleged "sieve Europe" (because the external frontier, according to the anti-immigration groups, is highly porous). Schengen became a *bête noire* for civil liberties organizations such as the UK-based Justice and Statewatch (which produces many valuable factual reports on the system), and for pro-immigration and antiracist groups. The main hostile arguments are that Schengen represents a European-wide repressive system; that it encourages governments to take an unnecessarily harsh line with clandestine immigrants; that it tends to criminalize clandestine immigrants and asylum seekers because they are entered in the same database as drug dealers, arms traffickers, and other "real" criminals; that it encourages racist attitudes because most of the immigrants it aims to keep out are nonwhite from poor countries; that it lacks transparency because many of its arrangements are negotiated confidentially and not subject to effective parliamentary scrutiny; that the data protection guarantees are faulty; and that the arrangements for legal and political accountability are weak.

These charges are of great concern to active minorities, some members of national parliaments (particularly in the Netherlands, the UK House of Lords, and the French

Senate), and members of the European Parliament; but public opinion remains overwhelmingly in favor of tight control of immigration. There is no sign that majority opinion in the major European countries is troubled by the frequently harsh treatment of asylum seekers, or indeed by the placing of countries such as Sri Lanka and Nigeria, which seem obviously dangerous for some people, on the so-called white list whose citizens will not be considered for asylum. The main difficulties for the system came from neighboring countries because Schengen,[17] seen from east central Europe, threatened to become a new Iron Curtain, a rigorously controlled frontier separating those within the system from those without. Although the Iron Curtain analogy is an exaggeration, the imposition of tight controls has important symbolic and psychological effects.

This separation initially affected countries negotiating for membership in the EU. Hungary and Slovenia were the two most offended because prior to the full implementation of Schengen, the Austrian–Hungarian and the Slovenian–Italian borders had been relatively open and, at least for the states directly concerned, relatively problem free.[18] The 1997 trial run of the application of Schengen norms to border controls on these borders caused indignation and widespread disruption. When the controls were instituted in 1998, modifications had been made for local traffic[19] and, although it is not publicly admitted, some local flexibility in the interpretation of Schengen. The general problem of introducing tight controls on persons and inspection of all vehicles is that it imposes costs on firms (all the candidate countries have otherwise open access for industrial products to the EU market), it disrupts local economic activities and markets, it inhibits normal transfrontier social relations, and it represents a symbolic exclusion.

The European Commission's Task Force on Enlargement now screens the legal provisions and practical measures taken by the six candidate countries. Although this process involves justice and home affairs as a whole, particular emphasis is placed on the Schengen system and matters relating to it—asylum policy; external borders; immigration controls; organized crime; drug trafficking; terrorism; and police, customs, and judicial cooperation.[20] The extent to which EU countries are willing to relax controls on their present eastern external border depends on the willingness of the candidate countries to impose Schengen norms at their borders.[21] The candidate states are thus coopted into the EU. The problem has now been displaced from the EU frontier to one between, on the one hand, the EU and the candidate countries and, on the other hand, the other countries of eastern Europe. There is a powerful sense of exclusion in the excluded countries, often focused on the tiresome bureaucratic process of acquiring visas (see Vachudová, this volume).

CONCLUSION

Several general propositions and arguments emerge from the remarkable evolution of border control regimes in Europe. The first is alluded to but not explored in this chapter. There is undoubtedly a connection between border controls and the nature of political regimes. To simplify: authoritarian, repressive regimes are threatened by open borders and cannot tolerate them. If compelled by circumstances to open their borders, they must either reform or collapse. This was as true of Japan in 1853, when Commodore Perry enforced access to the Japanese market for western goods, as it was for the Communist bloc countries after 1989. By contrast, liberal regimes, with a respect for human rights and based on a market economy, cannot impose an exclusive and rigorously enforced border control regime without compromising their basic purposes. One anxiety in Europe is that an EU regime of tight immigration controls will lead to a more controlled and policed society with increased surveillance of individuals and of certain geographical areas. In the United States, civil liberties concerns have acted as a constraint on certain forms of immigration control, and this is likely to also be the case in Europe.

Second, border controls necessarily vary according to the nature of international economic relationships. In simple terms, the full implementation of the "Four Freedoms" (for movement of capital, labor, goods, and services) contained in the 1957 Treaty of Rome inevitably led to the abolition of all border controls, including indirect limitations on the movement of persons and goods (such as nationally determined public health controls) that could be used to exclude them. The four freedoms were the fundamental requirement of a single market; but their political subtext was the ambition, stated in the preamble to the Treaty of Rome, for "an ever closer union" between the European peoples. A free trade area, such as NAFTA, does not carry with it the same implications or express the same political ambition. The European Economic Community (EEC) negotiated in 1963 a free trade agreement with Turkey and in the early 1990s the so-called Europe Agreements, which included free trade in industrial goods, with east central European countries. All excluded agricultural products and services; none abolished controls on either persons or goods at the border, and restrictions on entry and settlement of persons remained in place. In the case of Turkey, this situation could persist indefinitely.

Third, there has been a certain deterritorialization of border controls in the sense that controls are now exercised in the consulates located in most countries of the world, by transportation companies through the use of carrier liability legislation,[22] by third countries by the pressure on east central European countries to accept Schengen norms, by internal controls on identity by police and other public services, and by the Schengen external frontier and its associated arrangements. In other words, the controls that were formally concentrated at national border posts are now exercised by a variety of means. Also, immigration diplomacy to seek the cooperation of countries from which immigrants originate is becoming increasingly important for the EU and the United States as a means of controlling migration flows (see Mohar and Alcaraz, this volume). The fundamental difference between Europe and North America is that in the latter region no general agreement exists in NAFTA to cover all aspects of border controls. Such an agreement necessarily involves systematic police and judicial cooperation, as well as general policy coordination, both of which lie far beyond any existing political ambitions.

Fourth, the effectiveness of border controls on persons is open to question.[23] The United States and the EU share a similar problem of immigration crises provoked by political persecution, penury, and violence in other countries. Also, there are large numbers of undocumented immigrants in both the United States and the EU. Ways of dealing with this latter issue have varied across Europe. Some clandestine immigrants have been accepted as residents by large-scale amnesties in France, Italy, and Greece. Others have managed to establish themselves in countries, particularly in Germany, which have relied on the review of individual cases, by finding work and raising families while the system for processing their dossiers has been clogged by the numbers of asylum seekers/clandestine immigrants. They acquired entitlements by unauthorized residence and establishment. Many illegal immigrants enter on tourist visas and disappear in the informal economy. Uniformly stringent enforcement of controls is too disruptive and too threatening to human rights. Moreover, it runs counter to certain powerful economic interests. In the United States, some sectors in various areas of the country would suffer without illegal Mexican immigration (see Spener, this volume); this is also true for certain sectors in southern Europe. In the absence of effective controls, a certain myth of control is substituted. This myth is necessary to sustain the legitimacy of the EU and its member states.

Fifth, the modern state is inextricably bound to a clearly defined territory as well as a clearly defined membership. The clearly delimited territories of the modern state are of recent origin and there is no reason, in principle, why they should persist indefinitely. But we cannot, despite the progress of European integration, envisage a system in which all the security, protections, services, and benefits provided by the modern state can be organized without delimited territories. Health, education, and welfare services are provided within given territories to people who reside there and who are accorded rights of access to these services. Internal security and legal protections are guaranteed by the territorial state. In the EU, by contrast with the United States, this situation is evolving because responsibility for access to territory is being shared and an internal "security community" is being built. The extent to which the state can or must lose control of its regalian functions, in particular the police function, remains uncertain and controversial. However the "decoupling" of police from the state has, in Europe, become an issue for discussion.[24] The nature of the debate in North America is very different because it focuses more on the extraterritorial operations of U.S. law enforcement agencies.

Sixth, the concentration of frontier functions on the linear state border is beginning to break down in obvious ways such as the transfer of national border controls to the EU external border (and where possible to the borders of neighboring states) and the embryonic federalization of police cooperation. There are also less obvious ways—Thomas Faist has argued that the boundaries of welfare provision no longer correspond with the borders of the state, with the establishment of supranational rights and the different regimes for third country nationals within the EU.[25] Different frontiers are being established, in terms of direct or indirect effects of decisions, for different areas of policy. This is also happening in North America because, as Mexicans and Canadians are often sensitively aware, policy decisions taken in the United States have a direct impact on them.

Seventh, a normative debate has begun on the criteria for admission of persons to the EU, whether access to citizenship should be facilitated and made subject to common rules, whether immigrants officially resident in the EU should be able to move freely between the member states, and whether the civil liberties of immigrants should be more adequately protected. Without the implementation of common rules in these areas, EU immigration policy will remain an aspiration. The different traditions and different current practices make this a particularly difficult debate because national identities are strong and national sentiments are easily stirred. However, EU countries are committed to movement toward a common immigration policy—in NAFTA, this is considered as neither possible nor desirable.

These points show some overlap between European and North American concerns, but also that the debate in Europe is both wider and deeper because of the nature of the EU. The main analogy between the EU and North America is the problem of control of persons at the southern border of the United States and the external border of the EU. One feature of the U.S.–Mexico border experience that is almost bound to be reflected in Europe is that drives toward strengthening border controls in some places simply have a displacement effect—illegal immigrants are diverted to those sectors of the border where the enhanced controls are not in place (Spener, this volume). The U.S.–Caribbean sea frontier shows precise parallels with the EU Mediterranean frontier—persistent immigration pressure punctuated by crises (see Mitchell, this volume). What Nevins describes as the "NAFTAization" of the U.S.–Mexico border—the promotion of "extra-territorial opportunities for national territory-based capital" while "attempting to provide security against the social costs unleashed by globalization—especially immigration" approximates to what is happening between the EU and its neighbors (Nevins, this volume). Encouraging cross-border economic flows while enforcing strict border controls on persons is a delicate political task and one shared by the United States and the EU.

In general, however, in other regional groupings, where there is an explicit adoption of the EU model (such as MERCOSUR and the West African Economic Community), closer parallels with European border controls may eventually develop, although in both these cases there is still a long road to travel. In the nineteenth and first half of the twentieth centuries, ideas of state sovereignty and territoriality (and therefore of border controls) were diffused from Europe to the rest of the world. However, it is far from inevitable that European precedents will have the same trajectory in the future.

NOTES

1. Malcolm Anderson, *Frontiers. Territory and State Formation in the Modern World* (Cambridge: Polity, 1996), 34–36.

2. Malcolm Anderson, "Transfrontier Co-Operation—History and Theory," in *Grenzüberschreitende Zusammenarbeit in Europa. Theorie-Empirie-Praxis,* G. Brunn, Peter Schmitt-Egner, eds. (Baden Baden: Nomos, 1998); Malcolm Anderson, "Transfrontier Co-Operation: and Assessment," in *North European and Baltic Integration Yearbook* (Berlin: Springer Verlag, 2000).

3. The history of border controls remains to be written. A study of the wording of documents, formalities at the border, the signs and symbols used to demarcate territory, and the organization and control of agencies that police the border would reveal the symbolic representations of state authority. For an important contribution to this field see John Torpey, *The Invention of the Passport: Surveillance, Citizenship and the State* (New York: Cambridge University Press, 1999).

4. Roger Dion, *Les Frontières de la France* (Paris: Hachette, 1947), 6.

5. The China–Korea frontier consisted of a band of territory between fifty and ninety kilometers across which, although it had at one time been settled and cultivated, crossing was forbidden to both Koreans and Chinese. Death was the penalty for settling in this zone. Although vagabonds, outlaws, and itinerants were occasionally to be found there, it achieved its purpose of dividing Chinese and Koreans. This separation was a deliberate attempt to put an end to the interminable wars between the two peoples who, according to Richthofen, had as a result become so distant from one another that they had no accurate image of the physical appearance of the other—in the frontier region of China, Chinese people thought that Richthofen might be Korean. Ferdinand von Richthofen, *Entdeckungsreisen in China: 1868–1872: die Ersterforschung des Reiches der Mitte,* K.-D. von Petersen, ed. (Darmstadt: Wiss. Buchges, 1984).

6. For example, East German border guards always insisted on a list of addresses that would be visited and, if a foreigner were in transit, the border guards would make a reservation at special hotels. This was not the case in Poland. At least after 1960, checks on literature carried by foreigners was much stricter at East German, Soviet, and even Czech borders than it was in Poland and Hungary.

7. Hélène Ahrweiler, *Byzance et la mer* (Paris: Presses Universitaires Françaises, 1966); K. N. Ciggaar, *Western Travellers to Constantinople: the West and Byzantium 962–1204* (Leiden: E. J. Brill, 1996).

8. It was not completed until the second half of the nineteenth century in some places. For Germany, see John Breuilly, *The Formation of the First German Nation-State, 1800–1971* (London: Macmillan, 1996); John Breuilly, "Sovereignty, Citizenship and Nationality: Reflections on the Case of Germany," *The Frontiers of Europe,* in Malcolm Anderson and Eberhard Bort, eds. (London: Pinter, 1998), 36–67.

9. This was the historical precedent to which Winston Churchill and Ernest Bevin, both born in the nineteenth century, looked to in the dark days of World War II and its immediate aftermath. In a minute to Foreign Secretary Anthony Eden in 1942, Churchill suggested that there should be unrestricted travel in Europe after the war. Ernest Bevin, when asked what was his policy when he arrived in office in 1945, replied that he had only one: "to be able to buy a ticket at Victoria Station and go where I damned well please [without a passport]."

10. Malcolm Anderson et al., *Policing the European Union: Theory, Law and Practice* (Oxford: Clarendon, 1996); Didier Bigo, *Polices en Réseaux: l'Expérience Européenne* (Paris: Presses de Sciences Po, 1996).

11. Didier Bigo, "Security, Borders and the State," in *Borders and Border Regions in Europe and North America,* Paul Ganster et al., eds. (San Diego: San Diego University Press, 1997), 27–46.

12. Ole Waever et al., *Identity, Migration and the New Security Agenda in Europe* (London: Pinter, 1998); Jef Huysmans, "Dire et écrire la sécurité: le dilemme normatif des études de sécurité," *Cultures et Conflits,* nos. 31–32 (1998): 177–204.

13. Monica den Boer, ed., *Schengen's Final Days? The Incorporation of Schengen into the New TEU, External Borders and Information Systems* (Maastricht: European Institute of Public Administration, 1998); Monica den Boer, "The Incorporation of Schengen into the TEU: A Bridge too Far?" in Jens Monar and Wolfgang Wessels, eds., *The Treaty of Amsterdam; Challenges and Opportunities for the European Union* (London: Pinter, 2000).

14. There was difficulty in discovering the content of the Schengen *acquis.* See House of Lords, Select Committee on the European Communities, Session 1997–98 31st Report, *Incorporating the Schengen Acquis into the European Union* (The Stationary Office, 1998). A deadline of May 1, 1999, was set for incorporating the *acquis* into the treaty framework. The dispute between Britain and Spain over Gibraltar prevented the fulfillment of the original intention—the integration into Pillar I of the Schengen *acquis,* concerning free movement, immigration, and asylum, and the publication of the whole of the *acquis.* Elements of the Schengen *acquis* have—by virtue of a compromise typical of the EU—been scattered around in the Amsterdam Treaty. See, for example, OJ L 176, 10.7.99 (Council Decision of May 20, 1999). Charles Elsen has gathered together the Schengen *acquis,* which is available at public.info@consilium.eu.int "The Schengen *acquis* integrated into the European Union" (Council of the European Union General Secretariat, May 1, 1999).

15. The controls on goods were abolished through the EU "1992 programme" before Schengen was implemented.

16. In June 1998, the Schengen Executive Committee decided that certain Schengen documents should remain confidential. These included some decisions and declarations of the Executive Committee, some declarations of the Central Control Group, three annexes to the Common Visa Instructions, the SIRENE manual, three documents on the controlled delivery of drugs, and the strengthened external frontier guidelines. These moves toward official secrecy mark an important step toward the development of state-like characteristics in the EU.

17. The southern frontier mainly posed problems of control of migration and the spilling over of political violence from Algeria into France. There are also wider political issues concerning the maintenance of cooperative relations with countries on the southern shore of the Mediterranean while preventing the immigration of their nationals (*The Frontiers of Europe,* Malcolm Anderson and Eberhard Bort, eds.).

18. Allegations that Italian organized crime was investing in Slovenian casino and tourist developments had little to do with border controls, although the different regulatory regime in Slovenia could facilitate these investments.

19. Roberto Leo, "Schengen and Its Daily Practice on the Borders. The Particular Situation in Friuli Venezia Giulia," in *Schengen and the Southern Frontier of the European Union,* Malcolm Anderson and Eberhard Bort, eds. (Edinburgh: ISSI, 1998), 109–112.

20. *Bulletin Quotodien Europe,* February 26, 1999.

21. This also caused some real problems. Economic relations between Poland and Belarus were disrupted, with adverse effects on a relatively poor Polish region. Poland has also had historically close relations with Ukraine. The relations between Hungary and Hungarian minorities in Slovakia, Romania, and Serbia will be adversely affected by the imposition of the full rigor of the Schengen norms.

22. States imposing duties on carriers to verify the identity of passengers dates from the nineteenth century (Torpey, this volume) but shifting responsibility to nonstate actors for the implementation of immigration rules has only become general practice in the last two decades (Lahav and Guiraudon, this volume).

23. Didier Bigo, "Frontiers and Security in the European Union," in *The Frontiers of Europe,* Malcolm Anderson and Eberhard Bort, eds., 148–164; Russell King, "The Mediterranean: Europe's Rio Grande," in *The Frontiers of Europe,* Anderson and Bort, eds., 134; Russell King, "Towards a Pattern of Immigration into Southern Europe," in *Schengen and the Southern Frontier of the Europe Union,* Anderson and Bort, eds., 115–140; Koslowski, this volume.

24. Neil Walker, "The New Frontiers of European Policing," in *The Frontiers of Europe,* Anderson and Bort, eds., 165–186.

25. Thomas Faist, "Boundaries of Welfare States; Immigrants and Social Rights on the National and Supranational Levels," in *Migration and European Integration. The Dynamics of Inclusion and Exclusion,* Robert Miles and Dietricht Thränhardt, eds. (London: Pinter, 1995), 177–195.

3

States and the Regulation of Migration in the Twentieth-Century North Atlantic World

John Torpey

The enthusiastic reception recently accorded by many social scientists to the notion of "globalization" has been accompanied by a postmodern preoccupation with the fragmentation and proliferation of identities, and the corresponding sense that nation-states—as institutions capable of guarding their borders, bounding political communities, and commanding people's supreme political loyalties—are moribund. The claim about the decline of nation–states is frequently linked to the observation that the "hypermobility" of capital means that states are increasingly powerless to control their own economic futures. Indeed, some of this literature seems intent on updating Marx's dictum about the contradiction between the burgeoning capitalist forces and the retrograde feudal relations of production as an analysis of the fate of states in the contemporary world.[1] Those inclined toward these views argue that there is now afoot an irresistible global surge of voluntary migration, and that borders have been rendered largely irrelevant in the face of economic incentives that exert an overwhelming power of attraction on people from the world's more unfortunate areas. This baneful situation is exacerbated by the fact that, having once arrived, those people can claim the rights of citizens without actually being such and can only rarely be returned to their countries of origin, no matter which of the receiving countries' laws they may have violated.[2]

I want to suggest in what follows that this definition of the contemporary situation concerning international migration is misguided, at least in certain respects. Without question, the sluices of international migration have opened for many groups who were previously largely absent from the migratory stream, with the result that perhaps 120 million people, or roughly 2 percent of the world's population, can be counted as international migrants; their destinations tend to be more diverse than ever before, despite a pronounced preference for the countries of the "core" of the world system; and the saliency of "human rights" as an element in the interest calculus of liberal-democratic states, and thus as a constraint on state actions that may facilitate the arrival and persistence on their territories of noncitizens, has grown over time.[3]

But these incontrovertible facts should not be confused with a decline in "core" states' capacity, or their willingness, to police their borders and to restrict the movements of persons across them, or to regulate access to the rights of citizenship, when they choose to do so. As Gary Freeman has wryly put it, "Anyone who thinks differently should try landing at Sydney airport without an entry visa or go to France and apply for a job without a work permit."[4] Nor should these developments be regarded as a sign that the activities of states play a substantially declining role—relative to individual preferences and market forces—in shaping migratory flows. From a longer historical perspective than that typically adopted by those caught up in the "business school jargon"[5] of "globalization," we need to examine not why so many are moving and relocating (more or less) permanently, but so few.

Any adequate understanding of contemporary migration patterns in and around the "core" of the world system must therefore attend not just to economic processes and developments, but to the interests, policies, and activities of states as well. It should be emphasized at the outset, however, that these activities need not necessarily be consistent with one another or without unintended consequences, for the recent history of immigration to the North Atlantic world has been replete with unanticipated twists and turns. The potentially contradictory aspects of states' migration postures derive in part from the fact that "states" are not monolithic, but only the more or less well-coordinated executors of the desires of a conglomeration of diverse and competing interests.[6] Despite considerable opposition to large-scale immigration as expressed in public opinion polls in the countries of the North Atlantic world, for example, mounting evidence suggests that these preferences are routinely ignored by their governments, and that this reality is an important part of the explanation for the expansion of the rights of noncitizen residents in recent years.[7] Moreover, as Christian Joppke has recently noted, the perception that state sovereignty is being undermined by human rights constraints derives in substantial part from the fact that immigration into and asylum seeking in the states of the North Atlantic world "have activated the contradiction between the universalistic rights dimension and the particularistic identity dimension of nation–states."[8] In this sense, Joppke argues that the sovereignty of liberal-democratic states is inherently "self-limited"[9] in consequence of the tensions in such foundational documents as the Declaration of the Rights of Man and Citizen. Recent changes in the source regions of migrants to the "core" of the world system also have taken place against the background of a prior period of state actions designed to sharply limit access to non-white outsiders. Earlier restrictionism has thus artificially heightened the sense among the indigenous populations of the North Atlantic countries of the strangeness of many recent newcomers.

Our chief concern will be with states' efforts to circumscribe their populations and to regulate their borders in order to do so. The prerogative of determining who does and does not belong, which Hannah Arendt described as a central attribute of sovereignty a half century ago, remains so today.[10] Yet under certain conditions states may regard it as in their interest to voluntarily cede certain elements of their sovereignty to other entities. This should remind us that "sovereignty" is not and never has been an absolute quantity from which any subtraction must be regarded as a loss. To paraphrase Marx, states make their own policies, but they do not make them just as they please, "but under circumstances directly found, given, and transmitted" *from the outside.*[11]

During the period following World War II, many European states have thus deemed it desirable to "pool" some elements of their sovereignty in the European Union (EU) in the interests both of military-political reconciliation and of competing more effectively with their political-economic rivals, especially North America and Japan. Those states did not, in the process, relinquish their sovereignty, particularly their concern with regulating their borders; they merely modified the manner in which and the agencies through which that sovereignty was exercised. To be sure, the constraints imposed by EU institutions and agreements may lead to a curtailment of states' freedom to behave as they wish; this is one reason for the persistent British skepticism about the EU. Yet participation in the EU may strengthen attributes traditionally associated with sovereignty. Patrick Weil has noted that France has a strong "technical" interest in the execution of the Schengen Accords, which strive to create a region of borderless movement for citizens of EU member states, because "if the accord is properly implemented, France will be the primary beneficiary, with the border police of the other Schengen nations essentially screening all incoming visitors long before they reach France's land borders."[12]

Here it is necessary to introduce some distinctions, the lack of which tends to muddle analysis of contemporary states' activities with respect to "border control." Much of the discussion about immigration control concerns the ability of states to regulate *movement.* The stress here is on states' ability to locate, identify, and constrain the mobility of people (potentially) in motion, and this tends to focus attention on the extent and controllability of illegal immigration—whether this occurs by way of the surreptitious crossing of borders or the willful violation of visa stipulations (each of which accounts for approximately half of the illegal immigrants in the United States). But this is a very different problem from migrants' ability, once having entered, to *establish* themselves—to live, work, and persist in a particular territory, and perhaps ultimately to acquire full citizenship.

These two dimensions of "state control of borders" reflect the fact that states are at once *territorial* and *membership* associations.[13] The first dimension, *territorial access,* chiefly raises questions about the *capacity* of states to identify citizens, distinguish them from noncitizens, and regulate their movements in keeping with policy objectives. The second dimension, *establishment,* concerns the extent to which states may be able to exclude noncitizens from opportunities for work, social services, or simply unperturbed existence once they have already entered the territory. The two dimensions often overlap, of course, but they may be usefully distinguished for analytic purposes.

I will argue below that, seen from a longer perspective than that usually adopted by social scientists who study migration, the capacity of the states of the North Atlantic world to distinguish between citizens and noncitizens and to track the movements of both are now dramatically greater than they were, say, 100 years ago, and show no signs of diminishing. With respect to the issue of establishment, I agree with those who argue that the freedom of nonnationals to establish themselves and enjoy civil and social citizenship (a.k.a. "human") rights has grown during the post–World War II era, and that family unification policies have led to a substantial unexpected increase in permanent immigration in some countries. But I disagree that these developments should be regarded as instances of "policy failure" or loss of control over borders. Indeed, such experiences have sharpened the keenness of states (and suprastate entities such as the EU) to implement more effective border controls.

To put it rather crudely, the argument has heretofore been framed in terms of "*Brubaker* v. *Soysal*," as if only the "neonational" or "postnational" positions could be correct. In fact, what is happening is that both positions are valid in certain respects. It is precisely the development of patterns of membership that facilitate the establishment of noncitizens without their political incorporation in the states of the North Atlantic world that has stimulated a greater preoccupation on the part of states to enhance their capacity to regulate their borders. To the extent that there has been an expansion of nonnationals' ability to establish themselves on the territories of numerous states in the "core" of the world system, however, we should consider the implications of the fact that these countries now house substantial populations endowed with some, but not all of the rights normally associated with citizenship—lacking political rights, in particular.

In what follows, I first examine how states developed the authority to regulate movement and establishment, and then consider in broad outline the consequences of states' activities for migratory patterns in the twentieth-century North Atlantic world.

MONOPOLIZING THE LEGITIMATE MEANS OF MOVEMENT

In a well-known formulation, Max Weber argued that the modern state should be defined as an agency "that (successfully) claims the *monopoly of the legitimate use of physical force* within a given territory."[14] The notion of a *monopoly* on the legitimate use of force within a specific territory is meant to contrast with the situation, for example, in medieval Europe, where a variety of competing powers created a political geography of "inextricably superimposed and tangled" suzerainties, from which no international system of nominally equal states could emerge.[15] The achievement of this putative equality involved a gradual process whereby states claimed an exclusive "embrace" of their own subjects and the right to exclude all but those subjects from entry into their territories. In the course of securing for themselves the authority to "retain" their own citizens and to deny entry to those of other countries, modern states, and the international state system of which they are a part, expropriated from individuals, churches, and other private entities the legitimate "means of movement," particularly, though by no means exclusively, across international boundaries. This monopoly on the legitimate means of movement has been an essential corollary of the monopoly on the legitimate use of coercion in a world of states defined as nation–states.[16]

States have sought to monopolize the right to authorize the movements of persons—and to establish their identities in order to enforce this authority—for a great variety of reasons. In particular, states have been concerned with supervising the growth, spatial distribution, and social composition of their populations and with regulating access to whatever "public goods" may be on offer in their territories. These aims reflect the ambiguous nature of contemporary states, which are at once agencies of domination serving particular interests and organizations that may promote the security and well being of their members.

States' efforts to monopolize the legitimate means of movement have involved a number of mutually reinforcing aspects: the gradual definition of states everywhere as "national" (i.e., as "nation–states" comprising members understood as nationals); the codification of laws establishing which types of persons may move within or across their borders, and determining how, when, and where they may do so; the stimulation of the worldwide development of techniques for uniquely and unambiguously identifying each and every person on the face of the globe, from birth to death; the construction of bureaucracies designed to implement this regime of identification and to scrutinize persons and documents in order to verify identities; and the creation of a body of legal norms designed to adjudicate claims by individuals to entry into particular spaces and territories.

To be sure, despotisms everywhere frequently placed controls on movement before the modern period, but these states generally lacked the extensive administrative infrastructure necessary to carry out such regulation in a pervasive and systematic fashion. The *successful* monopolization of the legitimate means of movement by states had to await the creation of elaborate bureaucracies and technologies that only gradually came into existence, a trend that intensified dramatically toward the end of the nineteenth century. The process required the development of "cards" and "codes" that sought to identify people unambiguously and to distinguish among them for administrative purposes.[17] Such documents had existed previously, of course, but their more or less uniform dissemination throughout whole societies in the form of "ID," and the emergence of a worldwide expectation that people crossing borders would have "proper papers" (normally the passport), would be some time in coming.

Let me make clear that I am not arguing that states and the state system *actually* control all movements of persons, but only that they have monopolized the authority to restrict movement vis-à-vis other potential claimants, such as private economic or religious entities. Such entities may play a role in the control of movement, but they do so today at the behest of states. John Meyer has put the point succinctly: "A worker may properly be kept from crossing state boundaries, and may even be kept from crossing firm boundaries by the state, but not by the firm."[18] More precisely, firms may keep a worker from crossing the boundaries of the firm, but they do so under authority granted them by the state. Things have not always been this way. Where the right to authorize movement was controlled by particular social groups before the coalescence of the modern state system (and indeed in certain places until well after that system had come into being), these groups were as often private entities as political authorities. Indentured servants' mobility, for example, was under the control of their masters. Serfs' legal capacity to move rested in the hands of their landlords, who had jurisdiction over them. The slave system in the Americas and elsewhere entailed that slaveholders held the power to grant their slaves the freedom to move about.[19]

As modern states advanced and systems of forced labor such as slavery and serfdom declined, however, states and the international state system stripped private entities of the power to authorize and forbid movement and gathered that power unto themselves. The process through which states monopolized the legitimate means of movement thus took hundreds of years to come to fruition. It followed the shift of orientations from the local to the "national" level that accompanied the development of national states out of the panoply of empires, smaller city-states, and principalities that dotted the map of early modern Europe.[20] The process also paralleled the "nationalization" of poor relief, for communal obligations to provide such relief had been an important source of the desire for restraints on movement. Previously in the domain of private and religious organizations, the administration of poor relief gradually came to be removed from their purview and lodged in that of states. As European states declined in number, grew in size, and fostered large-scale markets for wage labor outside the reach of landowners and against the traditional constraints imposed by localities, the provision of poor relief also moved from the local to the national arena.[21] These processes, in turn, helped to expand "outward" to the national borders the areas in which persons could expect to move freely and without authorization. Eventually, the boundaries that counted most were those not of municipalities, but of nation–states.

My argument should not be confused with the claim that private actors now play no role in the regulation of movement—far from it. Yet private entities have been reduced to playing the role of "sheriff's deputies" who participate in the regulation of movement at the bidding of states. During the nineteenth and into the twentieth century, for example, governments in Europe pressed steamship companies into overseeing for them whether particular people should be permitted to travel to the destinations they had chosen. For example, an Italian passport law adopted in 1901 required all persons wishing to embark upon a transatlantic voyage to produce a passport before they were permitted to purchase steamship tickets.[22] Since the development of air travel, airline companies have been forced to fulfill similar obligations. Both shipping enterprises and air carriers have frequently resisted carrying out the sheriff's deputy function, however, mainly because they fear that their participation in such quasi-governmental activities will hurt their profitability. Not wanting to appear merely greedy, they are likely to say that they regard the regulation of movement as the province of the state—as indeed it is.[23]

In order to *implement* their monopoly on the legitimate means of movement, states must develop techniques to carry out the restrictions they adopt in this domain. That is, they must be able to construct an enduring relationship between the sundry agencies that constitute states and both the individuals they govern and possible interlopers. In other words, states must be able to determine who is eligible to cross their borders and to partake of social welfare benefits and other advantages available within the territory. Documents such as passports and identity cards, along with elaborate registration and information systems, have been crucial in states' efforts to sort out "who is who" and, more importantly, "what is what" in order to determine such eligibility. As Michael Mann has noted, the "unusual strength of modern states is infrastructural,"[24] and their capacity to identify their own subjects and to exclude unwanted others are the essence of that infrastructural power.

With the growth of social benefits and public goods more generally in the countries of the "core" of the world system by the late nineteenth century, these countries became both more attractive to others and more intent on restricting access to these advantages.[25] Nation–states—states of and for particular "peoples" defined as mutually exclusive groups of citizens[26]—thus crystallized roughly during the period of 1880–1920 through their efforts to sharply circumscribe their populations and to regulate the movements of persons across their borders more vigorously in terms of nationality. There was inevitably, of course, a certain amount of "seepage" of undesirable groups into national stocks, and what George Fredrickson once called "the anarchic nature of the human libido" posed intractable problems for those intent upon policing ethnonational boundaries. Those states seeking to restrict access to their domains or to their citizenship were nonetheless remarkably successful in doing so, with the result that foreign-born populations declined dramatically in certain countries. I now turn to an examination of the role of states in regulating migration in the twentieth-century North Atlantic world.

STATES AND MIGRATION IN THE TWENTIETH-CENTURY NORTH ATLANTIC WORLD

Although they have hardly become completely airtight, during the twentieth-century states have become considerably more successful than before in regulating population movements and constraining outsiders from crossing borders without authorization.

More broadly, states and their activities have decisively shaped the larger patterns of population movements in this century both by stimulating migration and by closing it off.

The period culminating in World War I and the subsequent interwar period saw the erection of high barriers to immigration in the United States and much of western Europe. Perhaps best known in this regard is the adoption by the United States in the 1920s of nationality-based quotas that sharply reduced immigration from Europe. Yet these laws only broadened a virtually complete bar against entry-and-establishment from Asia that had been gradually put in place during the preceding half century.[27] A crucial element of this restrictionist thrust in the United States was the development of a system of "remote control," whereby American consular officers in the country of departure assumed the responsibility for determining whether travelers and intending emigrants would be admitted upon their arrival on the shores of North America. The system operated so effectively that Ellis Island, the chief immigration inspection station in the United States since it was first put into service in the early 1890s, rapidly declined in usefulness and was eventually mothballed in 1954.[28]

Many European countries, too, adopted measures to stem or at least to regulate immigration during the years between the world wars. Wartime limitations on movement that had initially been instituted on a temporary basis gradually proved to be permanent.[29] Contrary to assumptions that its liberalism might lead it to be more resistant to restrictionism, the United Kingdom sought to constrain immigration long before the war and proved quite successful in doing so. Having begun to implement restrictive immigration policies as early as 1905 in nervous anticipation of an influx of Jews fleeing pogroms and revolution in eastern Europe, Britain had a foreign population (excluding those of Irish descent) of only 1 percent in 1930. The major exception to the interwar restrictionist wave was France, which welcomed foreigners as a way of making up for low population growth rates and the population losses it had suffered from World War I. Many of those who might have gone to Britain thus immigrated to France instead; this process of "deflection" constitutes a more general feature of migration patterns governed by the decisions of states about whom they wish to enter and whom they do not.[30] The resurrection of now-hoary restrictions on *exit* following the emergence of numerous authoritarian regimes— especially those in the Soviet Union, Italy, and Germany—further contributed to a climate of very low migration during the interwar years. As a result of these constraints on exit and on entry, "the great rivers of international migration [of the prewar years] dried to trickles."[31] This parching of the migrant streams helped to create an utterly unrealistic norm of "zero immigration" and corresponding nativist propensities among wide segments of the populations of the North Atlantic world's immigrant-receiving states (as well as that of Australia).

The advent of Nazi rule in Germany and the ensuing World War II brought on a whole series of new population movements. Despite its ferocity, however, the Nazi attempt to conquer Europe produced relatively small numbers of migrants, for several reasons. The potential receiving countries demonstrated little enthusiasm for accepting large numbers of Jews, as evidenced by the failure of the Evian Conference in June 1938 to resolve the problem of growing numbers of German and Austrian emigrants. Next, most of those who came to be trapped within German-controlled Europe after the onset of war in 1939 never had the opportunity to become refugees and never "imagined . . . that they would be murdered in history's greatest genocide."[32] During the war, of course, millions of Jews underwent deportations that ended in death rather than migration. The overall number of those displaced during World War II has been estimated at approximately 30 million, of whom some 11 million were outside their countries of origin at war's end. The principal movements of refugees following the cessation of general hostilities involved a group of roughly 13 million German expellees from eastern Europe, most of whom quickly found refuge in the territory of the two German states then in the process of formation. Yet postwar conflicts in such countries as Greece and Poland generated further flows that kept the refugee streams supplied with new recruits.[33]

The end of World War II marked the beginning of a major shift in the patterns of migration to northern and western Europe (increasingly understood as "the North"), the sources of which were now more frequently to be found in the poorer "South" than had previously been the case. The countries of northwestern Europe drew their new postwar population intakes chiefly from two sources: the immediate Mediterranean periphery and their own (former) colonial possessions. The prime example of the former pattern emerged in West Germany, which had been stripped of its colonial possessions in the Versailles peace settlement following World War I and therefore lacked the relevant ties to overseas populations. In their place, guest-worker programs brought 2.6 million Turks, Italians, Spaniards, Yugoslavs, and others to the country by 1973. Despite France's colonial connections, however, even France (through its *Office National d'Immigration*) recruited by 1970 some 2 million workers and 700,000 of their dependents, mainly from southern Europe.[34]

Meanwhile, changes in the relationship between the European metropoles and their colonies enabled large numbers to move from other areas of the "South" to Europe. Thus hundreds of thousands of Africans from both above and below the Sahara entered France by the early 1970s, along with a smaller number of "immigrants" from the *departements d'outre mer* who went uncounted because they were in fact citizens of France (but whose numbers have been estimated at around 250,000–300,000 as of 1972). Similarly, Britain absorbed large numbers of workers from the freshly independent countries of the New Commonwealth in the Caribbean, the Indian subcontinent, and Africa. From a figure of 541,000 in 1961, the population of those in Britain of New Commonwealth origins tripled to 1.5 million by 1981. This rate of increase was slowed considerably by the Commonwealth Immigrants Act of 1962, which sharply curtailed immigration from these regions, and the 1971 Immigration Act, which tightened previously liberal family unification provisions. Again, between 1945 and the early 1960s, the Netherlands likewise took in some 300,000 "repatriates" from the Dutch East Indies (now Indonesia).

Although Dutch citizens, many of those returning from the Netherlands' overseas possessions were of mixed ancestry.[35] These new immigrant populations, overwhelmingly nonwhite except for those returning colonial settlers and their descendants who had remained genetically aloof from the natives, transformed the face of these societies within a generation.

With an eye to the gap in wealth between sending and receiving countries and the post-World War II labor needs of the latter, it has been said that "foreign worker migrations to western Europe [during 1945–73] were caused primarily by economic considerations on the part of migrants, employers, and governments."[36] While this explanation accounts in part for the migration patterns in this period, there is considerably more to the story. The massive die-off (estimated at perhaps 55 million in Europe)[37] and widespread devastation brought about by World War II generated a great need for workers, to be sure. But it was the Marshall Plan subsidizing reconstruction in Germany, with the aim of transforming that country from an unpredictable enemy into a reliable ally, that made the hypothetical demand for labor an *effective* demand there. The large-scale importation of workers from the European periphery and beyond after World War II cannot be ascribed "primarily" to mere "economic considerations," for this completely obscures the context in which it occurred—namely, the demographic decline caused by the war and the political decision of the United States to finance the development of a flourishing, capitalist western Europe as a bulwark against Communism. The U.S.S.R had suffered the brunt of the wartime casualties—estimated at more than 25 million deaths[38]—and yet neither it nor its postwar satellites became substantial importers of labor. The reasons for this difference were primarily political, not economic.

In the United States during this period, immigration remained very small as a result of the low rates of admission of those from overseas that were established by the legislative initiatives of the 1920s and before (out of deference to employer interests, immigration from within the western hemisphere had been exempted from these restrictive policies).[39] As a result of these exclusionary laws, the percentage of foreign-born in the United States fell by around 1970 from its 1910 peak of 15 percent to only 5 percent, a level that had not been witnessed since the early nineteenth century.[40] The prohibitions on immigration with respect to those from overseas, as well as the de facto cut-off of immigration during World War I, helped to determine the timing of the "Great Black Migration," in the course of which millions of African Americans were drawn out of the agricultural South and into the industries of the Northeast and the Midwest. The legislation discriminating against unwanted outsiders thus helped to precipitate a massive population shift of the unwanted within, giving them for the first time any substantial toehold in the American middle class.

A further notable aspect of this constellation was that the importation of Mexicans—who had long been used as a substitute for the Chinese and other Asians who had been progressively excluded from immigration since the late nineteenth century—played a critical role in shoring up labor needs in agriculture, particularly in the Southwest. The *bracero* program, an operation run by the U.S. Departments of State, Labor, and Justice and mainly concerned to insure a reliable flow of seasonal employees, brought in some 5 million Mexican contract workers between the 1940s and the early 1960s.[41] Still, the government was able to reverse this flow if it wished. One million Mexicans were deported in 1954 in the course of "Operation Wetback," a program that replaced illegal aliens with legal *braceros* and that "had the effect of buttressing and entrenching a system of contract labor that was uniquely suited to agricultural production."[42]

Soon after the end of the *bracero* program, the immigration reforms of the 1965 Hart–Celler Act, reflecting the general fervor in support of civil rights and against racial discrimination, abolished the national origins quotas that had been in place for four decades. This change in the U.S. posture toward immigrants was apparently expected by its framers to rejuvenate the traditional flows of newcomers from Europe. Yet western Europeans living in countries that were now more prosperous and politically stable had less incentive to emigrate; most of eastern Europe, on the other hand, had fallen into a zone from which exit was nearly impossible. Along with these factors, the law's privileging of family unification and occupational qualifications stimulated a massive shift in immigration patterns. As a result, Asia and Latin America became the principal sources of voluntary migration to the United States. The policy has tended to promote a bimodal distribution of new migrants to the United States, dominated by the relatively less-skilled family members of Mexicans and people from the Caribbean basin who had already gained a foothold in the country, alongside a major influx of highly educated persons from Asia and the Middle East.[43] The difficulties that many of these groups have encountered in gaining access to the "American way of life" have sparked a shift in thinking about the processes of incorporation into American society, from older notions of a relatively undifferentiated "melting pot" to a more worrisome pattern of "segmented assimilation."[44]

This bimodal distribution of the immigrant population was reinforced by the Immigration Reform and Control Act (IRCA) of 1986, which regularized the status of at least 2.7 million illegal aliens, predominantly from Mexico, who had entered clandestinely in some part because the 1965 reforms had made almost no provision for the entry of short-term agricultural laborers.[45] An important element of IRCA was that employers were to face sanctions for using illegal labor, but the provision allowing them to accept almost any documents that look genuine has tended to nullify the effect of this part of the act. Inflows of illegal workers, deriving heavily from Mexico, continue at a rate of perhaps 300,000 per year.[46] Yet under the presumption that illegal immigration had been brought under control by IRCA, the Immigration Act of 1990 foresaw a substantial rise in the numbers of those to be admitted legally into the United States. As a consequence of the 1990 law, at least 675,000 permanent entrants were to be admitted each year beginning in 1995, with approximately two-thirds of these slots allocated to those coming in under family unification provisions. Above this minimum, however, immediate relatives of U.S.

citizens may be admitted without limit; in 1995, those immigrating under this clause numbered 220,000.[47] These provisions reflected the power of ethnic and pro-immigration lobbying groups—the latter often representing employer interests—in immigration policymaking.

With slumping economic conditions following the end of the Cold War, however, these liberal policies soon gave rise to a noisy backlash against immigration. This was especially true in California, home to fully one-third of the country's foreign-born population. In 1994, voters in that state, whose aerospace and other military industries were hard hit by the surrender of the Soviet enemy, adopted a referendum (Proposition 187) barring illegal immigrants from access to public services. The Clinton administration's "welfare reform" of 1996 went so far as to deny access to various welfare benefits, such as food stamps and Supplemental Security Income (SSI), even to legal immigrant noncitizens.[48] It is widely believed that this policy had the effect of stimulating applications for citizenship, the numbers of which rose significantly in subsequent years; it also contributed to the decisions of the Dominican Republic and Mexico to recognize dual citizenship.[49] In the meantime, some of the provisions denying welfare benefits to legally resident aliens—which President Clinton had indicated he regarded as inappropriate at the time he signed the bill— have been repealed.

Using refugee policy as a tool of Cold War foreign policy, the United States also took in as refugees substantial numbers of people from communist regimes in Europe and Asia, or from fellow-traveling countries in the Americas.[50] Direct U.S. military activities intended to ward off communist takeovers during this period generated many of the population flows that were ultimately destined for the United States as refugees. Notably, in the aftermath of the Vietnam War, some 837,000 Indochinese were given refuge in the United States, including 529,000 Vietnamese, 182,000 Laotians, and 126,000 Cambodians. The Vietnamese refugees formed the node of a substantial community in Orange County, California, that is now the largest enclave of Vietnamese outside their home country. In the late 1970s, the "boat people" fleeing communist policies—or, frequently, encouraged by the regime to leave, especially if they were ethnic Chinese—were set afloat. Many of the boat people were seen in U.S. government circles as further evidence of the perfidy of communism and admitted on that basis.[51] Despite the long-standing American resistance to adopting international standards concerning refugee admissions, the Refugee Act of 1980 committed the United States to the definition of refugees enshrined in the 1951 Refugee Convention, potentially widening substantially the U.S. commitment to take in those fleeing persecution from any country, not just communist ones.

This shift in refugee policy was pushed forward by the Mariel crisis of early 1980, in which Fidel Castro permitted some 18,000 Cubans to go to the United States in a boat lift organized by the Florida Cuban community (see Mitchell, this volume). The crisis revealed that the U.S. policy of accepting virtually all refugees from communism could unintentionally abet the aims of rulers seeking to expel unwanted subjects. In the process, it "shattered what remained of the cold war consensus on refugee policy. . . . Henceforth, Cubans were no longer welcome defectors, but 'bullets aimed at Miami.'"[52] When Cuban authorities subsequently made clear that they were inclined on occasion to let off further human steam, the United States indicated that it might undertake efforts to interdict those departing in order to prevent their landing on U.S. soil. Especially with the deterioration of conditions that followed the collapse of Cuba's patron, the Soviet Union, the specter of a mass exodus loomed large in Cuban–American relations. In order to avoid further such incidents, the two governments struck a deal in mid-1994 whereby the United States would accept 20,000 immigrants per year from Cuba, regularizing their entry. Combined with the refugee crisis resulting from the military coup overthrowing Jean-Bertand Aristide in Haiti, U.S. refugee policy was in flux by the mid-1990s. This policy shift has been especially irksome to the Florida Cuban community, much of which regarded the admission of Cubans into the United States as its birthright and thus mobilized vigorously on behalf of young Elián Gonzalez when he washed ashore in late 1999.

During the high Cold War days of the 1980s, and as the obverse of the policy that smiled on refugees from communism, the United States tended to turn a blind eye toward those running from murderous regimes that were considered friends or allies, such as Guatemala and El Salvador, so that most of those fleeing these regimes who reached the United States entered the country illegally. Only toward the end of the Cold War was this policy challenged. In the *American Baptist Churches* (a.k.a. *ABC*) case, the federal government conceded de facto to having discriminated unfairly against asylum seekers from Guatemala and El Salvador, and was compelled to reopen the cases of those who had entered the country before September/October 1990. Yet denials of their applications remained much higher than those of Nicaraguans.[53]

Gradually, however, U.S. refugee policy is coming to reflect post–Cold War realities. The U.S.–led force that invaded Haiti to restore Jean-Bertrand Aristide to power set a precedent by intervening in large part to forestall ongoing mass migration. Although the 1997 Nicaraguan Adjustment and Central American Relief Act (NACARA) reinforced the disparity in the legal situation of exiles from Castro and the Sandinistas in the United States compared with that of their counterparts from Guatemala and El Salvador, a recently announced change in U.S. policy will overturn this discrepant treatment. As a result of the new law, some 190,000 Salvadorans and 50,000 Guatemalans will benefit from protection from deportation and from a presumption of extreme hardship that virtually guarantees their eligibility for permanent residency under an immigration remedy called "suspension of deportation."[54] Although this shift constitutes a recognition of the de facto establishment of these groups on American soil, had the United States' posture toward refugees been in line with international norms at the time many of these people arrived—in other words, if the United States had previously acted less as a "sovereign" state—large numbers of them might have been accepted as legitimate refugees long before.

Be that as it may, the United States increasingly accepts refugees as individuals fleeing from oppressive regimes and human rights violations rather than as defectors from regimes to which it is intransigently opposed, in part because many of the latter simply no longer exist. In sum, although it may be true that "U.S. asylum policy has evidently not shed its close linkage with foreign policy" in the postcommunist era,[55] the decline of a bipolar world political order and the emergence of broad array of new "security" threats means that the refugees admitted into the United States are likely to come from more diverse regions than was the case during the Cold War.

Next to family unification processes, illegal migration and the absorption of refugees have played the most important role in immigration patterns to western Europe since the curtailment of labor recruitment in the early 1970s. People increasingly sought to gain asylum because there was no other legal path of entry for those without close relatives in the target countries. Between 1981 and 1992, the number of asylum seekers in European Organization for Economic Cooperation and Development (OECD) countries grew from 116,000 to 695,000. Few persons crossed from East to West during the Cold War, however, as communist regimes made such departures very difficult. Asylum seekers thus increasingly came from relatively unfamiliar places outside of Europe. When the Berlin Wall fell in 1989, there was considerable fear that a mass exodus from eastern Europe would take place as 340,000 people streamed out of East Germany in 1989, headed mainly for the Federal Republic. These fears failed to materialize, however, in part because the inhabitants of other East bloc countries lacked ties to the West comparable to those between East and West Germany, and in part as a consequence of successful measures to restrict the flow.[56]

After the outbreak of the Yugoslav wars, however, refugee flows gathered new strength as some 2 million people were displaced. Because of the liberal asylum policy inscribed in its quasi constitution, the Basic Law, Germany was particularly affected. It assumed the vast majority of the refugee burden, taking in some 350,000 people; another several hundred thousand were scattered among other European countries. They were all expected to be temporary sojourners, but they sharply drove up the numbers of new asylum seekers—those seeking to stay permanently—of whom there were 438,000 in Germany in 1992. As in the United States, this dramatic increase in intakes of foreigners led to a backlash against German asylum policy. After an agonized public debate about the country's responsibilities toward refugees inherited from its past, asylum provisions were tightened. In consequence of this revision, first applications for asylum in Germany fell dramatically, to 128,000 in 1995.[57] Joppke has noted that in this instance, ironically, it was Germany's membership in the EU, whose member states were busily attempting to "harmonize" their asylum policies, that gave Germany the opportunity to recover that portion of its sovereignty that had been sacrificed in the Basic Law in atonement for the sins of the Nazi period.[58]

As with most refugee crises, however, the majority of those displaced in and from Yugoslavia have remained relatively close to their homes. This has been the case with the roughly 800,000 Kosovar refugees, only a small percentage of whom were taken out of the area by the humanitarian evacuation program coordinated by the United Nations High Commissioner for Refugees (UNHCR), with the largest numbers going to Germany and Turkey.[59] Those who went to Germany were given three-month renewable temporary protected status and were not allowed to apply for asylum.[60] The overall numbers of Kosovar refugees that various countries agreed to accept—approximately 130,000 as of late May 2000[61]—represented only about one-sixth of the total, suggesting that large numbers of Albanians would not have found refuge elsewhere even if they had left the region. In any event, as of late 1999, some 760,000 Kosovars had returned to their homes "spontaneously"—that is, without the assistance of the "international community."[62] Despite the continuing conflict in the area, therefore, the Kosovo crisis resulted in only a very limited displacement of refugees to other countries.

In recent years, flows of immigrants have also begun to develop toward European countries formerly known chiefly as countries of emigration. In Italy, for example, the size of the legal immigrant population is said to have more than tripled between 1980 and 1995, from 299,000 to almost 1 million. In addition, 500,000 illegal immigrants are estimated to have entered in 1996.[63] Italy has been an especially appealing destination for many Albanians in recent years. The most recent large-scale efflux from Albania came in 1997 when substantial numbers sought to flee deteriorating economic conditions and political chaos in the aftermath of the collapse of a nationwide Ponzi scheme. Seeking to avoid a repetition of this Albanian exodus, Italy was quick to participate in the relief operations aiding the Kosovo refugees in Albania, building one of the first refugee camps there.

These various trends and pressures place Italy in an awkward position. With one of the lowest fertility rates in Europe, Italian population growth is now entirely dependent on immigration. In addition, the highly regulated character of the Italian labor market gives employers strong incentives to hire illegal immigrant workers, who can typically be paid much less than natives.[64] At the same time, much of the recent concern about unwanted immigration within the EU has been focused on Italy as the perceived "weak link" in Europe's outer defenses against undesirables (see below). In part to demonstrate its fitness for membership in the EU, Italy has recently sought to tighten documentary requirements, penalize both illegal immigrants and migrant smugglers, and make deportations of illegals more swift and certain.[65] The enforcement of documentary and registration requirements can severely constrain the possibilities for establishment of those who have entered a country illegally. As Dita Vogel has shown, this is central to explaining the difference in the numbers of illegal aliens in Germany and the United States, respectively.[66]

The loosening of the internal borders in the EU as a result of the 1985 Schengen Accords has intensified worries among the signatories of the accord about the vulnerability of the EU's outer boundaries. These concerns have led to stepped-up efforts to coordinate migration policies, documentary requirements, and policing and information systems. The Amsterdam Treaty, which went into effect on May 1, 1999, shifts responsibility for developing EU-wide migration policies from national governments to the European Commission. As of the same date, the strictures of the Schengen Accord rather than national preferences govern the issuance of visas that give foreigners access to "Schengenland" for up to ninety days. In the area of refugee policy, the Dublin Convention outlines rules for determining which state is responsible for an asylum application, "governed by the principle that the state of entry would be responsible for any given application," with the aim of reducing so-called "asylum shopping."[67] These changes have provoked considerable concern from refugee advocates about the growing tendency to assume that asylum applications are fraudulent.

European economic integration has had important consequences for the movements of persons, facilitating mobility for those within the EU and complicating it for those from the outside (see Freudenstein, Jesien, and Vachudová, this volume). The greater coordination of policies has made it more difficult for asylum seekers to gain access to EU territory, as a result of which "more foreigners who cannot obtain visas are being smuggled into Europe, where they apply for asylum—by one estimate, 80 percent of the asylum seekers in 1999 are smuggled or arrive with false documents."[68] The increasing visibility of human smuggling operations in recent years is directly traceable to the difficulties that would-be migrants encounter in their efforts to gain access to the countries of the "core" of the world system (see Koslowski, this volume). Their willingness to pay large sums and take extreme risks in order to circumvent border controls—whether these are in the destination country itself or in its consulates and embassies in the migrants' homelands—dramatically demonstrate the effectiveness of exclusionary policies in the countries of the "North."

These policies include "remote control" techniques that, as we have seen, substantially enhance the ability of states to regulate migration (see Lahav and Guiraudon, this volume). In both the United States and Europe, it is primarily those from the countries of the poor "South" that are likely to be subjected to visa restrictions that complicate their entry. The 1986 IRCA mandated the institution of a "visa waiver" system under which the nationals of more than twenty-five countries may enter the United States without visas. The list of countries whose nationals must fulfill visa requirements in order to gain entry into the countries of the EU looks roughly similar, covering most "Third World" countries. Such visa controls are extremely effective in seeing to it that would-be immigrants never have the opportunity to test the reach of "human rights norms" in the target countries. These kinds of policies have led one seasoned observer to conclude that "the most economically developed and affluent countries are banding together to protect their privileged position in much the same way that Afrikaners and others of European descent sought to maintain their dominance in South Africa."[69] The parallel with South Africa may be somewhat overdrawn, but the preoccupation of the wealthy countries of the "North" with protecting their islands of prosperity from potential interlopers from the "South" surely is not.

Against this background, it may be salutary to compare the process of European unification to that of German unification over a century ago. During that earlier attempt to weld the German lands into a cohesive economic and political entity, one of the first steps taken by the governing elite was to *abolish* passport controls on movement within or across the boundaries first of the North German Confederation and, subsequently, of the German Empire.[70] By adopting laws guaranteeing the freedom of movement, wrote the liberal Berlin *National-Zeitung*, "we shall retain the strength and ability which grow so abundantly in our soil, and we will attract from other nations the strength and ability which can and want to contribute in our commonwealth to our welfare, honor, and might."[71] At that time, the industrialists of the Ruhr valley were eager to find hands for their burgeoning factories, and their labor demands ultimately led Germany to draw in millions of workers from its European periphery during the period before World War I.[72]

Today, in contrast, European governments find themselves confronting sustained high unemployment rates that are the source of considerable political unease.[73] Under these conditions, the states of the EU are not inclined to open their borders as did the German Empire 125 years ago. Some countries, such as Italy, nevertheless tolerate a considerable number of illegal immigrants to ensure added flexibility in an otherwise rigid labor market. Similarly, although the front door of legal entry into the United States remains well regulated (if at present fairly generously so), the United States continues its long-standing policy of a relatively unregulated "backdoor" for immigrant workers from Mexico. Far from "failing to control unwanted migration," this policy achieves more or less adequately the aim of ensuring a steady supply of cheap labor in critical economic areas.[74]

CONCLUSION

Claims that states have lost control of their borders generally rest on either or both of two arguments. First, states are said to lack the administrative capacity to control inflows of people. Second, liberal states are allegedly hamstrung by humanitarian concerns such as pressures for family unification and the growing unpalatability of restrictive measures such as deportation, with the result that growing numbers of outsiders establish themselves in the territory in contravention of immigration policy.[75]

I hope to have shown that the first concern—failure of administrative capacity to control people's movements—is overblown, and that the second, although it has substantial merit, is hardly tantamount to saying that states lack the means to close their doors to unwanted immigrants or the will to use those means when they wish to do so. The United States adopted relatively expansive immigration policies in the 1990s, but it is hardly true that the doors have been flung open and cannot now be shut. This is particularly apparent with respect to the treatment of refugees in the

United States' Caribbean backyard, toward whom there has been a shift in attitude "from invitation to interdiction."[76] Moreover, the adoption by the U.S. Congress of the draconian Illegal Immigration Reform and Immigrant Responsibility Act (IIRIRA) of 1996 has led to an upsurge of deportations to approximately 100,000 annually.[77] Meanwhile, those same European states that have been relaxing border controls internally remain quite preoccupied with excluding nonnationals of the member states. If anything, the documentary controls and other bureaucratic defenses that states have erected against unwanted immigration and illegal establishment are constantly being strengthened. There seems little doubt that migratory movements would grow dramatically if this were not the case, especially in view of cheaper intercontinental transportation, greater awareness of higher standards of living elsewhere, and growing networks that facilitate both migration and adjustment to new surroundings.

Nor should the unexpected establishment and persistence of many migrants be seen as a matter of "policy failure," and hence as evidence that borders are "out of control." To be sure, there have been *unintended consequences* of immigration policies that have led to unexpected influxes of foreigners, as well as to the opening of migration flows from unexpected sources, as has occurred since the 1965 immigration reform in the United States.[78] It should be recalled, however, that family unification policies were initially instituted in at least two prominent labor-importing countries, Germany and Switzerland, not just for humanitarian reasons but as a response to competition for labor power from other states.[79] Finally, large-scale family unification immigration to the United States has been the stated policy of the government throughout the 1990s. Whether intentionally or not, this stance has proven to be perfectly attuned to a booming economy that has absorbed labor power at an impressive rate since the early post–Cold War slump. As a result of the remarkable demand for labor, in fact, the Immigration and Naturalization Service (INS) has recently been reported to be "looking the other way" with regard to much illegal immigration.[80] In all events, while the foreign-born population of the United States has risen from around 5 percent in 1970 to roughly 10 percent in the 1990s, this compares with a figure of some 15 percent in 1910, suggesting that immigration restrictions are still not entirely without force.

What *is* worrisome is that there are significant populations of noncitizens who have established themselves on the territory of the states of the North Atlantic world who may have no economic or legal reason to acquire citizenship. Despite the fact that some immigrants may engage in politics, especially of the "homeland" variety, this situation means that there are relatively small but growing elements of these countries' resident populations that are not part of the formal political process. These persons' access to *civil* rights is perfectly consistent with the neo-liberal thrust of recent years; as T. H. Marshall pointed out some time ago, capitalism requires a formally free and mobile labor force, which civil rights guarantee. But as the 1996 immigration reform in the United States demonstrated, their access to social rights may depend crucially on their possession of political rights. It was presumably easier for President Clinton to sign a bill denying certain welfare benefits even to *legal* resident aliens, because such persons were in no position to vote against him or his party. These strictures were subsequently relaxed, to be sure, but things might work out differently in the future.

States' control over their physical borders may involve tacit acceptance of apparently "uncontrolled" flows of illegal immigrants. Their control over access to membership rights may have been modulated in recent years by the spread of human rights norms, leading to a heightened preoccupation with border controls in the states of the North Atlantic world. But they can and may well reassert that control in coming years in response to anti-immigration backlashes and conditions of economic adversity; the stock market boom can't last forever. Joppke is right to point out that those who trumpet postnational membership make a virtue of necessity, and celebrate a form of political limbo—"denizenship"—that the denizens themselves find wanting.[81] Although it is surely desirable that immigrants be accorded the decency of legal treatment equivalent to that accorded to citizens, we would do well to take more seriously the difficulties raised by the presence in the states of the North Atlantic world of considerable numbers of persons excluded from participation in democratic politics.

NOTES

1. The feudal relations of production, Marx wrote in the *Communist Manifesto*, "became so many fetters. They had to be burst asunder; they were burst asunder." The chief exponent of this view has been Saskia Sassen; see, for example, *Globalization and its Discontents* (New York: The New Press, 1998).

2. This position is forcefully argued in Wayne Cornelius, Philip L. Martin, and James F. Hollifield, eds., *Controlling Immigration: A Global Perspective* (Stanford: Stanford University Press, 1994). The now canonical statement of the "rights without citizenship" position is Yasemin Soysal, *Limits of Citizenship: Migrants and Postnational Membership in Europe* (Chicago: University of Chicago Press, 1994), but see also David Jacobson, *Rights Beyond Borders: Immigration and the Decline of Citizenship* (Baltimore: Johns Hopkins University Press, 1996).

3. On this last point, see David Jacobson, "New Border Customs: Migration and the Changing Role of the State," *UCLA Journal of International Law and Foreign Affairs* 3:2 (Fall/Winter 1998–99): 443–462. On recent global migration patterns, see Stephen Castles and Mark Miller, *The Age of Migration: International Population Movements in the Modern World*, second edition (New York: Guilford, 1998); the estimate of the world's migrant population is on pp. 4–5.

4. Gary Freeman, "The Decline of Sovereignty? Politics and Immigration Restriction in Liberal States," in *Challenge to the Nation–State: Immigration in Western Europe and the United States*, Christian Joppke, ed. (New York: Oxford University Press 1998), 93.

5. John Gray uses the phrase in his review of Russell Jacoby's *The End of Utopia* in *Los*

Angeles Times Book Review, May 23, 1999.

6. See Theda Skocpol, *States and Social Revolutions: A Comparative Analysis of France, Russia, and China* (Cambridge: Cambridge University Press, 1979), 29.

7. On these points, see Freeman, "The Decline of Sovereignty?" and Virginie Guiraudon, "Citizenship Rights for Non-Citizens: France, Germany, and the Netherlands," in Joppke, ed., *Challenge to the Nation–State*.

8. Christian Joppke, "Asylum and State Sovereignty: A Comparison of the United States, Germany, and Britain," in *Challenge to the Nation-State*, 110.

9. Christian Joppke, "Immigration Challenges the Nation–State," in *Challenge to the Nation-State*, 15ff.

10. See Hannah Arendt, *The Origins of Totalitarianism* (New York: Harcourt, Brace, 1973 [1948]), 278.

11. Marx, "The Eighteenth Brumaire of Louis Napoleon," in *The Marx-Engels Reader*, second edition, Robert Tucker, ed. (New York: Norton, 1978), 575.

12. Patrick Weil, *The State Matters: Immigration Control in Developed Countries* (New York: United Nations Department of Economic and Social Affairs, Population Division, 1998) (ESA/P/WP/146), 17.

13. See Rogers Brubaker, *Citizenship and Nationhood in France and Germany* (Cambridge, Mass.: Harvard University Press, 1992), chapter 1; see also John Crowley, "Where Does the State Actually Start? Border, Boundary & Frontier Control in Contemporary Governance," paper presented at the Annual Meeting of the International Studies Association, Minneapolis, MN, March 18–20, 1998.

14. Max Weber, "Politics as a Vocation," in *From Max Weber*, Hans Gerth and C. Wright Mills, eds. (New York: Oxford University Press, 1946), 78.

15. Perry Anderson, *Lineages of the Absolutist State* (New York: Verso, 1974), 37.

16. For a detailed discussion, see John Torpey, "Coming and Going: On the State Monopolization of the Legitimate 'Means of Movement,'" *Sociological Theory* 16:3 (November 1998): 239–259.

17. See Gérard Noiriel, *La Tyrannie du national: Le droit d'asile en Europe, 1793–1993* (Paris: Calmann-Levy, 1991) and *The French Melting Pot: Immigration, Citizenship, and National Identity*, trans. Geoffroy de Laforcade (Minneapolis: University of Minnesota Press, 1996), chapter 2. In her work on laws relating to naming, Jane Caplan speaks similarly of the emergence of a "culture of identification" during the nineteenth century. See Caplan, "'This or That Particular Person': Protocols of Identification in Nineteenth-Century Europe," in Jane Caplan and John Torpey, eds., *Documenting Individual Identity: The Development of State Practices in the Modern World* (Princeton N.J.: Princeton University Press, forthcoming).

18. John Meyer, "The World Polity and the Authority of the Nation-State," in George Thomas, et al., eds., *Institutional Structure: Constituting State, Society, and the Individual* (Newbury Park, Calif.: Sage, 1987), 53.

19. For a comparative analysis of slavery and serfdom as systems of control over movement, see Peter Kolchin, *Unfree Labor: American Slavery and Russian Serfdom* (Cambridge, Mass.: Belknap/Harvard University Press, 1987), esp. chapter 1, "Labor Management"; for a broad comparative study of slavery as entailing the "social death" of its victims, see Orlando Patterson, *Slavery and Social Death: A Comparative Study* (Cambridge: Harvard University Press, 1982).

20. On this process, see Charles Tilly, ed., *The Formation of National States in Western*

Europe (Princeton N.J.: Princeton University Press, 1975).

21. See Philip Gorski, *The Disciplinary Revolution: Calvinism and State Formation in Early Modern Europe, 1550–1750*, Ph. D. dissertation, Department of Sociology, University of California, Berkeley, 1996; Gorski, "Sixteenth-Century Social Reform: Why Protestantism Mattered." Typescript, Department of Sociology, University of Wisconsin, Madison, 1997; and George Steinmetz, *Regulating the Social: The Welfare State and Local Politics in Imperial Germany* (Princeton: Princeton University Press, 1993).

22. For a discussion of this law, see John Torpey, *The Invention of the Passport: Surveillance, Citizenship, and the State* (New York: Cambridge University Press, 2000), chapter 4.

23. On this issue, see Janet Gilboy, "Regulatory Relaxation: International Airlines, the Immigration Service, and Illegal Travelers," paper presented to the Annual Meeting of the Law & Society Association, St. Louis, Missouri, May, 1997. On recent developments in the modalities of the "sheriff's deputy" function carried out by private entities, see Lahav and Guiraudon in this volume.

24. Michael Mann, *The Sources of Social Power: The Rise of Classes and Nation-States, 1760–1914*, vol. 2 (New York: Cambridge University Press, 1993), 60.

25. For two versions of this argument, see Aristide Zolberg, "International Migration Policies in a Changing World System," in *Human Migration: Patterns and Policies*, William McNeill and Ruth Adams, eds. (Bloomington: Indiana University Press, 1978), stressing "public goods," and Leo Lucassen, "Eternal Vagrants? State Formation, Migration, and Travelling Groups in Western Europe, 1350–1914," in Jan Lucassen and Leo Lucassen, eds., *Migration, Migration History, History: Old Paradigms and New Perspectives* (New York: Peter Lang, 1997), emphasizing "poor relief."

26. See Brubaker, *Citizenship and Nationhood in France and Germany*.

27. For an excellent comparative discussion, see Sucheng Chan, "European and Asian Immigration into the United States in Comparative Perspective, 1820s to 1920s," in *Immigration Reconsidered: History, Sociology, Politics*, Virginia Yans-McLaughlin, ed. (New York: Oxford University Press, 1990).

28. Aristide Zolberg, "The Great Wall Against China: Responses to the First Immigration Crisis, 1885–1925," in Lucassen and Lucassen, eds., *Migration, Migration History, History: Old Paradigms and New Perspectives* (New York: Peter Lang, 1997), 308–309 and Torpey, *Invention of the Passport*, chapter 4.

29. See John Torpey, "The Great War and the Birth of the Modern Passport System," in *Documenting Individual Identity: The Development of State Practices in the Modern World*, Caplan and Torpey, eds. (Princeton N.J.: Princeton University Press, forthcoming).

30. James Hollifield, "Immigration and Republicanism in France," in *Controlling Immigration: A Global Perspective*, Wayne Cornelius, Philip L. Martin, and James F. Hollifield, eds. (Stanford: Stanford University Press, 1994); Leo Lucassen, "The Great War and the Origins of Migration Control in Western Europe and the United States (1880–1920)," in *Regulation of Migration: International Experiences*, Anita Böcker et al., eds. (Amsterdam: Het Spinhuis, 1998), 59; Zolberg, "Matters of State: Theorizing Immigration Policy," in *The Handbook of International Migration: The American Experience*, Charles Hirschman, Philip Kasinitz, and Josh DeWind, eds. (New York: Russell Sage, 1999), 92n20.

31. Eric Hobsbawm, *Nations and Nationalism* (New York: Cambridge University Press, 1990), 132.

32. See Aristide Zolberg, Astri Suhrke, and Sergio Aguayo, *Escape from Violence: Conflict*

and the Refugee Crisis in the Developing World (New York: Oxford University Press, 1989), 18–20; William D. Rubinstein, *The Myth of Rescue: Why the Democracies Could Not Have Saved More Jews from the Nazis* (New York: Routledge, 1997), 17. The question of the role of the western countries' immigration barriers in the destruction of European Jewry has recently resurfaced as an extremely contentious issue after having been apparently resolved by the work especially of David Wyman; see his *The Abandonment of the Jews: America and the Holocaust, 1941–1945* (New York: The New Press 1998 [1984]). For a dissenting view that stresses political obstacles to loosening immigration restrictions, see Peter Novick, *The Holocaust in American Life* (Boston: Houghton Mifflin, 1999), chapter 3.

33. Zolberg et al., *Escape from Violence*, 21–22.

34. Castles and Miller, *The Age of Migration*, 70–71.

35. Castles and Miller, *The Age of Migration*, 73–74.

36. Castles and Miller, *The Age of Migration*, 76.

37. Rüdiger Overmans, "55 Millionen Opfer des Zweiten Weltkrieges? Zum Stand der Forschung nach mehr als 40 Jahren," *Militärgeschichtliche Mitteilungen* 48 (1990): 103–121. I am grateful to Professor Robert Moeller of the UC Irvine History Department for this reference.

38. See Ronald Grigor Suny, *The Soviet Experiment: Russia, the U.S.S.R. and the Successor States* (New York: Oxford University Press, 1998), 331.

39. See Zolberg, "International Migration Policies in a Changing World System," 277.

40. See Roger Waldinger and Mehdi Bozorgmehr, "The Making of a Multicultural Metropolis," in *Ethnic Los Angeles*, Roger Waldinger and Mehdi Bozorgmehr, eds. (New York: Russell Sage Foundation, 1996), 9.

41. Kitty Calavita, *Inside the State: The Bracero Program, Immigration, and the I.N.S.* (New York: Routledge, 1992), 1.

42. Calavita, *Inside the State*, 55.

43. Alejandro Portes and Rubén Rumbaut, *Immigrant America: A Portrait* (Berkeley: University of California Press, 1990), 62–65; see also Waldinger and Bozorgmehr, "The Making of a Multicultural Metropolis."

44. For an overview, see Min Zhou, "Segmented Assimilation: Issues, Controversies, and Recent Research on the New Second Generation," in Charles Hirschman, Philip Kasinitz, and Josh DeWind, eds., *The Handbook of International Migration: The American Experience* (New York: Russell Sage, 1999).

45. Sharon Stanton Russell, "Migration Patterns of U.S. Foreign Policy Interest," in *Threatened Peoples, Threatened Borders: World Migration and U.S. Policy*, Michael S. Teitelbaum and Myron S. Weiner, eds. (New York: Norton, 1995), 27; Portes and Rumbaut, *Immigrant America*, 235.

46. Waldinger and Bozorgmehr, "The Making of a Multicultural Metropolis," 12. Citing an INS statistical report, Waldinger and Bozorgmehr claim that the number of those regularized under the provisions of IRCA has exceeded 3 million.

47. Russell, "Migration Patterns of U.S. Foreign Policy Interest," 29; Castles and Miller, *The Age of Migration*, 95.

48. See Castles and Miller, *The Age of Migration*, 84, 95.

49. See David Jacobson, "New Border Customs," 454.

50. On the use of refugee policies as a tool of American foreign policy, see Gil Loescher and John A. Scanlan, *Calculated Kindness: Refugees and America's Half-Open Door, 1945–*

Present (New York: The Free Press, 1986).

51. Russell, "Migration Patterns of U.S. Foreign Policy Interest," 48; and Aristide Zolberg, "From Invitation to Interdiction: U.S. Foreign Policy and Immigration Since 1945," in *Threatened Peoples, Threatened Borders: World Migration and U.S. Policy*, Michael S. Teitelbaum and Myron S. Weiner, eds. (New York: Norton, 1995), 132–133.

52. Zolberg, "From Invitation to Interdiction," 142–144.

53. Russell, "Migration Patterns of U.S. Foreign Policy Interest," 51; and Zolberg, "From Invitation to Interdiction," 152.

54. Joel Brinkley, "New Protection for Refugees from Right-Wing Oppression," *New York Times* (West Coast edition), May 21, 1999: A14, and interview with Scott Busby, a former official in the INS. General Counsel's office, March 10, 2000. One wonders whether the INS decision was not prompted in part by the defeat only a few days earlier of a Guatemalan referendum on constitutional reforms that proposed to give "official recognition to Guatemala's 24 Indian groups" and to "strengthen civilian control over police forces, limit presidential powers and bolster the judiciary." See Associated Press, "Guatemalan Indians Lament Recognition Measure's Defeat," *New York Times* (West Coast edition), May 18, 1999: A5.

55. Christian Joppke, "Asylum and State Sovereignty: A Comparison of the United States, Germany, and Britain," in *Challenge to the Nation–State: Immigration in Western Europe and the United States*, Christian Joppke, ed. (New York: Oxford University Press, 1998), 121.

56. See Castles and Miller, *The Age of Migration*, 104–111.

57. Castles and Miller, *The Age of Migration*, 88–99, 109.

58. See Joppke, "Asylum and State Sovereignty," 122–130.

59. See the UNHCR Web site, http://www.unhcr.ch, May 25, 1999.

60. *Migrant News*, June 1999, "Kosovar Refugees."

61. See David Rohde, "Despairing of Getting Home, Kosovars Yearn to Go Abroad," *New York Times* (West Coast edition), June 1, 1999: A1, A13.

62. See United States Institute of Peace, "Balkan Returns: An Overview of Refugee Returns and Minority Repatriation" (Washington, D.C.: United States Institute of Peace, 1999), 1–2.

63. Castles and Miller, *The Age of Migration*, 82–83.

64. On these issues, see Kitty Calavita, "Italy and the New Immigration," in *Controlling Immigration: A Global Perspective*, Wayne Cornelius, Philip L. Martin, and James F. Hollifield, eds. (Stanford: Stanford University Press, 1994), 303–326. Spain faces a similar situation; see Wayne A. Cornelius, "Spain: The Uneasy Transition from Labor Exporter to Labor Importer," in *Controlling Immigration*, 331–369, and Marlise Simons, "Between Migrants and Spain: The Sea that Kills," *New York Times* (West Coast edition), March 30, 2000: A3.

65. See "Centri speciali prima dell'espulsione," *Corriere della Sera*, February 20, 1998: 3.

66. See Dita Vogel, "Employer Sanctions and Identification in the Labour Market of Contemporary Germany," in *Documenting Individual Identity: The Development of State Practices in the Modern World* (Princeton, N.J.: Princeton University Press, forthcoming).

67. Rey Koslowski, "European Union Migration Regimes, Established and Emergent," in *Challenge to the Nation–State: Immigration in Western Europe and the United States*, Christian Joppke, ed. (New York: Oxford University Press, 1998), 169.

68. "EU: Schengen, Asylum," *Migrant News*, June 1999.

69. Anthony Richmond, *Global Apartheid: Refugees, Racism, and the New World Order* (New York: Oxford University Press, 1994), 213, 216.

70. See Torpey, *Invention of the Passport*, chapter 3.

71. Theodore Hamerow, *The Social Bases of German Unification, 1858–1871: Ideas and Institutions* (Princeton, N.J.: Princeton University Press, 1969), 160–161.

72. See Ewa Morawska and Wilfried Spohn, "Moving Europeans in the Globalizing World: Contemporary Migrations in a Historical-Comparative Perspective (1955–1994 vs. 1870–1914)," in *Global History and Migrations*, Wang Gungwu, ed. (Boulder, Colo.: Westview, 1997).

73. For an intriguing analysis that suggests that unemployment rates in the United States are actually comparable to those in Europe, a fact that is hidden by the high rate of incarcerations in the American penal system, see Bruce Western and Katherine Beckett, "How Unregulated Is the U.S. Labor Market? The Penal System as a Labor Market Institution," *American Journal of Sociology* 104: 4 (January 1999): 1030–1060.

74. For a compelling discussion of the extent to which the United States' apparently laissez-faire migration policies toward its southern neighbor actually constitute a conscious policy, see Zolberg, "Matters of State."

75. On these points, see Cornelius et al., eds., *Controlling Immigration*.

76. To borrow the title of Zolberg's article, "From Invitation to Interdiction."

77. Interview with Scott Busby, March 10, 2000.

78. In his comments on the "declining control" argument advanced in the volume edited by Cornelius, Martin, and Hollifield (1994), Rogers Brubaker also speaks of "unintended consequences" rather than "policy failure." See Rogers Brubaker, "Are Immigration Control Efforts Really Failing?" in *Controlling Immigration: A Global Perspective* (Stanford: Stanford University Press, 1994), 228.

79. Switzerland and Germany were presumably in a strong position in this competition, and hence their position would likely have had a strong influence on the policies of other countries. See Castles and Miller, *The Age of Migration*, 70–71.

80. See Louis Uchitelle, "INS Is Looking the Other Way As Illegal Immigrants Fill Jobs," *New York Times* (West Coast edition), March 9, 2000: A1, C14.

81. Christian Joppke, "Immigration Challenges the Nation-State," in *Challenge to the Nation–State: Immigration in Western Europe and the United States*, Christian Joppke, ed. (New York: Oxford University Press, 1998): 28.

4

Comparative Perspectives on Border Control: Away From the Border and Outside the State

Gallya Lahav and Virginie Guiraudon

In May 1999, in Douglas, Arizona, rancher Roger Barnett rounded up thirty Mexicans who had crossed the border illegally and called the U.S. Border Patrol. The local mayor, Ray Borane, invoking the 1996 federal immigration law, wrote to U.S. Attorney General Janet Reno to ask her to give local police and sheriff's deputies the right to work as Border Patrol agents. The reporter of the story noted that the image of ranchers patrolling their property for intruders is "as old as the Old West."[1] At the same time, the reason why there are so many illegal crossings in Douglas is recent: the stepped-up border control in Texas and California has redirected flows to the Arizona border.

The Douglas story contains elements of the new and the old. It reflects a renewed commitment to migration control in the late twentieth century, at a time when liberal norms and free trade have made this a difficult task. It also evokes remnants of previous centuries when local and private actors enjoyed significant prerogatives over the movement of persons. This chapter discusses these reinvented forms of control in the United States and Europe that occur away from the border and that involve noncentral state actors. It argues that old actors are being incorporated at new sites, to respond more effectively and efficiently to changing constraints and opportunity structures. Relying on a historical and comparative analysis of policy instruments, we identify the cultural and geopolitical factors that account for variations in domestic outcomes between Europe and the United States.

Control over who enters and exits one's territory has long been associated with the prerogatives of the modern nation–state, an essential component of the post-Westphalian concept of national sovereignty.[2] Yet, as we document, liberal democratic nation–states seeking to select incoming migrants have enlisted the help of an extended "playing field" of local, transnational, and private actors outside the central state apparatus to forestall migration at the source or uncover illegal migrants.

55

Conversely, public law and order officials in charge of migration control have also begun operating in local and international venues, designed to allow the state to regulate migration by "remote control" and to circumvent judicial constraints on migration policy *senso stricto.*

This chapter proceeds in three parts. First, we seek to contextualize the current involvement of nonstate actors in migration policy and the increasing vertical and horizontal character of migration policymaking. We argue that state agencies are responding to a particular "control dilemma" in an era where liberal norms, free trade, and cheap travel have burdened border control. We then scrutinize empirical developments whereby European and American state agencies have developed policy instruments that target migrants (1) before they reach the border (external controls) and (2) inside state territory (internal controls). Our research focuses on the United States and the European Union (EU) since the 1980s, as discourse and policies became more "control-oriented" on both sides of the Atlantic. The comparative analysis allows for both an explanation of the variations that emanate from cultural and geopolitical factors, and for general conclusions about the implications for border control *and* state power in liberal democracies.

THE DETERMINANTS OF REMOTE CONTROL

In historical terms, the state "monopoly over the legitimate means of movement" is fairly recent (see Torpey in this volume). Still, in the modern nation–state era where nation–states acting in concert in the international system set up the modern passport system to control movement, the role of local and private actors was limited.[3] Most of the twentieth century has been characterized by national control over the entry and stay of foreigners. This began to change during the 1970s in Europe, and during the 1980s in the United States. The new trend grew from a renewed will to control migration (labor migration, family unification, asylum seekers, and refugees), itself rooted in public concerns about societal security. This situation has allowed central state agencies in charge of law and order to link migration and security issues in such a way as to extend their realm of action.[4] There are therefore both electoral incentives and bureaucratic support for the stemming of migration flows.

Two important countervailing trends condition this extension of state power. First, there are a number of *normative constraints* on the administrative discretion of state control agencies. Formal constitutional guarantees as well as activist administrative and constitutional courts have significantly circumscribed both the authority and the capacity of states to prevent family unification or to dispose of migrants at will.[5] The "liberal epoch" of human rights norms that facilitated humanitarian migration alongside labor recruitment (family unification and asylum) contrasts with the preceding period. One only needs to recall the expulsions of 400,000 Poles from Germany in 1885–1886,[6] or the exclusion of Chinese immigrants before the turn of the century in the United States to realize the normative evolution that has taken place in the migration policy domain.[7] Second, states concerned with fostering modern trade and commerce cannot unambiguously embrace policies that hinder the movement of people across borders. The desire to prevent the entry and stay of "unwanted migrants" coincides with the wish to support booming tourist industries.[8] More generally, free trade requires a degree of openness that impedes calls for tighter border controls.[9]

These pressures present state actors with two dilemmas. First, on the one hand, the issue of border security opens special opportunities for state actors to extend their authority; on the other hand, they are constrained by norms and laws that treat precisely this issue. Second, the wish to appeal to public opinion contradicts the desire to support and reassure business constituencies. By focusing on state responses to these dilemmas, we show that central state agencies have reinvented control over migration. They have done so by shifting the level of policymaking at the international and local levels and by co-opting and cooperating with a range of players that include private actors and sending or transit countries. These actors have assumed "sheriff's deputy" functions in an enlarged playing field. Scholars have interpreted the migration control dilemma that states face as a sign of their "losing control,"[10] or as evidence of a "gap" between the stated goals of migration control and its outcomes.[11] We disagree with these claims to the extent that they overlook the variety and subtlety of policy responses. State agencies in charge of migration control have sought to solve the control dilemma in cost-effective ways, in ways that could at once appease public anxieties over migration, short-circuit judicial constraints on migration control, and still promote trade and tourist flows.

Several chapters in this volume focus on recent changes in border control policies (see for example Nevins and Spener). Peter Andreas's work on the U.S.–Mexico border has documented the strategy that seeks to restore the appearance of control. In his words, the recent buildup at the border "has less to do with actual deterrence and more to do with managing the image of the border."[12] The 1996 Illegal Immigration Reform and Immigration Responsibility Act promotes measures such as the building of a fourteen-mile triple-layer fence south of San Diego and the doubling of the size of the border patrol by 2001. It reinforces a 1990s trend that has seen the Immigration and Naturalization Service (INS) budget and personnel skyrocket.[13]

Nonetheless, this strategy of visibility can only achieve one policy goal: focusing the public's attention on efforts that should appease their anxieties about migration while diverting it from unregulated flows.[14] State control agencies also have to take into account some of the consequences of globalization: sustained migration pressures, global tourism, freer trade flows. The solution that arose in the 1980s consisted of two parts. First, states sought to prevent migration at the source. In practice, this means "externalizing" control so that prospective unwanted migrants or asylum seekers do not reach the territory of the receiving countries. As we will see, this has been achieved through the incorporation of various actors for the creation of "buffer zones" via the development of visa regimes, carrier sanctions, transnational cooperation, and international and bilateral agreements (see Jesien, this volume). Second, when migration has already occurred, states have sought to uncover illegal migrants by "internally" delegating control to local and private actors (such as municipalities, regional authorities, employers, or other private actors through sanctions, for instance) who have more direct access to migrants.

This strategy can be construed as a two-pronged effort that entails shifting the level at which officials in charge of migration control operate, allowing them to find a favorable context in terms of procedures and participants.[15] The co-opting of nonstate actors in the performance of the migration control "function" (i.e., security agencies working for airline companies) serves to "shift liabilities" from the central state to private actors such as employers, carriers, and travel agencies, services such as universities for foreign students, and even individuals as sponsors.[16]

Our argument posits that the extension of this delegation of policy elaboration and implementation functions to noncentral state actors coincides with the interests of national control agencies. In considering the incentives and constraints that keep these processes in motion, we thus examine the empirical developments from the particular perspective of the state. In order to systematically delineate these institutional structures and outcomes, we pose a playing field of two spatial axes (public–private; international–domestic) where various actors are positioned (see figure 4.1).

The following section provides an overview of the four types of actors—international, transnational, local, and private—as they are located along the two sets of

Figure 4.1.   Vertical and Horizontal Dimensions of the Immigration "Playing Field"

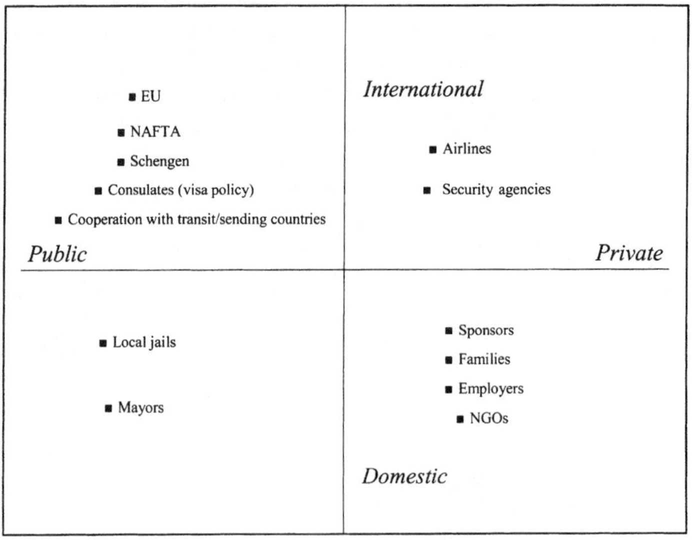

axes. It considers their roles in monitoring external and internal sites, including the control of entry, work, stay, and deportation of foreigners. As we show, few states have devised new tactics to address the problem, but more of them are joining the crusade exacerbated by a mounting control dilemma with greater urgency.

EMPIRICAL FRAMEWORK:
ENLISTING INTERNATIONAL, LOCAL, AND PRIVATE ACTORS

External Control Sites

The establishment and universalization of a visa regime laid the groundwork for a more complex system in extending the area of what Aristide Zolberg calls "remote control" immigration policy.[17] With visas, the first immigrant relationship to the host country became established at home, in the country of origin, and the barriers of control were thereby established in the sending countries. A major thrust of more recent policy efforts in many countries is "interdiction," defined broadly as activity directed at preventing departure.[18] Interdiction initiatives take various forms, including information campaigns to deter potential migrants, visa requirements, carrier sanctions, and liaison with foreign control authorities, as well as the physical interception of persons traveling on fraudulent documents. Remote control also implies the establishment of "buffer zones" beyond the national borders of receiving countries. It includes harmonization of policies through (1) transgovernmental cooperation, (2) cooperation with transit and sending countries, and (3) the help of private actors, namely travel carriers.

Transnational Actors and Transgovernmental Cooperation

Since the early 1980s, European migration control officials operate not only at national but also transnational levels. This has allowed them to avoid the judicial scrutiny that they face nationally, and to short-circuit other domestic actors with contending views. During the early- and mid-1980s, immigration and asylum issues emerged in the discussions of supranational organizations—among civil servants and police officials dedicated to other policing themes such as drugs or terrorism (the Club of Berne in 1984, the STAR group in 1984).[19] In 1985, the Schengen Agreement was signed by France, Germany, and the Benelux countries. The agreement, which also contained three articles on immigration (see Anderson, this volume), provided an important impetus for cooperation.

At that point in time, there were various flexible, informal groupings involving various countries. They served to evade the scrutiny of bodies of supervision such as parliaments and courts, and to promote trust between officials from different countries through nonbinding interactions. Moreover, these groups enabled law and order officials to set the agenda on transnational cooperation on migration issues and thereby become the main actors involved. Schengen is a paramount example, in which the interior and justice ministries replaced the foreign ministries originally in charge of negotiating the implementation agreement between 1985 and 1990.[20] The issues, their framing, their justifications, and the very language discussed today were already set by 1989.[21]

The fact that cooperation started in the early 1980s is instructive for its rationale. It occurred before the fall of the Berlin Wall. The end of the Cold War did not precede—let alone cause—these cooperative developments. Migration and refugee pressures from the East led to a significant rise in the number of asylum seekers only between 1989 and 1993. In fact, one of the lowest points in numbers of entries in Europe is the period 1982–1985 with flows comprising mostly family members.[22] Therefore one cannot attribute cooperation to a simple convergence of national interests in the face of geopolitical changes.

The single market project of the EU has been used *post facto* as a justification for cooperation on border controls, migration, and asylum. Analytically, however, it is arduous to speak of a functional spillover effect of the yet-to-be-achieved single market. Moreover, not all EU member states that supported and participate in single market policies partake in EU negotiations about migration (the UK, Ireland, and Denmark have opted out of Amsterdam's Title IV, which concerns the harmonization of migration and asylum regulations).

Deserving of emphasis is the margin of maneuver that justice and interior ministers gained in transgovernmental settings, as compared to national venues where they have to compromise with other ministries representing different interests. The lack of transparency of intergovernmental cooperation forums still makes it difficult to obtain the minutes of meetings, or copies of documents adopted before they are implemented, sometimes without domestic legislation.[23] Some national parliaments have criticized this *politique du fait accompli*. The French Senate set up a control commission after the Schengen implementation agreement, because both houses of parliament had access to its contents only a few weeks before ratification, had little knowledge about their implications, and had to ratify the final version without amendments.

In 1992, the Treaty on European Union (articles K 1–9) created the third pillar on Justice and Home Affairs with one full group (GD1) of the K4 committee dedicated to asylum, visa, and migration.[24] These groups were not obliged to answer to a representative body (such as the European Parliament) nor to an international court such as the European Court of Justice (ECJ). Other national ministries have been notably absent from the negotiating tables.

Title IV of the Amsterdam Treaty (which came into force on May 1, 1999) states that an "area of freedom, security and justice" will be established progressively. This entails the adoption by the European Council of measures aimed at ensuring free movement of persons, as well as steps related to external border controls, immigration, and asylum, within a period of five years. The so-called Schengen *acquis* will be incorporated into the EU framework.

Since European Council decisions will need to be unanimous and the Parliament and the Court of Justice have limited roles, justice and interior ministers still control the agenda in the migration control policy domain. Procedurally, the European Commission will have exclusive right of initiative after five years, while the European Council will act unanimously. After the European Parliament has been consulted, co-decision will only be extended to cover all or part of the areas covered by Title IV if all the council members agree.[25] The role of the European Court of Justice has also been circumscribed with respect to the "preliminary ruling" procedure. Furthermore, the court will not have jurisdiction over national measures adopted to restrict border crossings in order to maintain law and order and safeguard internal security. Therefore, the exclusion of certain national actors (such as courts, parliaments, and other ministries) at the European level is not compensated by the presence of strong supranational actors. For instance, the commission will need to elaborate proposals likely to gain unanimous support in a way that diminishes its role as an agenda setter or an "entrepreneurial bureaucracy."[26]

In these ways, policy elaboration in international venues serves to solve the "control dilemma" by excluding the actors that hinder control (such as courts that assert liberal norms). The outcome of intergovernmental bargains on external controls further limits the migrants' access to the judicial system. For instance, decisions taken among European states on "manifestly unfounded claims" and safe third countries prevent asylum seekers from having their claims fully examined by the legal system.[27] Moreover, the decisions taken in international forums such as Schengen have sanctioned all types of remote control policymaking. These include the elaboration of a common visa policy and the adoption of carrier sanctions (i.e., Article 26 of the Schengen Agreement, for instance, requires signatory states to establish carrier sanctions).

The construction of a "frontier regime" (Anderson, this volume) among EU states is in the making and remains unique. It is doubtful that countries in other regional integration projects will have the incentives to go in this direction, especially in North America, since NAFTA is but a free trade agreement and does not involve equal partners but rather a mix of sending and receiving countries.

International Actors: Cooperation with Sending and Transit Countries

Even though transgovernmental cooperation to harmonize policy instruments has essentially been a European phenomenon, cooperation with sending and transit countries of immigration developed on both sides of the Atlantic in the 1980s and 1990s. In North America, as the issue of migration control gained salience in the 1990s, it became linked to free trade issues during the debate on NAFTA in the United States. Indeed, while the U.S.–Mexico Binational Commission, established in 1981, included working groups such as the Border Relations Action Group, the frequency of meetings increased after 1994 with the Working Group on Migration and Consular Affairs. This group serves as a forum of cabinet-level officials to resolve border problems of mutual interest.[28] On the ground, the new strategy at the border has included the creation of joint U.S.–Mexican border task forces. With the launching of Operation Gatekeeper III in October 1997, U.S. and Mexican officials formed a multiagency group that focuses on warning migrants of the danger of illegal border crossing, protecting them against bandits, reviewing medical emergency procedures, and cracking down on smugglers. The relationship between Mexico and the United States is still fraught with distrust and misunderstanding (Mohar and Alcaraz, this volume). For this and other reasons, one should not equate U.S.–Mexican cooperation on the border with Franco-German mobile units at Schengen's internal border.

The United States has also developed its cooperation with Haiti and Cuba to guarantee the effectiveness of its interdiction policy off the coast of Florida, following a number of "migration crises." As Christopher Mitchell documents (in this volume), the United States' decision to back a regime change in Haiti by deploying U.S. armed forces to restore Aristide in 1994 made it easier to intercept and repatriate Haitians. Similarly, since Cuba and the United States signed an agreement in 1995 whereby Cuba would accept unauthorized migrants found at sea by U.S. vessels, Cubans are routinely repatriated.

In Europe, cooperation has evolved from the signing of bilateral readmission agreements that mostly relied on pecuniary incentives to a more sophisticated multilateral policy toward central and eastern Europe. These arrangements now link accession to the EU with the adoption of stricter migration controls (see also Vachudová and Jesien, this volume). This strategy was particularly pursued by the German government, which signed readmission agreements with eastern European countries and Vietnam, trading deutsche marks for the return of unwanted migrants. Yet the phenomenon was widespread and took different forms. In 1993, Morocco agreed with the Netherlands to check the identity of offenders susceptible to expulsion to Morocco and readmit them. In the summer of 1994, France and Algeria signed a confidential agreement stipulating that Algeria would readmit expelled illegal aliens whom the French believe to be Algerians even if they have destroyed their papers.[29] New immigration or transit countries are increasingly bound by such arrangements.[30]

Applicants to the EU remain a special case. Prospective EU member states are now expected to "Westernize" in a number of areas, including human rights, asylum, refugees, illegal migration, the entry and stay of foreigners, and visas. They should also develop institutions for border control and internal controls such as employers' sanctions.[31] Conforming to the EU's "third pillar" and to Schengen norms is also a requirement. Central and eastern European states have tried to adopt treaties and pass legislation in the area of migration and asylum to conform to elusive EU norms, even when doing so conflicted with their own state interests.[32] EU institutions and other international organizations are imposing a set of standards and norms on central and eastern European countries *as if* the latter were written in stone and *in lieu of* nation–states. It is no longer about Germany exchanging money for the repatriation of illegal migrants but rather about the EU Commission assessing the compliance of central and eastern European aspiring member states with respect to justice and home affairs matters in the context of Agenda 2000.[33]

These developments are evidence of the increasing delegation of policymaking: Western states delegate border control to their eastern neighbors and transfer the monitoring of the agents' compliance to EU institutions. Both on the ground and at the government level, working with countries on the other side of what Roland Freudenstein calls the "frontier of poverty" (this volume) has been a consistently emerging trend among developed liberal countries in Europe and North America.

Private Actors: Carrier Sanctions

A core actor in the enlarged control system at the external level has been the transport or carrier company. To migrants, these industries represent a resource of personnel, services, and access. To states, they are cheap ways of applying sanctions and penalties. With minimal training investment, private actors provide the state with the means to effectively differentiate between the "legal" passages for travelers or economic tourists and would-be overstayers or migrants.[34] This shift in the locus of responsibility represents the development of a public–private relationship within which the resources of private actors are deployed to the benefit of the state and cooperation is secured through sanctions and penalties.

The role of air carriers in immigration control was envisaged long before "globalization" of the twentieth century. It has been secured since the Paris Conference in 1919, which in effect placed airspace, the domain through which airlines must travel, under sovereign control. By virtue of owning airspace, airlines became subject to national restrictions, and dependent on state actors for market operation. The practice of sanctioning carriers does not in itself represent a precedent in legislation governing the rules of entry. In the United States, carriers have been obliged, at their own expense, to transport inadmissible passengers back to their countries of departure since the Passenger Act of 1902. In accordance with guidelines established by the 1944 Convention on International Civil Aviation (ICAO), transport companies have been forced to assume the role of international immigration officers. Standards 3.35 to 3.38 of the ICAO established the responsibility of the airline to ensure that passengers possess the necessary travel documents. Nonetheless, whereas the burden of assuming expenses at one time amounted to the costs of retransport, increasingly countries have introduced laws to raise the responsibilities of carriers to pay fines. In the United States, the Immigration and Nationality Act (8 U.S.C) penalizes international air carriers with a $3,000 assessment for each infraction, in addition to the cost for removal for each inadmissible individual (U.S.C., se. 1323).[35]

Although the United States was a pioneer in establishing the liability of transport companies during the steamship era, in 1994, all EU countries, with the exception of Spain, Ireland, and Luxembourg, passed laws increasing the responsibilities of carriers.[36] The contents, interpretation, and application of laws on carriers' liabilities have varied greatly among states,[37] but they all represent similar efforts of states to extend the burden of implementation *away* from the central government and *to* the sources of migration, thereby increasing efficacy and decreasing costs. The private actors whose help is enlisted can valuably supplement state efforts at direct monitoring of wrongdoing.[38] The state thus reaps the rewards of a more effective migration control system, while enlisting more technical support to defuse the political and economic costs of regulating the border. These methods also permit states to circumvent constraints imposed by judicial and civil rights groups, which may be present at the national or international level. In this vein, airline cooperation on matters of same-day removals of inadmissible foreigners on the "carrier's next regularly scheduled departure" is critical. It allows the state to avoid the costs of detention, which also include the prevention of access to lawyers.[39]

The international transport industry occupies a unique role in the late twentieth century, not only because air travel has increased (in contrast to railroads and ships), but also because the industry provides a critical service in the movement of people from one national jurisdiction to another. Considering that passenger traffic has increased dramatically with globalization, airlines have changed the economic face of many countries, generated by the tourism boom. Ireland, for example, one of the least developed EU countries, has been named the fastest growing tourist destination in Europe over the last ten years, because it experienced a 129 percent increase from 2.4 million *overseas* visitors in 1988 to 5.5 million in 1998.[40] These developments are welcomed equally by national business actors and states, who manage their "control dilemma" by appealing to economic interests and incorporating them more effectively.

Similar to international agreements made by ICAO signatories, and the Paris Convention earlier, the role of these private actors is sanctioned by international agreements, which have served to diffuse policy instruments such as carrier sanctions. In the EU, member states refer to their obligations to Article 26 of the 1990 implementation agreement of the Schengen Convention in relying on carriers to serve as immigration officers.[41] More stringent security checks at airports—identity cards, tickets, boarding passes, baggage and so on—have made the absence of passport controls virtually irrelevant, and to some degree have offset regional integration efforts. Thus, the effects of these reinvented actors vary greatly in the changed context of twentieth-century globalization, namely in order to redress the control dilemma.

Just as they first realized consulates abroad could play an important role in preventing migration at the source through the visa regime, states have found an array of actors with whom to cooperate. Such cooperation is based on a mixture of sanctions (in the case of carriers) and incentives (the prospective of EU membership for ECE states) to meet state goals.

Internal Control Sites

Remote control policy has also been used to shift liabilities closer to the source and away from the central state, internally, at the domestic level. Just as third states, international, and transnational actors are enlisted in external control, local actors are significant players within national territories. In addition, the extended playing field makes private actors equally important for internal control as they are for external control. Despite striking cross-cultural differences, the increasing incorporation of these types of agents reflects the political will of states to enforce migration rules.

Private Actors: Employer Sanctions and Liabilities of Other Nonstate Actors

Private actors or independent authorities, who rely on market forces, have become crucial immigration agents in extending the area of "remote control" immigration policy. The role and liabilities of private actors in sharing the burden of regulation are manifest in the use of a varied repertoire of actors and more stringent deterrent methods such as sanctions (see table 4.1). At the domestic level, private actors include employer groups for work; detention centers for deportation; as well as individuals, migrant families, and sponsors.

Often compelled by international and regional agreements, these actors are either incorporated by liberal states, or "privatized" in the sense that their functions have

Table 4.1   Third Party Nonstate Actors in Immigration Regulation
(in select liberal democracies)

Country	Transport Companies (sanctions)	Employers (sanctions)	Immigrants (punishment for illegal)	Civil Society (sanctions for harboring illegal)
UK*	Yes	Yes	Yes	Yes
Belgium*	Yes	Yes	Yes	Yes
Denmark*	Yes	Yes	Yes	Yes
Finland*	Yes	Yes	Yes	No
Germany*	Yes	Yes	Yes	Yes
Italy*	Yes	Yes	Yes	No
Netherlands*	Yes	Yes	No	Yes
Sweden*	Yes	Yes	Yes	Yes
Canada+	Yes	Yes	Yes	Yes
United States+	Yes	Yes	Yes	Yes

*Member of EU
+Member of NAFTA
Source: Authors' tabulations

evolved from contractors into regulators, from the public to the private sphere. Although there are differences between the U.S. and European cases that stem from cultural norms regarding state intervention in the economy, the cost-benefit logic of this exchange is similar.

At the internal level of immigration control, the private counterpart to admissions regulation lays in the employment sector, where immigration control may be equally effective. Strategies to stem illegal migration at the work site have developed to redistribute the liabilities of migration control outside of the central state, and these strategies make employer groups more significant actors. In the early to mid-1970s, when external borders were closed, most European countries had already instituted similar provisions adopted by the French as early as 1926, by adopting and refining employer sanctions.[42] Despite considerable structural variations, the labor agency, the organization with the most labor market expertise, has been responsible for detecting and removing unauthorized workers from the workplace. This means that in contrast to the United States, where before the 1986 IRCA, illegal aliens were considered to violate federal law by entering the country and working (but employers were not), in much of Europe, employer sanctions have long been part of labor laws. Employers in Europe are thus more vulnerable to liabilities than their American counterparts. In addition, the combined influence of the business, the family, and ethnic lobbies on congressional committee politics in the U.S. federal system has in effect taken many of the teeth out of employers' sanctions through antidiscrimination clauses, and has no equivalent in Europe.[43]

Strategies for enforcement have evolved over time, and have been marked by both the increase of legal arsenal and the number of actors.[44] Although much of the enforcement capacities of work control systems depend on the verifiability of documentation, there are dramatic differences between the U.S. and European countries that stem from different civic traditions and political cultures. Although European countries like France do not have a mandatory national identification document system, it is believed that more than 90 percent of Frenchmen carry a national identity card.[45] Lacking in such traditions, American strategies to regulate the workplace have been hampered in addressing the problem of fraudulent documents. Moreover, a political culture adverse to state intervention in business makes the role of employers less vulnerable to liabilities than their European counterparts.

Nonetheless, there are incremental changes on this front. In 1989, the INS revised the "green card," and in 1996 began to replace some of the older work authorization forms with a new "tamper-resistant" Employment Authorization Document, based on a Social Security number and on improved breeder documents to establish identity. The INS has also been developing and testing databases and access systems for businesses to use in verifying employment eligibility. The adoption of a worker authorization system has been viewed as a first step toward a national ID card, and unsurprisingly has come under substantial fire from civil rights advocates and those who oppose the expansion of federal government power to give employers permission for hiring.

Decentralizing trends have included "outsourcing" of enforcement to labor inspection agencies, security services, or police. Private actors such as security agencies have also been increasingly incorporated for deportation purposes. A recent uprising that erupted at a detention center for illegal immigrants exposed a trend in supervisory functions: the "contracting out" of detention centers and guards to private for-profit security services. In 1996, private contractors ran approximately one-third of national centers holding illegal immigrants or asylum seekers.[46]

States have shifted the onus of regulation to private individuals and civil actors in monitoring stays through deportation and enforcement of exit rules.[47] Since 1989, the United States has added liability for the costs of detention fees for inadmissible passengers pending trial; where air carriers have historically been liable, the 1989 Immigration User Fee Law added a $5 charge to travelers entering the United States to defray the costs.[48] Furthermore, the 1996 U.S. bill increased penalties for document fraud on illegal migrants, such as civil fines and the barring of future entry (a serious penalty for someone with close family members). In France, a 1997 government bill aiming to prevent illegal immigration proposed that French hosts who have foreign guests on special visas inform the town hall when their guests leave, allowing the French government to compile computer records on the movements of foreigners. Although as a result of heavy protests the article of the bill was amended and finally eliminated in 1998, efforts to extend the burden of regulation were shifted to the foreigner, who would have been required to submit his certificate of accommodation upon leaving the country.

At the core of privatizing regulations for immigrant stays has been the role of the family. In the United States, the burden on families has emerged in the form of more restrictive sponsorship rules and practices that are now enforceable. New rules affect legal immigrants who are typically sponsored by relatives or by a business.[49] Until the recent immigration bills, sponsors of immigrants were typically required to assure that anyone they brought into the country would not become a "public charge." Because these pledges had become unenforceable in court, recent bills aimed to make this support binding. Sponsors, rather than taxpayers, are required to provide a more substantial safety net for immigrants by making the sponsor's affidavit of support a legally enforceable document. For the first time, the notion of "becoming a public charge" has been carefully defined with the intention of making this a realistic ground for deportation.

The incorporation of private actors through sanctions and the privatization of migration regulation through "contracting out" of implementation functions both involve the extension of state control over migration away from the border and outside of the central state. On the one hand, these shifts in liabilities represent an incorporation of private actors in state regulatory functions; on the other, they shift the externalities of policymaking outside of the central government.[50]

Local Actors: Decentralization and Localization

Since the 1980s, policy reforms have also tended to give local or regional governments certain prerogatives in migration control.[51] This is most pronounced in unitary states that have been "decentralizing," such as France and the Netherlands. In federal states, the relationship between state and federal governments had been more clearly laid out prior to that period. Yet, both in Germany and in the United States, the states that receive the largest share of migration have expressed disgruntlement with existing institutional and financial arrangements and called for stricter rules or stricter application of existing law.

In France, the law passed on December 30, 1993, which included measures against "marriages of convenience," gave mayors the right to call on the *Procureur de la République* to suspend or annul a wedding involving a foreigner. A 1995 Ministry of Justice survey revealed that 82 percent of the cases were concentrated in twelve *tribunaux de grande instance* while 69 percent of the courts were not called upon at all.[52] In 1993, the *certificat d'hébergement*, a housing certificate first created in 1982, became necessary in order to obtain a short-term visa that had to be approved by the mayor (it was eliminated in 1997). A 1996 study compared 945 municipalities to see how they applied the law of August 24, 1993, on housing certificates for visa applicants. They reported vast disparities across the territory: 50 percent of the mayors requested papers that were not required by law; others refused to give out the application forms or to sign the certificates.[53]

In the Netherlands, since the 1980s, municipalities have had a growing role in the control of "bogus" marriages and in the verification of conditions for family reunification. In the 1990s, the new laws on newcomers linking welfare allowances with the attendance of training and language classes also require local monitoring of migrants. Similarly, there is no longer a designated budget for ethnic minorities since a 1980s decentralization law gave that responsibility to local governments.[54] In other words, both migration and immigrant policy has been partly devolved to the local level. In interviews, Dutch Immigration and Naturalization Division officials acknowledged that mayors interpreted their new mandates diversely: from annoyance to too much severity.[55]

In the United States, federalism has tended to take the form of federal agents applying federal laws and state agents, state laws. In the area of migration, states until the mid-to-late nineteenth century still carried a number of prerogatives including the rights granted to aliens and the bestowing of nationality.[56] Part of the explanation comes from the fact that states with slave populations wanted control over the latter. Courts took away some of these state rights after the Civil War. During most of the twentieth century, Supreme Court decisions have emphasized the exclusive federal prerogatives in the area of immigration regulation, through the plenary power doctrine, and the dangers of state encroachment. Political demands in the 1980s and 1990s for a state role in immigration policy turn back the clock.[57] Peter Spiro has argued that the devolution of immigration policy to the states is a growing reality.[58]

It is ultimately up to Congress to authorize states to play a role in immigration policy. The 1996 Illegal Immigration Reform and Immigrant Responsibility Act also permits the INS to train and deputize local police officers to enforce immigration laws. Salt Lake City Police Chief Ruben Ortega, himself of immigrant origin, asked the city council to deputize twenty police officers in 1998. He argued that immigrants were responsible for 80 percent of felony drug arrests. Although the city council voted four to three on September 1 to oppose, this case showed the willingness of local police to get involved, especially in cities where immigrants are a more recent phenomenon and are not very organized.[59]

In Germany, states implement federal laws such as the federal aliens' law. In cases where the law is not clear about jurisdictional boundaries (as is the case for rules governing detention centers for foreigners), they have great leeway in doing so.[60] In 1981, the federal government issued recommendations about the granting of residence permits for foreign spouses of second-generation resident aliens. Two states (Bavaria and Baden-Wurtemberg) set a three-year waiting period for family unification instead of one. Ruling on three appeals by non-EC citizens in 1987, the Federal Constitutional Court found the change excessive and a disproportionate injury to the right to a family life guaranteed under Article 6.[61] However, according to the judges, the fact that states applied federal guidelines differently did not in itself constitute a violation of equality before the law or federalism.[62]

Divergent state attitudes toward immigrant policy have long been a feature of the German case. To a large extent, this was made possible by the prerogatives of the states in areas such as culture and education.[63] In the area of migration control, the federal aliens' law has been disparately interpreted and applied. In the 1990s, differences arose in expulsion policy. In 1994–1995, some Social Democratic Party (SPD) state governments suspended the expulsion of Kurds and Syrian-Orthodox Christians to Turkey.[64] Recently, when fighting erupted in Kosovo, the German federal representative for the Balkans urged the interior ministers of the sixteen states to continue to deport rejected asylum seekers.[65] Lower Saxony, North Rhine-Westphalia, Hessen, Saarland, and Brandenburg had stopped deportations to Kosovo. However, on March 13, 1998, after the German federal government refused to impose a nationwide ban on deportations, Lower Saxony said it would resume the deportation of rejected asylum seekers to Kosovo. Regional disparity not only reflects partisan differences but also proximity to the (southern) border. The German *Bund* however has shown in the Kurdish case that it can rein in recalcitrant states. Even if it was unclear whether the federal government could force states into expelling again, lower court decisions invalidated orders to suspend expulsions.[66]

Therefore, the localization of control has the advantage that the national government can control local elected actors should they not behave as expected. At the same time, the central government can rely on regions or municipalities that are electorally motivated to make examples out of illegal migrants, especially those that are more likely to be in contact with them "at the source" than state border patrols.

Sometimes local actors also have financial motives. It should be pointed out that local authorities have been "contracted out" to detain illegal migrants. In the United States, nine national centers holding illegal aliens or asylum seekers in 1996 were run by local and state actors with the support of government funds, and the INS rents thousands of beds in local jails. In fact, two-thirds of the 16,000 foreigners detained by the INS in 1998 were in local jails. A York county commissioner, when asked about the aggrandizement of a Pennsylvania prison to detain immigrants, reported that they had a $26/day profit margin per detainee.[67]

Subnational governments are also involved in supranational police cooperation. As early as 1972, Bavaria belonged to *Arbeitsgruppe Südost* with Austria, Canada, and eastern European countries. In 1978 and 1979, other *Länder* became involved in the *Arbeitsgruppe Nord* and *Arbeitsgruppe Südwest*, respectively.[68] States with external borders have been particularly active in border control policy. Large German states are increasing their presence in Brussels, as migration control becomes an "EU affair."[69] In the United States, California has developed its diplomatic relations with Mexico on migration issues. In fact, one of the first acts of the new governor in 1998 was to visit Mexico and discuss migration issues. In brief, the vertical dimension to migration management presents an important axis of the extended "playing field" and should not be overlooked.

CONCLUSION

Some of the subsequent chapters concentrate on the evolution of border policy, documenting the visible changes that constitute part of what we have called the "control dilemma" story. States seek to reconcile competing interests between the requirements of economic integration and their will to assert their "monopoly over the control of movement" to appease public anxieties. Yet, even as the issue of migration becomes a nexus for the visible advance of state power, liberal democratic states are operating under new normative and legal constraints. Other chapters provide suggestions of the repertoire of old, new, and borrowed control instruments states have exploited to meet their policy goals while circumventing these constraints.

The purpose of this chapter has been to offer a general framework of an enlarged migration "playing field," an attempt to reconceptualize state and public regulatory modes by identifying the actors available to policymakers in controlling migration on both sides of the Atlantic. Actors are located along two axes: public–private; and international–domestic/local spaces. These horizontal and vertical dimensions of policymaking allow us to visualize the variety of actors enlisted in regulating cross-border flows. International, transnational, local, and private actors pervade both the external and internal control sites, including questions of entry, work, stay, and deportation of foreigners. They provide the state with a range of actors to whom control functions may be delegated in a cost-effective manner. This view uncovers new opportunity structures available to liberal states in an interdependent world, while explaining how similar incentives and instruments can produce diverse historical and cross-cultural outcomes. To a large degree, policy tools have been transferred across the Atlantic. Thus, U.S. carrier sanctions, for example, appear to have traveled eastward while employers' sanctions have migrated westward. Nonetheless, substantial structural and cultural differences between the EU and the United States mediate policy organization, implementation, and effectiveness.

These differences taken into account, the general insight that bureaucrats and elected officials in both the EU and the United States can look "away from the border and outside the state" reveals the prematurity of mourning the decline of the state (as globalization scholars sometimes do). While acknowledging the constraints to states in a global liberal era (i.e., humanitarian, civil rights, economic interests, public opinion), this argument underscores the capacity of liberal democratic states to reinvent forms of border control. By delegating policy functions, states have been able to reconcile their contradictory interests, defuse public anxiety, reduce the costs of regulation, and occasionally circumvent even the most basic of liberal rights.

True, some forms of delegated control belong to an old repertoire of strategies employed when nations look to impose more stringent control over migration. Even so, their renewed attraction in the 1970s and 1980s, and widespread use in the 1990s, suggests a formalization and institutionalization that is quite new. Moreover, the old "playing field" of indirect methods of border control has expanded; and its enlargement should be seen as part and parcel of "globalization." This proliferation of actors and levels available to states seems to keep pace with contemporary migration pressures, allowing central governments to strengthen their capacity to control migration despite new constraints. State actors can calculate that the cost of relinquishing some of their autonomy over policy will be compensated by the benefits of efficacy in reducing unwanted migration, reduction of judicial oversight, and defraying of financial costs. If one defines sovereignty as the authority and the capacity to rule, states may have regained the latter in exchange for forsaking the appearance of the former.

NOTES

1. *Chicago Tribune*, May 12, 1999.
2. Stephen Krasner, "Westphalia," in *Ideas and Foreign Policy*, Judith Goldstein and Robert Keohane, eds. (New York: Cornell University Press, 1993); Alexander Wendt, "Anarchy is What States Make of It: The Social Construction of Power Politics," in *International Organization* 46 (1992): 391–425; Thomas Biersteker and Cynthia Weber, *State Sovereignty as Social Construct* (Cambridge: Cambridge University Press, 1996).
3. John Torpey, "Coming and Going: On the State Monopolization of the 'Legitimate Means of Movement,'" in *Sociological Theory*, 16, no. 3 (1998a): 239–259. For instance, a 1753 Prussian law required innkeepers to inform authorities of foreigner lodging, as did a

1813 passport law that also imposed sanctions on carriage personnel and employers; see John Torpey, "Le Controle des passeports et la liberte de circulation: le cas de l'Allemagne au XIXe siecle," in *Geneses*, 30 (1998b): 55–57. Hotel registration was later revived as a means of surveillance in Europe's Schengenland. Similarly, the U.S. Passenger Act of 1902 required steamship companies to transport inadmissible passengers ("likely to be a public charge") back to their country of departure. Local and regional authorities sometimes kept some migration control prerogatives in certain federal settings.

4. Didier Bigo, *Polices en Reseaux; L'experience Europeene* (Paris: Presses de la Fondation Nationale de Sciences Politiques, 1996).

5. See Peter Schuck "The Politics of Rapid Legal Change: Immigration Policy in the 1980s," in *Studies in American Political Development*, 6 (1992): 37–92; Peter Schuck and Theodore Hsien Wang, "Continuity and Change: Patterns of Immigration Litigation in the Courts, 1979–1990," in *Stanford Law Review*, 45 (1992); Stephen Legomsky, *Immigration and the Judiciary: Law and Politics in Britain and America* (Oxford: Clarendon, 1987); James Hollifield, *Immigrants, Markets, and States: The Political Economy of Postwar Europe* (Cambridge: Harvard University Press, 1992); Gerald Neuman, "Immigration and Judicial Review in the Federal Republic of Germany," in *New York University Journal of International Law and Politics* 23, no. 1 (1990): 35–85; John Guendelsberger, "The Right to Family Unification in French and United States Immigration Law," in *Cornell International Law Journal*, 21 (1988): 76–81; Christian Joppke, "Asylum and State Sovereignty," in *Comparative Political Studies*, 30, no. 3 (1997): 259–298; *Immigration and the Nation-State* (Oxford: Oxford University Press, 1999); Virginie Guiraudon, *Policy Change Behind Gilded Doors: Explaining the Evolution of Aliens' Rights in Contemporary Western Europe* (Ph.D. dissertation, Cambridge: Harvard University, 1997); "European Courts and Foreigners' Rights," *International Migration Review* (2000b). In the United States, Gary Freeman has argued that migration control policymaking has also been captured domestically by strong sectoral interests (in particular business, ethnic, and family lobbies) that do not want restrictive entry policies, "The Decline of Sovereignty?" in Joppke, *Challenge to the Nation-State* (1998): 86–108.

6. Ulrich Herbert, *A History of Foreign Labor in Germany* (Ann Arbor: University of Michigan Press, 1990).

7. Some scholars have argued that international human rights norms have also constrained state action. See Yasemin Soysal, *Limits of Citizenship* (Chicago: Chicago University Press, 1994); Saskia Sassen, *Losing Control?* (New York: Columbia University Press, 1996); David Jacobson, *Rights across Borders: Immigration and the Decline of Citizenship* (Baltimore: Johns Hopkins University Press, 1996). However, as we have shown elsewhere, they have had less tangible effect on domestic migration policies. See Guiraudon, "European Courts and Foreigners' Rights" (2000b), and Viriginie Guiraudon and Gallya Lahav, "The State Sovereignty Debate Revisited: The Case of Migration Control," in *Comparative Political Studies*, 33, no. 2 (March 2000): 163–195.

8. Gallya Lahav, "The Role of Non-State Actors in the Movement of People: Promoting Travel and Controlling Migration in the European Union," paper presented at the European Community Studies Association Sixth Biennial International Conference (Pittsburgh, Pennsylvania, 1999).

9. Sassen, *Losing Control?*

10. Sassen, *Losing Control?*

11. Wayne Cornelius, Philip Martin, and James Hollifield, *Controlling Immigration* (Stanford: Stanford University Press, 1994).

12. Peter Andreas, "The Escalation of U.S. Immigration Control in the Post-NAFTA Era," in *Political Science Quarterly*, 113, no. 4 (1999): 591–615.

13. Gallya Lahav, "The Evolution of Immigration Policy in Liberal Democracies since 1965: Changing the Gatekeepers or 'Bringing Back the State,'" paper presented at the German American Academic Council (Berlin, 1997). Outside the United States, new migration countries in southern Europe have also diligently shown their will to be good citizens of Europe by raising fences and mobilizing personnel at the border. For a description of the ways in which southern Europe has copied the northern European migration regime, see Martin Baldwin-Edwards, "The Emerging European Immigration Regime: Some Reflections on Implications for Southern Europe," *Journal of Common Market Studies*, 35, no. 4 (1997): 497–519. The Spanish government has so far spent 340 million dollars on a double fence along the 8.3-kilometer-long border separating Morocco and the enclave city of Ceuta. *Migration News Sheet*, March 1999: 5.

14. Or from developments that contradict political statements about "zero-immigration" policies such as the recruitment of seasonal workers, or, as in Germany, contract workers.

15. Guiraudon (1997); "European Integration and Migration Control: Vertical Policy-Making as Venue Shopping," in *Journal of Common Market Studies*, 38, no. 2 (2000a). This view derives from the literature on "policy venues," defined as "institutional locations where authoritative decisions are made concerning a given issue"; see Frank Baumgartner and Bryan Jones, *Agendas and Instability in American Politics* (Chicago: Chicago University Press, 1993), 32. It stems from E. E. Schattschneider's work on the expansion of the scope of conflict in policy debates and on the "mobilization of bias" (*The Semisovereign People*, New York: Holt, Rhinehart and Winston, 1960).

16. Gallya Lahav, "Immigration and the State: The Devolution and Privatisation of Immigration Control in the EU," in *Journal of Ethnic and Migration Studies*, 24, no. 4 (1998): 675–694.

17. Aristide Zolberg, "Matters of State: Theorizing Immigration Policy," in *The Handbook of International Migration: The American Experience*, Charles Hirschman, Philip Kasinitz, and Josh DeWind, eds. (New York: Russell Sage, 1999), 71–93.

18. United Nations, *World Population Monitoring: Issues of International Migration and Development* (New York: Population Division, 1997).

19. The Club of Berne included representatives from the EC and Switzerland and focused on antiterrorism whereas the STAR group (*Standige Arbeitsgruppe Rauschgift*) concentrated on drug trafficking and involved the German BKA, France, the Netherlands, Austria, Denmark, Switzerland, and Luxembourg (Bigo, *Polices en Reseaux*, chapter 2).

20. Vendelin Hreblay, *Les Accords de Schengen: Origine, Fonctionnement, Avenir* (Brussels: Bruylant, 1998).

21. See Tony Bunyan for a compilation of these texts: *Key Texts on Justice and Home Affairs in the European Union, Volume 1, From Trevi to Maastricht, 1976–1993* (London: Statewatch, 1997).

22. OECD, *SOPEMI, Continuous Reporting System on Migration: Trends in International Migration* (Paris: OECD, 1995); Chien-Yi Lu, "Harmonization of Migration Policies in the European Union: A State-Centric or Institutionalist Explanation?" paper presented at the European Community Studies Association Sixth Biennial International Conference (Pittsburgh, Pennsylvania, June 1999), 4.

23. Tony Bunyan and Frances Webber, *Intergovernmental Cooperation on Immigration and Asylum* (Brussels: Churches Commission for Migrants in Europe, 1995).

24. The Justice and Home Affairs council has so far agreed on one joint position on the common definition of a refugee and on five legally binding joint actions, regarding school travel for third country national children, airport transit procedures, a common format for resident permits, burden sharing for displaced persons and human trafficking. On the "Europeanization" of migration control and transgovernmental cooperation, see Michael Anderson and Monica den Boer, eds., *Policing across National Boundaries* (London: Pinter, 1994); Didier Bigo, ed., *L'Europe des polices et de la securite interieure* (Bruxelles: Complexe, 1992); Bigo (1996); Simon Hix and Jan Niessen, *Reconsidering European Migration Policies* (Brussels: Churches Commission for Migrants in Europe, 1996); Baldwin-Edwards, "The Emerging European Immigration Regime," 497–519.

25. Member state responsibilities with regard to the maintenance of law and order and internal security are upheld. During a five-year transitional period, notwithstanding a few exceptions, there will be joint initiative by the Commission or the Member States, the consultation of the European Parliament (EP), and unanimity in the Council.

26. Andrew Geddes, "The Representation of 'Migrants' Interests' in the European Union," in *Journal of Ethnic and Migration Studies*, 24, no. 4 (1998): 695–713.

27. The relevant texts include Schengen, Dublin, the 1992 London resolutions, and the nonbinding yet by then almost redundant 1995 "Resolution on Minimum guarantees for asylum procedures" in the third pillar.

28. Saskia Sassen, "The *de facto* Transnationalizing of Immigration Policy," in Joppke, ed., *Challenge to the Nation-State* (1998): 49–85.

29. *Le Monde*, October 18, 1994.

30. In 1992, Morocco signed an agreement with Spain whereby it would take back aliens that had entered Spain illegally. In 1998, Italy and Tunisia signed a readmission agreement whereby Tunisia accepted the return of illegal Tunisians apprehended in Italy. In return, Italy promised to invest $50 million a year for three years in Tunisia to create jobs and discourage emigration.

31. Sandra Lavenex, *Safe Third Countries: Extending the EU Asylum and Immigration Policies to East and Central Europe* (Budapest: Central European University Press, 1999); Rey Koslowski, "European Union Migration Regimes, Established and Emergent," in Joppke, ed., *Challenge to the Nation-State* (1998a): 153–188.

32. Rey Koslowski, "European Migration Regimes: Emerging, Enlarging, and Deteriorating," *Journal of Ethnic and Migration Studies*, 24, no. 4 (1998b): 735–749; and in this volume. See also Vachudová, this volume.

33. See the "Commission's Opinion on [Estonia, Hungary, Poland, the Czech Republic, Slovenia]'s Application for Membership in the European Union," in *Agenda 2000* (Brussels: Commission of the European Communities, 1997).

34. Frank Paul Weber, "Participation of Carriers in the Control of Migration: The Case of Germany," paper presented at the Annual Meetings of the International Studies Association (Minneapolis, Minnesota, March 1998).

35. While these private actors are mostly compelled to partake in the enlarged regulation system through negative constraints—the avoidance of sanctions and penalties—more recently, there have been some positive incentives for compliance. In the United States, for example, the Immigration and Nationality Technical Corrections Act of 1994 mitigated fines for "good performance" of airlines—in other words a reward for efficacy, if an air carrier can show that it has appropriately screened all passengers in accordance with regulations.

See Constance O'Keefe, "Immigration Issues and Airlines: An Update," in *Journal of Air Law and Commerce*, 63, no. 28 (1997): 17–65.

36. In Spain, an interministerial working group has been established to examine the feasibility of following the example of the other member states of the Schengen Group. For obvious reasons, Luxembourg has not been confronted by the problem of inadmissible passengers by air, but under a new bill drawn up with the aim of bring its Aliens Law in line with the Schengen Agreement, there is a provision on carriers' liability. See Antonio Cruz, *Carrier Liability in the Member States of the European Union* (Brussels: Churches Commission for Migrants in Europe, briefing paper 17, September 1994): 7.

37. Cruz, *Carrier Liability*.

38. Lahav, "The Role of Non-State Actors in the Movement of People: Promoting Travel and Controlling Migration in the European Union"; Reiner Kraakman, "Gatekeepers: The Anatomy of a Third-Party Enforcement Strategy," in *Journal of Law, Economics, and Organization*, 2 (1986): 53; Janet Gilboy, "Compelled Third-Party Participation in the Regulatory Process: Legal Duties, Culture and Noncompliance," in *Law and Policy*, 20, no. 2 (1998): 135–136.

39. Janet Gilboy, "'Third-Party' Involvement and Regulatory Enforcement Behavior," Working Paper #9408 (Washington, D.C.: American Bar Association, 1994).

40. *The New York Times*, September 11, 1999, A4.

41. Cruz, *Carrier Liability*.

42. France decreed employer sanctions again in 1976. The United Kingdom adopted legislation prohibiting the harboring of illegal aliens, though not their employment (out of fear of fueling discrimination) in 1971. Switzerland has had antiharboring statutes since 1931 and adopted an employment statute in 1984. West Germany first prohibited the employment of clandestine aliens in 1975; the Netherlands did so in 1974, as did Austria in 1981; and Italy, Spain, and Belgium have followed suit. See Mark Miller, "Employer Sanctions in France: From the Campaign against Illegal Alien Employment to the Campaign against illegal work," research paper (Washington, D.C.: U.S. Commission on Immigration Reform, 1995).

43. Freeman, "The Decline of Sovereignty?"

44. Miller, "Employer Sanctions in France"; Lahav, "Immigration and the State." In Spain, in 1993, the Employment and Social Security Inspectorate launched a campaign by increasing the number of work site inspections and reinforcing the control of social security registrations. Following this campaign the number of illegal cases brought to justice was reported to fall dramatically (OECD, *SOPEMI* 1995: 45).

45. Miller, "Employer Sanctions in France," 26.

46. *The New York Times*, July 7, 1997.

47. In the United States, the number of illegal aliens deported in 1995 reached a record level of 51,600, up 15 percent from 1995, and up nearly 75 percent from 1990.

48. Janet Gilboy, "Implications of 'Third-Party' Involvement in Enforcement: The INS, Illegal Travellers, and International Airlines," *Law and Society Review*, 31, no. 3 (1997): 505–529; O'Keefe, "Immigration Issues and Airlines."

49. The new immigration bills change the legal admissions system by increasing the minimum income a sponsor must have to sponsor relatives for admission (to 125 percent of the poverty line in the Senate bill, and 200 percent in the House). *The New York Times*, May 28, 1996.

50. See Gallya Lahav, "The Rise of Non-State Actors in Migration Regulation in the United States and Europe," in *Immigration Research for a New Century: Multidisciplinary Perspectives*, Nancy Foner, Ruben Rumbaut, and Steven Gold, eds. (New York: Russell Sage, 2000); Lahav, "Immigration and the State"; Harvey Feigenbaum and Jeffrey Henig, "The Political Underpinnings of Privatization: A Typology," in *World Politics*, 46 (January 1994): 185–208.

51. Michael Olivas, "Preempting Preemption: Foreign Affairs, State Rights, and Alienage Classification," in *Virginia Journal of International Law*, 35 (Fall 1994): 217–236; Jeffrey Passel, "Recent Efforts to Control Illegal Immigration to the United States," paper presented at the OECD Working Party on Migration (Paris, 1996).

52. Patrick Weil, *Mission d'etude de la legislation de la nationalite et de l'immigration, Rapports au Premier Ministre* (Paris: La Documentation Francaise, 1997), 67.

53. The study was conducted by the Cimade (a Protestant nongovernmental organization). See *Le Monde*, February 19 and December 13, 1997.

54. Guiraudon interview with Ben Koolen, Director of the Coordination of Minority Policy unit, Ministry of Interior (The Hague, Netherlands, 1995).

55. Guiraudon interviews with Natalie Jonkers, Nicolas Franken, and Gerard de Boer, IND, Ministry of Justice (The Hague, Netherlands, 1995).

56. Peter Schuck, "The Re-Evaluation of American Citizenship," in *Challenge to the Nation-State*, Joppke, ed. (1998); Gerald Neuman, "The Effects of Immigration on Nationality Law," paper presented to the European Forum series (Florence: European University Institute, 1998).

57. The politicization of the migration issue under certain governors such as Pete Wilson of California may signal changes over time in the handling of migration control within a single region in cases of state leadership changes.

58. And a legitimate one, given that a handful of states are the major fiscal and political stakeholders of immigration and are also playing a more independent role internationally. See Peter Spiro, "The States and Immigration in an Era of Demi-Sovereignties," *Virginia Journal of International Law*, 35 (1994): 121–178.

59. Guiraudon interview, Frank Sharry, Immigration Forum, Washington, D.C., February 1999.

60. Frank Paul Weber, "Expulsion: genese et pratique d'un controle en Allemagne," *Cultures et Conflits* (1997): 107–151.

61. Decision of May 12, 1987, in *Entscheidungen des Bundesverfassungsgerichts* 76: 1.

62. Neuman, "Immigration and Judicial Review in the Federal Republic of Germany," 59. At the operational or logistical level, differences are even greater. Frank Paul Weber's work on detention centers for foreigners has shown that rules and conditions vary from one state or locality to the next (1997).

63. Bavaria, for instance, maintained a separate school track for foreign children. For a comparative assessment of intranational differences in incorporation policy, see Didier Lapeyronnie, ed., *Immigres en Europe* (Paris: La Documentation Francaise, 1992).

64. See *Frankfurter Allgemeine Zeitung*, March 18, 1995, 1.

65. 140,000 of the 400,000 ethnic Albanians whose demand for asylum had been rejected in Germany by 1998 are from Kosovo. Source: migration.ucdavis.edu, *Migration News*, April 1998.

66. This was the case, for example, in Hessen where the administrative court found the Hessen Interior Ministry's suspension of orders to expel Kurds unlawful (*gesetzswidrig*). See

ZAR Aktuell, July 28, 1995, 1. On the federal government's capacity to force states into compliance, see Ralph Göbel-Zimmerman, "Handlungsspielräume der Landesregierungen für den Erlaß von Abshiebungsstoppregelungen," in *ZAR,* January 10, 1995, 28.

    67. Quoted in *The New York Times,* July 7, 1997.

    68. Bigo, *Polices en Reseaux,* 94.

    69. Roland Bank, "The Emergent EU Policy on Asylum and Refugees," paper presented in the European Forum seminar series (Florence: European University Institute, 1998).

Part Two

U.S. Border Controls

5

The Political Costs of State Power: U.S. Border Control in South Florida

Christopher Mitchell

South Florida was one of the first regions of the United States where relatively strong border controls were put into effect, beginning in 1980. United States Coast Guard vessels began patrols that in most years have dramatically curtailed illegal migration from two major migrant-source nations, Cuba and Haiti.[1] With significant exceptions (especially in 1991, 1992, and 1994), U.S. picket vessels in the Straits of Florida and the Windward Passage reduced unauthorized immigration by as much as 90 percent, as displayed in table 5.1. Later, in the 1990s, highly publicized initiatives to restrain unauthorized migration were launched along the U.S. land border with Mexico, such as Operations Hold the Line and Río Grande in Texas, Safeguard in Arizona, and Gatekeeper in California. At their most effective, however, these revised frontier-patrol policies reduced the number of arrests by only 50 percent.

At first blush, one might attribute these dramatic cutbacks to Florida's technical advantage—having no land border with a foreign nation. Unauthorized migrants seeking to enter by sea, we might surmise, are likely to be concentrated in relatively few, and highly visible, vessels that can be impounded or deflected relatively simply. However, this would be an erroneous, or better stated, an incomplete assumption. The circumstance of facing a largely maritime migrant flow has indeed proven advantageous for border control in Florida, but to mobilize and actualize that advantage, standard "frontier control" resources such as the Coast Guard and airborne patrols have proven inadequate by themselves. To supplement them and make them effective, the U.S. government has had to venture deep into the realm of international relations, utilizing bilateral and multilateral diplomacy, and in one instance a major deployment of the U.S. armed forces (in Haiti in 1994). In addition, to employ these diplomatic, military, and naval policy tools successfully, Washington has needed to contend with influential domestic political forces, including some that are centered in South Florida and some with more diverse national roots.

Table 5.1   Cubans and Haitians Arriving in the United
States in 1980, and Coast Guard Interceptions at Sea
Near South Florida, 1981–1998

	Nation of Origin	
Calendar Year	Cuba	Haiti
1980	124,776	24,530
1981	NA	64
1982	NA	158
1983	47	687
1984	19	1,951
1985	43	2,327
1986	27	3,176
1987	44	3,588
1988	59	4,699
1989	391	3,368
1990	467	1,131
1991	2,203	9,941
1992	2,557	31,401
1993	3,656	2,329
1994	37,139	24,917
1995	626	1,969
1996	403	700
1997	406	587
1998	1,047	1,206

Author's tabulations on the basis of several sources.[2]

In describing and analyzing U.S. border control policy in South Florida since 1960, this chapter will assert that state power over frontiers may rest on three basic resources. Those assets are technical means (both tangible and organizational), domestic political support, and diplomatic understandings with foreign governments (especially migrant-source nations). In addition to helping to clarify our specific case, this approach will make it easier to compare the U.S. experience in South Florida with the tasks Washington faces in seeking to control the nation's long land frontier with Mexico.

We will begin with a brief overview of South Florida's remarkable population growth, economic development, and mounting political complexity—all of which have been intimately related to migration from the Caribbean area. The chapter then surveys the record of population movement from abroad into the area before 1980, and explores why U.S. policy toward those flows changed so crucially in that year. We will examine how implementing stronger border controls led Washington to bargain diplomatically with Cuba and Haiti during the 1980s, and helped bring the United States to intervene militarily in the latter nation in 1994. As a domestic counterpoint, this chapter will outline the complex interplay among local, state, and national currents of public opinion, which helped to determine the political sustainability of sea patrols against migrants heading for South Florida. Finally, we will speculate on the future effectiveness of U.S. frontier controls, both in Florida and along the Mexican border.

THE SOUTH FLORIDA REGION

South Florida is dominated by the Miami–Fort Lauderdale metropolitan area, the twelfth largest in the United States (see table 5.2). The southern section of Florida, in turn, houses nearly 40 percent of the 14,654,000 people living in the nation's fourth most populous state. South Florida has grown rapidly: the population of Miami–Dade County nearly quadrupled between 1950 and 1990, although its growth rate has slackened in recent years.[3] Indeed the region mushroomed from virtual emptiness to intense urban and suburban growth during the twentieth century alone; Miami was a tiny settlement when the extension of Henry Flagler's Florida East Coast Railway to the locality in 1896 launched the city's headlong development.

Miami's economy has largely been shaped by its location.[4] Lacking extensive mineral or agricultural resources, it earns its living from its climate, from its proximity to the Caribbean and Latin America, and from the production and consumption of the people who have been attracted to the area. Economic activity is centered on services including tourism, shipping, banking, and insurance; the Port of Miami handles more cruise-ship passengers, for example, than any other port in the world. Miami–Dade County also includes an active light-manufacturing sector, largely made up of small enterprises; there are 3,000 establishments employing 80,000 workers.

Migration from elsewhere in the United States, and especially from the Caribbean and Central America, have been the chief engines of recent demographic expansion in South Florida. As figure 5.1 indicates, between 1950 and 1990 Hispanic residents rose from 4 percent of the county's population to more than 49 percent, while the slower-growing African American segment of the population included more

Table 5.2   Population of Principal Metropolitan Areas in South Florida, 1997

Metropolitan Area	Population
Fort Myers–Cape Coral	387,091
Miami–Fort Lauderdale	3,515,358
Naples	195,731
Sarasota–Bradenton	538,783
West Palm Beach–Boca Raton	1,018,524
Total	5,655,487

Source: United States Department of Commerce, Bureau of the Census, "Metropolitan Area Rankings," 1997. Internet: www.census.gov/Press-Release/metro01.prn

Figure 5.1   Population Growth and Ethnicity in Miami–Dade County, 1950–1990

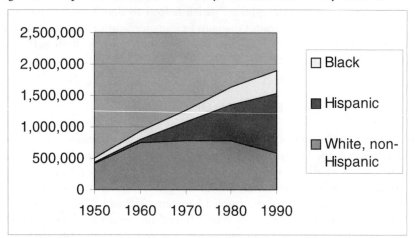

Source: Alejandro Portes and Alex Stepick, *City on the Edge: The Transformation of Miami* (Berkeley and Los Angeles: University of California Press, 1993), calculated from Table 8, p. 211.

than 60,000 Haitians. Major component groups within the Hispanic community in 1995 included Cuban Americans (600,000), Nicaraguans (74,000), Puerto Ricans (73,000), Colombians (54,000), and Mexicans (23,000).[5]

Like many other regions in the United States, South Florida is politically ambivalent about immigration. A good deal of the area's economic and cultural dynamism has resulted from international population flows. Major immigrant groups, especially Cubans, Haitians and Nicaraguans, have often importuned the U.S. government to admit more of their compatriots who would probably settle in the area. On the other hand, the inflow of numerous migrants has produced sometimes painful dislocations, as the traditional Anglo power-holders were sharply challenged by Cuban American elites, and non-Hispanic residents watched the unquestioned hegemony of Anglo culture erode. Nor did U.S.–born African Americans and recently arrived Haitians usually feel a quick mutual kinship or shared political interests.

In addition, South Florida has experienced repeated "migration emergencies," in which scores of thousands of new and often needy immigrants have disembarked within a matter of months. As a result of these varied and intensely felt aspirations and experiences, South Florida is probably more sensitive to immigration policy questions than any other U.S. region except possibly San Diego. In 1994, the Florida state government even declared an "immigration emergency," and threatened to detain "raft people" arriving from Cuba, if the U.S. government did not act to restrain that alarming inflow.[6] In 1998, the U.S. Immigration and Naturalization

Service (INS) signed a formal agreement to cooperate with Florida in responding to "any mass influx of aliens within the state."[7]

CARIBBEAN MIGRATION TO SOUTH FLORIDA
AND THE CRISES OF 1980

The first major waves of migration from the Caribbean to South Florida originated from Cuba during the 1960s and 1970s, and they came with the assent and even encouragement of the U.S. government. As part of its hostility after mid-1960 to the Cuban Revolution, Washington welcomed Cubans who came to the United States in two major movements (1960–1962 and 1965–1973). Almost all these migrants traveled by air, and they were classified as refugees from communism. Many received federal financial help in adapting to their new locations, and in 1966 the Cuban Adjustment of Status Act granted them the right to apply for permanent U.S. residency. U.S. policymakers viewed these first emigrants from Cuba—a good many of whom were skilled, affluent, or both—as valuable both symbolically and practically. In U.S. eyes, their departure represented a rejection of Cuban socialism and a subtraction of human resources from the Castro government's support base. Havana, on the other hand, was willing to permit the departure of more than 600,000 to the United States during these years, to remove a source of potential opposition whose repression would be costly and might undercut international respect for the regime.

A second, far less welcomed migrant stream began to enter South Florida in the early 1970s from Haiti, which had been dominated for more than fifteen years by the Duvalier family dictatorship. The Haitians were far poorer and less educated than Cuban refugees, and they arrived in small boats, often simply walking ashore at South Florida beaches. (Sometimes bodies of Haitians washed ashore from boats that had foundered in the surf, or because emigrants had been simply dumped by unscrupulous smugglers.) From 1972 through 1979, 7,837 undocumented Haitians arrived via this route.[8] In part because they were fleeing a government that was profoundly repressive but not politically radical, and in part because they were poor black migrants entering a U.S. southern city less than twenty years after the advent of the Civil Rights movement, the U.S. government quickly showed hostility to the Haitian boat people. If apprehended, they were often detained in harsh stockades reminiscent of concentration camps, and many were deported to Haiti on the grounds that they were "economic" rather than "political" refugees, who should simply seek immigrant visas rather than claim to be the victims of political violence and persecution.

In the spring of 1980, seaborne migration to South Florida suddenly changed from an episodic and manageable problem to a full-blown crisis with national ramifications. Following seven years of little direct emigration from Cuba to the United States, the Cuban government announced in April 1980 that Cuban Americans who wished to transport friends and relatives to the United States could come to the port of Mariel, a few miles west of Havana, and pick them up. The revolutionary government took this step to recoup some of the political damage it had suffered when more than 10,000 Cubans had flocked to the grounds of the Peruvian embassy in Havana upon hearing that any who did so would be allowed to depart from Cuba. A "freedom flotilla" to Key West quickly developed. Seeking to further discredit the emigrant surge, the Cuban government obliged boat captains to transport a number of hard-core criminals, mental patients, and agents provocateurs (problematic migrants who together made up about 10 percent of the total). Castro described "those who are leaving from Mariel" as "the scum of the country—antisocials, homosexuals, drug addicts, and gamblers, who are welcome to leave Cuba if any country will have them."[9] In all, nearly 125,000 migrants, dubbed *marielitos* even by the U.S. media, reached the United States by sea in 1980. At the same time, the flow of boat people from Haiti burgeoned to twenty-five times the rate of the 1970s.

Alarmed by the size, speed, and apparent social characteristics of the migrant inflow from Mariel, U.S. public opinion quickly changed from its traditional stance of welcoming Cubans to one of hostile restrictionism. The Carter administration, locked in a difficult election campaign that it eventually lost, was sharply criticized for what appeared an indecisive and weak response. Florida state politicians demanded strict screening before *marielitos* were released from custody, and federal assistance in meeting the social costs of absorbing the new arrivals. In Miami, even Cuban Americans joined non-Hispanic whites and blacks in viewing those coming in the flotilla as socially detrimental; they were concerned that the highly negative public image of Mariel would tarnish the positive public reputation they had labored to build within the United States.[10]

Improvising quickly in the face of a novel policy crisis, the U.S. government tried to end the sealift. Arriving Cubans were classified not in the relatively privileged category of "refugees," but simply as "entrants" who would not receive immediate federal assistance.[11] The Coast Guard warned boats departing from U.S. shores for Cuba that they faced confiscation and a $1,000-per-migrant fine if they returned with undocumented Cubans; more than 1,000 boats were actually impounded. Washington also fruitlessly urged the Cuban government to switch to an airlift, or to let the United States send larger vessels to evacuate political prisoners who had been prescreened in Cuba. In late September the revolutionary government finally closed Mariel to further emigration, partly because its own international image had been damaged by the protracted spectacle of a boatlift under miserable conditions.

IMPLEMENTING STRONGER BORDER CONTROLS AFTER 1980

The Reagan administration began a U.S. policy of limiting and deterring unauthorized migration to South Florida that has been continued and elaborated on for nearly twenty years. The major instrument of this policy was the tactic of stationing Coast

Guard vessels near source nations in the Caribbean to "interdict" migrant-carrying vessels in international waters. The first target of this new approach was Haiti. In 1981 the United States began routinely posting a Coast Guard cutter in the Windward Passage, to find and stop migrant-smuggling boats, which were often haphazardly built and unseaworthy. Passengers would be transferred to the U.S. vessel, and interviewed in summary fashion to determine whether they could plausibly claim "a well-founded fear of persecution" in Haiti.[12] (During the 1980s, these shipboard reviews adjudged only about one in a thousand U.S.–bound Haitians to be legitimate asylum seekers.) Then the smuggling boat would be burned, and all passengers deemed to be "economic migrants" would be returned quickly to a Haitian port.

This policy was rooted in both political and legal considerations. Since the major public relations costs of appearing to have lost control of U.S. borders were incurred in the politically strategic state of Florida, it was far preferable to deflect migrants at sea rather than to round them up and detain them within range of newspapers and TV stations in Miami. Legally, Washington wished to deal with Haitian migrants outside U.S. territory, since if they reached U.S. shores they could often delay deportation through a series of claims within the U.S. administrative and court systems. If apprehended in international waters, boat people could legitimately be returned anywhere.[13]

These maritime tactics were supplemented by active U.S. diplomacy in Port-au-Prince. In 1981 the United States negotiated an agreement with the Duvalier regime, under which Haiti sanctioned the Coast Guard patrols, and agreed to restrain the smuggling trade and to accept returned migrants without retribution. Even Haiti's relatively chaotic dictatorship—then entering its last five years of dominance—proved quite effective in suppressing the launching of vessels for clandestine migration. The U.S. strategy of negotiating with Caribbean migrant-source countries—seeking "migration control allies" in the terms used by Gallya Lahav and Virginie Guiraudon in their chapter in this volume—was extended to Cuba in 1984. Following negotiations precipitated by a visit of Jesse Jackson to Havana, the Cuban government agreed to accept several thousand *marielitos* whom the United States had imprisoned as "excludable," and the United States agreed to accept 20,000 Cubans annually as legal migrants. Washington hoped the latter measure would "make another . . . Mariel unnecessary."[14]

The importance of supplementing sea patrols with diplomatic agreements became fully clear during the 1990s, when both Haiti and Cuba relaxed their efforts to prevent boats from leaving their shores. The renewed Haitian outflow stemmed from the reimposition of harsh authoritarian rule. The Duvalier dictatorship had fallen in 1986, and after numerous weak military and civilian governments came and went, in 1990 a radical populist, Father Jean-Bertrand Aristide, was overwhelmingly elected president. He was overthrown seven months later by a brutally repressive junta led by General Raoul Cédras, and in the following two years almost 44,000 Haitians fled by sea and were picked up by U.S. patrol ships. In 1994, a new spurt of departures by sea began from Cuba, where the government once again permitted emigration in order to lessen and discredit domestic discontent. Perhaps in recognition that Cuban Americans would probably not send another flotilla of vessels, this time the Castro regime encouraged Cubans to construct makeshift rafts on which to float to U.S. waters. During this crisis, almost 25,000 *balseros* ("raft people") were intercepted by the U.S. Coast Guard.

These emergencies demonstrated three important weaknesses in the policy of Coast Guard interdiction alone, when the source nation was not cooperating. First, the number of small boats and rafts might overstrain the Coast Guard's resources. When dozens of vessels may depart in a single day, a higher proportion is likely to evade detection, costs rise dramatically, and other tasks of the service have to be subordinated. As the wave of boat people grew following President Aristide's overthrow in 1991, for example, fifteen Coast Guard cutters were assigned to the Haitian patrol out of thirty-three available for the whole eastern U.S. seaboard. Previously only one vessel had been needed.[15] The costs of patrolling also more than tripled during the same period, from an annual rate of $30 million to $103 million.[16]

Second, the very presence of U.S. ships—especially if they are visible from land—may act as a "magnet," attracting even more vessels from shore. Both the State Department and the INS criticized the Coast Guard for sending too many patrol craft close to Haiti; the Coast Guard responded that one of its core missions was to rescue those in distress at sea.[17]

Third, when migrants are apprehended during a large outflow of sea craft, major problems present themselves: how and where to care for the migrants, whether and where to land them, and under what legal status or justification. Early in both the Haitian and Cuban emergencies of the 1990s, those intercepted were kept on the decks of Coast Guard cutters, under jury-rigged tarpaulins to ward off sun and rain. Conditions on the vessels quickly became unmanageable, however, and camps for the migrants were hurriedly constructed at the nearest offshore U.S. facility: the Guantánamo Bay Naval Base in eastern Cuba! At other times, detained refugees were held on U.S. bases in Panama, and on a hospital ship anchored in the harbor at Kingston, Jamaica. In all these locations, the emigrants were depressed and discontented, and their advocates and families in the United States maintained a drumbeat of criticism at their indefinite detention with no access to legal due process.

In a painful policy evolution that we will describe more fully in the section that follows, the U.S. government gradually determined that it needed to help create a more legitimate political regime in Haiti to replace the Cédras junta. Only such a government would be an effective interlocutor with Washington on what had become the key issue of migration. The United States never recognized the de facto Haitian government that replaced Aristide, and in effect continued to treat him as the lawful Haitian leader. Working through both the United Nations and the Organization of American States (OAS), U.S. diplomats crafted a trade embargo to pressure the Haitian generals, but met only truculent defiance. In September 1994, facing imminent invasion by a U.S.–led OAS military force, General Cédras and his colleagues agreed to depart after talks with a delegation led by former President Jimmy Carter. President Aristide was restored to office in mid-October.

Migration diplomacy continued with Cuba into the mid-1990s as well. The 1984 migration agreement had proven vulnerable to the multiple disputes about other issues that bedevil U.S.–Cuban relations. Havana suspended cooperation under the accord in mid-1985, retaliating for the creation of Radio Martí to beam U.S. propaganda to the Cuban people. The agreement was reactivated in 1987, but Cuba complained that the United States dragged its feet in admitting legal migrants as it had agreed to do.[18] At the height of the 1994 "raft crisis," Washington in effect promised to exert itself so that 20,000 Cubans would actually enter the United States legally each year, and Cuba undertook to discourage any more rafters from embarking. The following year, the two governments agreed that Cuba would accept, without reprisal, future unauthorized migrants found at sea by U.S. vessels. They would no longer be admitted to the United States, or quarantined elsewhere; they would routinely be returned to Cuban control.

DEALING WITH DOMESTIC POLITICAL FORCES

One should not exaggerate the autonomy enjoyed by U.S. diplomacy on the issue of Caribbean migration after 1980. In fact, the 1980s and 1990s demonstrated that varied domestic political constituencies exerted notable influence over the government's actions in the field of international relations, actions aimed at countering migration by sea from the Caribbean to South Florida. In this lobbying over migration policy, there was an interplay among local political views expressed in South Florida, and pressures from public opinion in the state of Florida and nationally. Both the Haitian and Cuban cases chronicle the imposition of restrictive immigration policies—favored by most pressure groups at the state level in Florida and in the national arena—on coethnics in Miami. However, the Miami groups were able to influence specific U.S. strategies, affecting their detailed provisions, the speed of their implementation, and many of their political costs to Washington.

From 1981 to 1991, the Haitians in Miami were in a very weak position in pressing for better governmental treatment for themselves and for Haitians intercepted at sea. They were a small and poor minority in a section of the nation where blacks suffered special disadvantages, and their key weapon—bringing lawsuits—was plagued with delays and disappointments. With aid from sympathetic lawyers both locally and nationally, they gradually won court decisions to alleviate conditions of confinement and to increase their opportunities to demonstrate genuine political motivations for fleeing Haiti. But they were never able to overturn the government's legal basis for repatriating migrants who could not reach U.S. territory, losing a key lawsuit by a 1993 Supreme Court vote of 8 to 1. State and national sentiment to restrain Haitian migration firmly held sway during these ten years.

The 1990 election in Haiti and the coup that sought to cancel it the following year decisively altered the domestic terms of debate within the United States about Haiti and unauthorized Haitian migration. President Aristide's government was arguably the first in Haiti's entire history that could plausibly claim full democratic legitimacy. General Cédras's junta attacked both democracy and human rights, which were two of the most important pillars of proclaimed U.S. policy in inter-American relations. In addition, the brutality and lawlessness of the regime Washington came to call "the *de factos*" lent strong credence to the claim by Haitian boat people that they were fleeing not poverty but the prospect of torture and murder. The U.S. government was in a difficult bind for the three years that followed Aristide's overthrow in September 1991. It appeared callous and hypocritical if it repatriated Haitian migrants to the rule of an especially violent and corrupt regime, but it was unwilling to release thousands of Haitian refugees in South Florida or elsewhere.[19]

The makeshift solution chosen by President Bush and affirmed by president-elect Clinton—confining Haitian boat people in offshore "safe havens," mainly at Guantánamo Bay—proved only temporarily effective. It provided an almost ideal target for a growing national network of backers for the Haitian cause, including the Congressional Black Caucus and prominent individuals including African American dancer and choreographer Katherine Dunham and tennis star Arthur Ashe. These articulate allies engaged in civil disobedience and hunger strikes, pressing home the question of why black migrants from a brutal right-wing regime were kept in harsh tent cities at Guantánamo Bay, while (before August 1994) Cubans fleeing from left-wing authoritarianism were routinely being admitted to the U.S. mainland.

The strain upon a U.S. Democratic administration of appearing racist while countenancing Haitian dictators who abused human rights ultimately became unbearable. A dynamic was created that pushed President Clinton toward action that would restore a passably democratic government in Haiti. The combination of OAS military threat and U.S. diplomatic persuasion that crystallized in September 1994 achieved Aristide's restoration. Once that was accomplished, both interception and repatriation became far easier to defend in the arena of U.S. public opinion, and most of the Haitians at Guantánamo were returned to Haiti.

Cuban Americans in South Florida were in a far stronger position to influence United States immigration policy after 1980, and they organized effectively to increase that leverage. They were far more numerous and affluent than the Haitians and—increasingly obtaining U.S. citizenship—they came to represent a potent swing-voting bloc in a state with a rich cache of electoral votes. Florida's presidential primary, as well, was often viewed as pivotal during the 1970s and 1980s. The Cuban American National Foundation (CANF), organized by Miami businessmen in 1981, adroitly utilized a political action committee (Free Cuba PAC) and dogged lobbying to maintain and sharpen the U.S. embargo of Cuba. Most Cuban Americans did not want to see a repetition of the Mariel sealift that had been used to stigmatize them, but they argued strongly that Cubans who reached the United States on their own should be permitted to remain as legal residents. For fourteen years after Mariel, no administration in Washington challenged that basic approach.

State-level and national response to the 1994 rafters' crisis, however, finally pushed U.S. decision makers to treat Cubans found at sea in the same way that Haitians had been dealt with since 1981. Florida Governor Lawton Chiles, a Democrat, was seeking reelection in a year that proved to be disastrous for his party in Congress and in many other state races. He foresaw defeat if "another Mariel" was permitted in South Florida, and prodded the federal government to detain and screen *balseros* rather than releasing them to sponsoring Cuban American families. After urgent White House consultations including a meeting between President Clinton and half-a-dozen Cuban American leaders, the United States announced that, in future, intercepted raft people would be interned at Guantánamo Bay. In Miami, "Spanish talk radio shows blazed against the policy change and the word on the lips of hosts and callers was 'betrayal,'" but other Cuban Americans expressed reservations. Portrait photographer Mario Cabriera, who arrived during the 1960s, observed: "These same people [the *balseros*] are the ones who until quite recently were Castro supporters and forced us to leave our homeland."[20]

With opinions in Miami's "Little Havana" divided, and state and national opinion strongly averse to admitting more unauthorized Cuban migrants, militant Cuban American organizations were reduced to ineffective critics of the new maritime interdiction policy. When Washington took what seemed to be the logical next step in 1995, and agreed to return Cuban boaters and rafters directly to Havana's jurisdiction, the CANF and other organizations sponsored demonstrations that blocked the Dolphin Expressway in Miami and the Holland Tunnel between New York and New Jersey. They could not change the U.S. government's basic course of action at sea, although Washington did ultimately agree to admit most of the Cuban ex-rafters from their tent-city purgatory at Guantánamo Bay.

The South Florida anti-Castro forces did retain a significant legal resource: the 1966 Cuban Adjustment of Status Act. This U.S. legislation stipulates that migrants from Cuba who succeed in entering the United States may, after one year, receive permanent resident status.[21] Cuban rafters who—quite literally—set foot upon U.S. shores enjoy dramatic legal advantages over those seized while still afloat (and over unauthorized entrants of all other nationalities). No U.S. administration has shouldered the political costs of seeking to repeal this law, and from time to time Cuban emigrants receive wide publicity as they desperately dash for the Florida shores, sometimes contending with government patrol vessels.[22] The CANF and other exile organizations—supported by elected political leaders in Miami and in Dade County—invoked the Adjustment Act in the highly contentious case of six-year-old Cuban raft survivor Elián González in 1999–2000. They stubbornly resisted the boy's return to his Cuban father in the face of pressure from the INS and Attorney General Janet Reno, who were supported by U.S. public opinion.

CONCLUSION

In our review of recent U.S. frontier policy in South Florida, we have seen that state power over the border grew and became effective—albeit at considerable local political cost—in a process that required more than fifteen years. Technical means, diplomatic arrangements, and domestic political backing all contributed to this process. The effective use of patrol vessels and aircraft proved to be a necessary but not sufficient condition for blocking most seaborne unauthorized migrants; the cooperation of governments in source nations was also vital for successful interdiction. In addition, domestic public opinion played an important role, with national sentiments for restriction serving as both prod and support for Washington's post-1980 initiatives in South Florida. Smaller "special publics" in U.S. localities that favored continued admission of undocumented migrants were neutralized or defeated, but only over time and after substantial political concessions including some in the realm of foreign policy. In South Florida, U.S. policymakers could afford to concentrate on frontier control, unhindered by any crosscutting desire to develop strong trade and investment ties with migrant-sending nations. Trade with Haiti carried no political weight, and since the early 1960s Washington has sought to isolate Cuba economically not only from the United States but from the rest of the world as well.

We can now consider some implications of our findings, first for future developments in the South Florida, and second for frontier control along the Mexican border. In Florida, this study implies that future sudden changes—of policy or politics—in key source nations such as Cuba and Haiti could alter what currently seems to be stable U.S. border control. The United States could ill afford to do without the collaboration of Havana and Port-au-Prince in restraining unauthorized migration by sea, but the level of that cooperation in the future is uncertain at best.

The prospect of a future migration emergency seems especially plausible in the case of Cuba. In a recent lottery for U.S. immigrant visas (under the 1995 bilateral immigration accord), approximately 5 percent of the entire Cuban population entered their names; there were thirty lottery participants for every winner. This continuing demand for migration is voiced under a regime that depends—for its policy dynamism if not for its fundamental legitimacy—on an aging leader whose successors are neither well identified nor likely to consolidate their authority easily.

The United States is not well positioned to take proactive steps to sustain future joint action with the Haitian, and especially the Cuban, governments in the field of migration. Washington tends to react to alterations in political stability or foreign policy in major Caribbean nations, rather than anticipating those changes and their implications for migration and migration policy. (Although bilateral migration agreements with both Haiti and Cuba have tried to provide for future contingencies, they have had to be renegotiated following coups and policy reversals in source nations.) This reactive pattern is partly rooted in the low prestige and priority that migration considerations command in the planning and coordination of U.S. diplomatic initiatives.

The United States is especially hampered in dealing with Cuba about migration by the rigidity of its nearly forty-year-old policies toward Fidel Castro's government. The United States has a major interest in ensuring that Cuba's policy of emigration control remains sustained and continuous, as political authority evolves in that nation. Yet Washington's overall policy toward Cuba is basically to oppose and weaken the regime, with little evidence of reflection or maneuvering to help shape a successor government. This inflexible policy—extensively codified into law by the Helms-Burton Act—was reaffirmed in order to mollify Cuban Americans angry at the forced return of *balseros* to Cuba.

Our study also suggests several observations about the future of efforts to control unauthorized migration across the U.S. land frontier with Mexico. Along the 2,000-mile U.S.–Mexico border, several of the key elements we have found to be important to frontier control in South Florida are also significant policy considerations. These include the design and cost of technical control measures, the importance of persuading source nations to moderate emigration, and U.S. public opinion expressed at the local, state, and national levels. However, the character and configuration of some of these elements are notably different in the Southwest from the pattern they displayed in South Florida.

Technical Measures

Strengthening the land border is probably substantially more costly and less effective than deploying ships and planes to ward off undocumented seaborne migration. The U.S. government maintains the Coast Guard and the Navy for reasons that go far beyond border control, and so many of the "overhead costs" of expanding the latter mission have already been provided. Building fences, ditches, banks of lights, and sensor networks, and staffing the frontier with more Border Patrol agents and support workers, are major new investments. Moreover, as David Spener's chapter in this book indicates, more effective U.S. surveillance in some border sectors may simply redirect migrants to less well-patrolled stretches of the frontier.

Domestic Politics and Public Opinion

In South Florida, the Miami metroplex includes politically vocal residents of Cuban and Haitian background, who often vigorously oppose strict sea patrols against their compatriots. In the U.S. Southwest, the pattern of public opinion is quite different. The dominant public views—both near and distant from the border itself—tend to advocate a hard line toward unauthorized migration.[23] When antirestrictionist demonstrations take place in states such as California, they generally focus on U.S. policies toward migrants already in the United States, not toward those still abroad. If anything, then, stronger enforcement along the U.S. land border probably accrues clear political dividends in most arenas of public opinion, although that policy is not favored by agribusiness and other employers of unauthorized migrants.

The political impact of U.S. public opinion also suggests why Washington policymakers may not be especially perturbed when special border-control operations largely re-channel unauthorized migrants to different parts of the frontier. Segments of the border that have been reinforced are close to large population centers such as San Diego and El Paso. If restrictionist groups are placated there—and we found in South Florida that we must define "public opinion" on immigration in relation to its specific locality—then the political costs of extensive immigrant flows far from U.S. population centers may be quite acceptable to the U.S. government, at least in the short and medium terms.[24]

Diplomatic Cooperation

It appears much more difficult to persuade Mexico and migrant-source nations in Central America to restrain land migration than it was to induce Cuba and Haiti to limit the departure of boat people. Land frontiers are far more penetrable at modest individual cost than is even a narrow stretch of open sea. To limit emigration, Mexico and the nations of Meso-America would have to take the difficult and unlikely step of strengthening their own borders extensively, against their own citizens. (The chapter in this volume by Gustavo Mohar and María-Elena Alcaraz indicates that Mexico is willing to strengthen its frontier vigilance against Central Americans wishing to cross Mexico into the United States. But the Mexican government is much less activist in dealing with its own U.S.–bound fellow countrymen and women. Beyond combating the smuggling trade, which it considers dangerous, Mexico simply warns its compatriots of travel hazards, and advises them of their rights once they are within the United States.) To induce Mexico and Central American nations to take stronger action, the United States would probably have to offer proportionately attractive concessions, in varied fields including trade, debt, and the treatment of migrants already in the United States. If these speculations are realistic, it seems hardly surprising that the North American Free Trade Agreement (NAFTA) negotiations in the early 1990s studiously skirted the issue of migration. Although a Regional Conference on Migration (RCM) links the United States with its neighbors across the southern border, thus far the RCM's action plans are modest and relatively noncontroversial.[25]

In short, it may be that U.S. border control against unauthorized migration in South Florida is quite effective at present, but remains vulnerable to the loss of its key diplomatic support in coming years. Along the Mexican border, effective migration control has not yet been established, and it may never have meaningful support from source nations. But because technical means have been marshaled in such a way as to maximize their visibility to generally restrictionist U.S. public opinion in the Southwest, state power in that region enjoys a somewhat unearned reputation for increasing mastery over the border.

NOTES

1. During major migration-by-sea crises in the Caribbean, such as the Cuban emergency of 1994, U.S. Navy ships have also been used to patrol for migrants or to transport them once intercepted.

2. For Cubans in 1980, María Cristina García, *Havana U.S.A.: Cuban Exiles and Cuban Americans in South Florida, 1959–1994* (Berkeley: University of California Press, 1996), 46. For Haitians in 1980, Alex Stepick, "Unintended Consequences: Rejecting Haitian Boat People and Destabilizing Duvalier," in *Western Hemisphere Immigration and United States Foreign Policy*, Christopher Mitchell, ed. (University Park: Pennsylvania State University Press, 1992), 135. For years since 1980, U.S. Coast Guard, "Migrant Interdiction Statistics (by calendar year)," published on the Internet at: www.uscg.mil/d7/d7pa/AvgPage.htm

3. The Miami metropolitan area gained more than 322,000 residents—10 percent—between 1990 and 1996. Internet: www.census.gov/population/estimates/metro-city/ma96-09.txt

4. For an excellent overview of Miami's society and social challenges, see Alejandro Portes and Alex Stepick, *City on the Edge: The Transformation of Miami* (Berkeley: University of California Press, 1993). Chapter 9 focuses particularly on the implications of Miami's emergence for the geographic theory of cities; Portes and Stepick argue (204–205) that Miami's origin was "economically underdetermined," and its growth through migration since 1959 has been "politically overdetermined."

5. These estimates are by the Miami–Dade County Planning and Zoning Department, in Deborah Ramirez, "Study Praises Miami as Model of Diversity," *South Florida Sun-Sentinel*, October 16, 1998, 5B. For a perceptive discussion of politics and culture among Cuban émigrés in South Florida, see David Rieff, *The Exile: Cuba in the Heart of Miami* (New York: Simon and Schuster, 1993).

6. Mireya Navarro, "For Now, Florida Tries to Go It Alone," *The New York Times*, August 19, 1994.

7. In announcing the new accord, the INS stated that "while U.S. policy to interdict migrants at sea and process them offshore remains unchanged, this plan provides a mechanism for apprehending and detaining those aliens who evade interdiction and arrive on our shores in violation of federal law." Governor Lawton Chiles remarked: "Four years ago, I declared a state of emergency in South Florida. Today, I'm declaring victory because the federal government will assume full responsibility for future mass migration response operations." U.S. Department of Justice, "INS and Florida Sign Historic Agreement on Response to a Mass Migration," INS News Release, Washington, D.C., October 19, 1998.

8. See Christopher Mitchell, "U.S. Policy toward Haitian Boat People, 1972–93," *The Annals of the American Academy of Political and Social Science*, 534 (July 1994): 70.

9. Quoted in Portes and Stepick, *City on the Edge*, 21.

10. García, *Havana U.S.A.*, 46–80; Portes and Stepick, *City on the Edge*, 18–37.

11. Haitians who arrived—only during 1980—were accorded the same legal status as the Cubans, since other classifications might appear racist in the glare of national publicity. Only Cubans, however, were later accorded some federal economic assistance through special legislation. A detailed analysis of U.S. policymaking during the Mariel emergency is provided by Mario Antonio Rivera, *Decision and Structure: U.S. Refugee Policy in the Mariel Crisis* (Lanham, Md.: University Press of America, 1991).

12. This was the criterion for receiving political asylum in the United States, under the Refugee Act of 1980 (passed before the Mariel–Haitian crisis of the same year). As Patricia Weiss Fagen dryly remarked, it was not legally sufficient for an asylum applicant to demonstrate a well-founded fear of *death* from generally repressive conditions; elaborate documentation that a migrant had been *specifically* threatened by political authorities was demanded. Fagen, "Applying for Political Asylum in New York: Law, Policy and Administrative Practice," *Occasional Papers* #41 (New York University: Center for Latin American and Caribbean Studies, April 1984).

13. The key decision of the U.S. Supreme Court on this subject came in *Sale v. Haitian Centers Council* (1993).

14. Jorge I. Domínguez, "Cooperating with the Enemy?: U.S. Immigration Policies toward Cuba," in *Western Hemisphere Immigration*, Christopher Mitchell, ed., 64. The Cuban government has been willing to negotiate with the United States over migration because at times the regime stood to gain discrete objectives from such bargaining, and because Havana often views specific, focused talks with Washington as a means to undermine the U.S. trade embargo.

15. Testimony of Rear Admiral William P. Leahy, Jr., Chief, Office of Law Enforcement and Defense Operations, U.S. Coast Guard, in U.S. Congress, House, Judiciary Committee, Subcommittee on International Law, Immigration, and Refugees, Cuban and Haitian Immigration, Hearing, One Hundred and Second Congress, First Session, November 20, 1991, 92.

16. Mitchell, "U.S. Policy toward Haitian Boat People," 75.

17. Howard French, "Flight of Haitians Suddenly Resumes," *The New York Times*, May 16, 1992.

18. Statistics lend credence to the Cuban contention. For example, in fiscal year 1990, the INS recorded admission of only 9,436 Cuban immigrants. Of these, fully 6,994 had been refugees and those given asylum who were already living in the United States, who had simply "adjusted status" to be officially considered immigrants. U.S. Department of Justice, INS, *1990 Statistical Yearbook*, table 8, 65.

19. If the Cédras government had acted more vigorously to restrain emigrant boats from leaving Haiti, they might have changed the whole dynamic of U.S. debate on the subject. It was chiefly the question of how to treat intercepted Haitian boat people that pressed two U.S. administrations, of different political parties, toward the unprecedented steps of recognizing a government in exile, and intervening to restore that government to office in Haiti.

20. Jon Nordheimer, "Cuban-Americans Ambivalent on Shift," *The New York Times*, August 20, 1994.

21. U.S. Congress, House Judiciary Committee, Immigration and Nationality Act with Amendments and Notes on Related Laws, seventh edition (Washington, D.C.: U.S. Government Printing Office, 1980), 155.

22. The INS's 1998 agreement with Florida on handling migration emergencies (discussed earlier in this chapter) does not invalidate the Adjustment of Status Act. Instead, it promises some federal funding for Florida's administrative costs in the event of a migration emergency, and more active medical and criminal background checks on arriving migrants. As INS Commissioner Meissner stated upon signing the agreement, "the real objective here is to deter [emergency] migration." Internet: www.cnn.com/U.S./9810/20/mass.migration/index.html

23. Thomas J. Espenshade and Maryann Belanger present recent poll data that indicate two-thirds of respondents in the United States view illegal immigration as a major problem, and that "Mexico and illegal immigration are highly intertwined in the public's mind." "Other evidence suggests," they continue, "that Americans feel that the United States has a problem with border security, that the federal government should and can be doing more to cope with the problem, and that the public is willing to support doing more." Espenshade and Belanger, "Immigration and Public Opinion," in *Crossings: Mexican Immigration in Interdisciplinary Perspectives*, Marcelo M. Suárez-Orozco, ed. (Cambridge, Mass.: David Rockefeller Center for Latin American Studies, 1998), 375–376.

24. For a similar interpretation, see Peter Andreas, "The U.S. Immigration Control Offensive: Constructing an Image of Order on the Southwest Border," in *Crossings*, Suárez-Orozco, ed., esp. 351–352.

25. RCM members are Mexico, the seven Central American nations, the United States, and Canada. Colombia, the Dominican Republic, Ecuador, Jamaica, and Peru recently attended as observers, plus several intergovernmental organizations (IGOs) and nongovernmental organizations (NGOs). Conference plans for action stress goals including studying existing migration policies, examining migration's connection with development, combating migrant-smuggling rings, and returning unauthorized migrants from beyond the region (e.g., ship-borne emigrants from Asia). RCM documents include: Regional Conference on Migration, "Draft Joint Communiqué," Puebla, Mexico, March 14, 1996, available on the Internet at: www.quicklink.com/mexico/gob96mar/imi14mar/htm>; and Citizenship and Immigration Canada, Press Release on "Conclusion of the III Regional Conference on Migration," Ottawa, March 2, 1998, available on the Internet at: cicnet.ci.gc.ca/english/press/98/9813-pre.html

6

The Remaking of the California–Mexico Boundary in the Age of NAFTA

Joseph Nevins

The U.S.–Mexico border is an area of enormous economic and demographic activity and growth, making it one of the most dynamic border regions in the world. This has resulted in intensifying levels of regional integration, formalized by the North American Free Trade Agreement (NAFTA).[1] The population of the U.S.–Mexico border region is now about 12 million and is expected to grow to reach 24 million in 2020.[2] Currently, nearly 300,000 Mexican workers cross the boundary *legally* on a daily or weekly basis to work in the United States. The number of annual authorized crossings of the boundary is in the several hundreds of millions—largely between the series of "twin cities" that straddle the international divide. Annual transboundary financial transactions total more than $6 billion.[3]

The U.S.–Mexico integration process is most intensive in the San Diego–Tijuana area, the westernmost section of the international divide. This transboundary urban zone is the fastest growing metropolitan region in North America.[4] The current population of San Diego–Tijuana, for example, is an estimated 4 million people, and demographic projections predict that it will reach 5.7 million by the year 2020.[5] About 60 million people and 20 million cars per year now enter San Diego from Mexico through the San Ysidro port of entry—making it the busiest land crossing in the world.[6] And an estimated 40,000 people cross the border each day to work, including several thousand who manage and work in *maquiladoras* in Tijuana, but live in the San Diego area.[7] For many, such trends would seem to indicate that the California–Mexico boundary is becoming increasingly irrelevant. Indeed, some even argue that the boundary is disappearing. As San Diego City Manager Jack McGrory explained in 1993, "Frankly, we're starting to operate as if the border didn't even exist, and it's paying off—in both directions."[8]

There is another seemingly contradictory trend, however. Over the last several years, the California section of the U.S. boundary with Mexico has seen an unprecedented infusion of resources from the U.S. Immigration and Naturalization Service (INS). As a result, historically unparalleled levels of law enforcement—aimed at restricting unsanctioned immigrants and contraband—characterize the California–Mexico boundary. In this regard, the California–Mexico boundary has never been as pronounced as it is today in its more than 150-year history. Although more generally this is true of the U.S.–Mexico boundary, the section of the international divide in the San Diego area is where the state's boundary enforcement capacity is greatest. Not surprisingly, it is also the area in the U.S. border region where official and grassroots activism in favor of enhanced boundary enforcement and of greater immigration restriction is strongest.

In this chapter I explore the relationship between the strengthening of boundary enforcement by U.S. authorities as it relates to immigration and their simultaneous "opening" of the boundary to trade and investment in the San Diego–Tijuana region. I contend that it is a combination of shrinking distance, in the form of growing economic transboundary integration, significant (if diminishing) sociocultural differences, and wide wealth and income disparities between California and Mexico that have provided fertile ground for populist efforts to achieve higher levels of boundary enforcement.

I also briefly consider the practical tensions between enhanced immigration enforcement and increased economic deregulation, demonstrating that although transboundary integration has helped to fuel calls for enhanced boundary enforcement, the sociopolitical and economic factors that underlie such integration have also served to undermine efforts to increase the effectiveness of boundary enforcement.[9] Finally, I argue that greater levels of boundary enforcement and intensifying transboundary economic development are manifestations of the contradictions between two of the key functions of the modern territorial state—contradictions which become more pronounced in an age of increasing transboundary flows,[10] especially along boundaries between countries with widely divergent levels of socioeconomic development.

BUILDING UP THE BOUNDARY

A trip today to the California–Mexico boundary in the area of the City of San Diego reveals a very different scene than one would have found at the beginning of the 1990s. What existed then in terms of a boundary fence had gaping holes. Large crowds of migrants and smugglers gathered each afternoon along the boundary waiting to cross at nightfall into the U.S. extralegally. "Banzai runs" of unauthorized immigrants through the official ports of entry into the United States were also common. And there were frequent attacks against unauthorized migrants and crimes (mostly against property) by "border bandits."[11] As a journalist from the *Los Angeles Times* described the situation,

Until 1994, the San Diego sector[12] commonly fielded fewer than one hundred [United States Border Patrol] agents per shift against several thousand border-crossers lining the riverbanks and canyons. The sector recorded as many as three thousand arrests on busy Sundays. Every night was a potential riot, a journey into the battle theater of the absurd. The steel fence on the river levee had not yet been built, so agents routinely used their vehicles to herd back crowds, speeding at them, churning up clouds of dust.[13]

Even though the journalist overstates the case—the construction of the steel barrier on the river levee, for example, took place in 1991[14]—the appearance of the present-day boundary in San Diego is unquestionably radically different. As one analyst recently stated, "the entire border along San Diego is now eerily quiet and peaceful. It's the quiet that comes from control."[15] Thus, a semblance of order has replaced the image of chaos that once seemed to reign in the urbanized border region of San Diego.

These changes are the outgrowth of a massive infusion of resources into the enforcement division of the INS in recent years, especially along the U.S.–Mexico boundary. The INS budget for enforcement efforts along the Southwest boundary, for example, grew from $400 million in fiscal year (FY) 1993 to $800 million in FY 1997.[16] The number of border patrol agents rapidly expanded from 4,200 in 1994 to approximately 8,000 agents as of August 1999.[17] Underlying the significant growth in state efforts to control the U.S.–Mexico boundary is a dramatically heightened consciousness on the part of the United States public vis-à-vis the boundary and the putative problem of unauthorized immigration from Mexico—matters that rarely received significant national attention prior to the 1970s. Beginning in the late 1960s, however, there was growing public perception of the international boundary with Mexico as "out of control," as a dangerously porous line of defense against unprecedented numbers of unauthorized immigrants entering the United States from Mexico.

A number of factors came together to precipitate the perception of a crisis of boundary control, one associated mostly with immigrants from Mexico. The advent of a Chicano civil rights movement in the late 1960s, whose most notable accomplishments took place in the border region, led many American elites to fear the rise of an "American Quebec" in the U.S. Southwest.[18] At the same time, the early and mid-1970s saw the emergence of the energy crisis and an economic downturn in the United States. As in the past, economic recession proved to be an important factor facilitating the rise of immigration restrictionist sentiment.[19] Simultaneously, apprehensions of unauthorized immigrants by the U.S. Border Patrol were rising rapidly. In this context "illegal immigration" and "border control" emerged as topics of intense media interest around 1973. Indeed, all the major media, beginning in the 1970s, featured stories highlighting the putative problems associated with unauthorized immigration, and largely that from Mexico.[20] Most importantly, a variety of federal government officials and national politicians, along with a compliant media, helped to construct the perception of the crisis and to stoke public fears.[21] The

growing concerns of state officials and the public at large, as well as increased legislative activism surrounding unauthorized immigration, had significant effects on the
U.S.–Mexico boundary, leading to an unprecedented growth in federal resources
dedicated to boundary policing beginning in the late 1970s. Combined with a "war
on drugs" begun during the Reagan administration, efforts to fight unauthorized
immigration in the border region had a transformational effect on the nature and
scale of boundary policing.[22]

These national-scale changes began to manifest themselves in the late 1970s in
San Diego, dovetailing with the local reality of a rising number of violent crimes
committed by so-called border bandits. San Diego media coverage of boundary-re-
lated issues increased considerably during that time, resulting in heightened concerns about unauthorized immigration and border region crime. Although much of
the initiative for heightened boundary enforcement measures came from Washington, D.C., local officials played a significant role in raising the boundary's profile as
it related to a whole host of issues surrounding extralegal immigration and its effects on San Diego County.[23]

These concerns continued to grow in the mid-1980s as the influx of unauthorized migrants from Mexico into the United States increased significantly in the
context of a serious downturn in Mexico's economy. Such factors facilitated increasing
calls by a number of local politicians for the deployment of U.S. troops to stymie
drug smuggling, unauthorized immigration, and potential terrorist attacks.[24] By this
time, San Diego stood out among U.S. border cities for the level and intensity of
pro-boundary enforcement activism, a trend that greatly intensified in the late 1980s
and early 1990s.

What makes San Diego unique—in comparison to other American locales in the
U.S.–Mexico borderlands—is its racial–ethnic composition. San Diego stands out
in stark contrast to Tijuana as a predominantly "Anglo" city whereas other major
U.S. border cities are predominantly composed of people of Mexican origin.[25] In
this regard, San Diego was less equipped culturally and politically to deal with
Mexico, especially as Mexico (broadly construed) failed to confine itself to south of
the international boundary.[26]

The racial and ethnic disparity in northern San Diego County, with the exception of isolated pockets, is even more pronounced and is heavily intertwined with
economic class distinctions.[27] As a 1988 report in the San Diego edition of the *Los
Angeles Times* described the local human geography,

> Northern San Diego County is today a land unlike any other along the U.S.–Mexico
> border. . . . A place where squalid, plywood-and-cardboard shacks sit in the shadow of
> $1-million mansions, where the BMW and Volvo set rubs elbows at the supermarket
> with the dusty migrants fresh from the fields, where the haves run routinely head-on
> into the have-nots.[28]

It is thus not surprising that a number of the more notable clashes between "natives"
and immigrants that were symptomatic of a growing preoccupation with the

Map 6.1

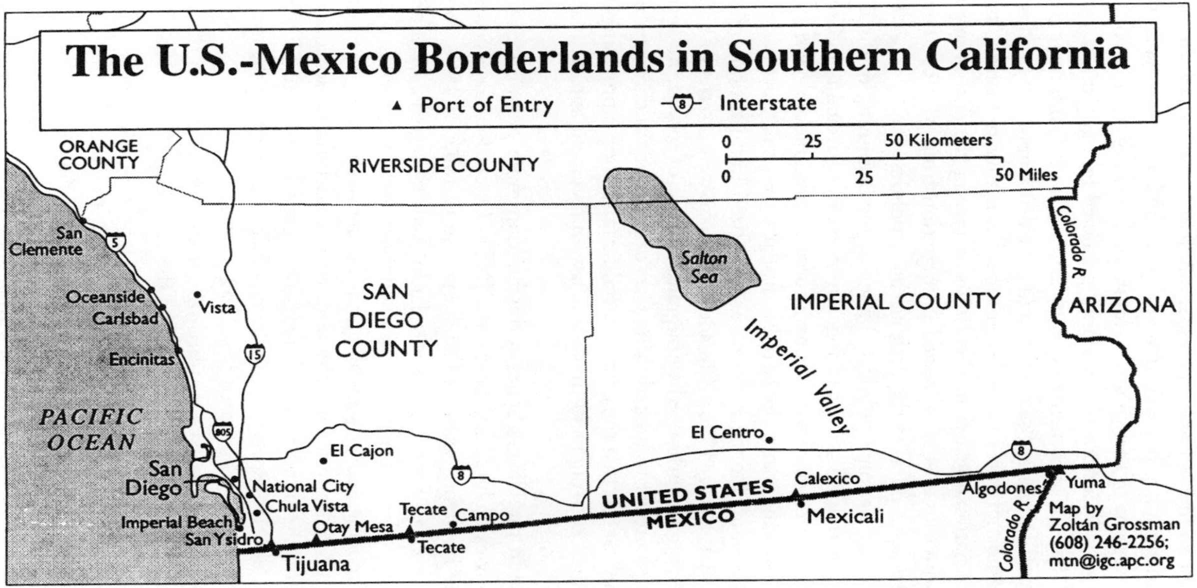

The U.S.-Mexico Borderlands in Southern California

▲ Port of Entry   —⑧— Interstate

0   25   50 Kilometers

0   25   50 Miles

ORANGE
COUNTY

RIVERSIDE COUNTY

SAN
DIEGO
COUNTY

IMPERIAL COUNTY

ARIZONA

Colorado R

Salton
Sea

Imperial Valley

El Centro

Calexico

Yuma

Algodones

Colorado R

Mexicali

El Cajon

National City
Chula Vista
Otay Mesa
Tecate Campo
Tecate

San
Diego
Imperial Beach
San Ysidro

Tijuana

Tecate

Vista

Oceanside
Carlsbad

Encinitas

San
Clemente

*PACIFIC
OCEAN*

UNITED STATES
MEXICO

Map by
Zoltan Grossman
(608) 246-2256;
mtn@igc.apc.org

U.S–Mexico boundary and unauthorized immigration took place in northern San Diego County.[29] By the early 1990s, California was experiencing a serious recession (one that hit southern California especially hard), the breakdown of local government, a widening gap between rich and poor, and a massive racial recomposition. California was one of the whitest states in the United States in 1960; today it is the most diverse, with a nonwhite majority predicted for early in the twenty-first century.[30] All these developments dovetailed neatly with California's long and sordid history of anti-immigrant sentiment and provided ample fuel for demagogic politicians and a host of anti-immigrant groups.[31] It is thus not surprising that California was the national leader in the 1990s in raising the anti-immigration banner, focusing primarily on unauthorized immigration from Mexico. These California-based efforts soon infected the national body politic.

Although the national political climate at the beginning of the decade did not seem favorable to immigrant bashing, sentiment was hardening in Congress and the White House to crack down on unauthorized immigration. Most importantly, efforts by conservatives and the Republican Party over the years had provided fertile ideological ground for the issues of unauthorized immigration and boundary enforcement by the early 1990s.[32] In addition, there were a series of high-profile incidents involving unauthorized immigrants—none of whom, however, were from Mexico—that greatly facilitated rising fears of a country under siege from without.[33] It was in this context that the Clinton administration began providing unprecedented levels of resources to augment the federal law enforcement apparatus along the U.S.–Mexico boundary.

Nowhere in the United States is this buildup more pronounced than along the California–Mexico boundary where the INS's "Operation Gatekeeper" takes place. Prior to the implementation of Gatekeeper on October 1, 1994, for example, the San Diego Sector of the U.S. Border Patrol had 980 agents; by June 1998, it had 2,264 agents, a level it has roughly maintained until the present. Meanwhile, the amount of fencing and/or walls along the border in the sector increased from 19 to more than 45 miles in length, the number of underground sensors rose from 448 to 1,214, and the number of infrared scopes grew from 12 to 59. Concomitantly, the number of INS inspectors,[34] those responsible for working the three official ports of entry in the sector, increased from 202 to 504.[35]

These developments have resulted in a significant decline in the number of apprehensions of unauthorized crossers by the San Diego Sector of the Border Patrol. Whereas in FY 1994 the San Diego Sector had been responsible for 46 percent of the apprehensions of unauthorized migrants in the United States, the sector's apprehensions were only 16 percent of the national total in FY 1998. The Tucson Sector, on the other hand, was responsible for 26 percent, and the El Centro Sector was responsible for 15 percent of the apprehensions in FY 1998.[36] The INS has presented this as proof of Gatekeeper's success in thwarting would-be unauthorized crossers in the San Diego area.[37]

Undoubtedly, Operation Gatekeeper has been a considerable success in helping to bring a certain order to the most urbanized sections of the border region in San Diego. Yet, it is not at all clear that Gatekeeper has had a significant effect in reducing the overall number of unauthorized crossings of the boundary in southern California or along the U.S.–Mexico boundary more generally. It is probable that, as in the case of Operation Hold the Line in El Paso,[38] Gatekeeper has succeeded in curtailing local migrants (especially day workers or street vendors and so-called "juvenile crossers") but has not seriously diminished the crossings by long-distance or long-term migrants, many of whom increasingly rely on professional smugglers and/or now cross at more remote, albeit more arduous, points along the boundary.[39] Even a May 1999 report by the U.S. General Accounting Office declared itself unable to conclude whether or not the new Southwest boundary strategy is successful, stating that "available data do not yet answer the fundamental question of how effective the strategy has been in preventing and deterring illegal entry."[40]

An unintended consequence of Operation Gatekeeper and the increased resources dedicated to boundary enforcement more generally may well be that unauthorized migrants are staying in the country longer.[41] Traditionally, many Mexican migrants have been seasonal workers, migrating back to Mexico in the off-season. But, "by raising the costs and risks of reentering the United States, heightened border surveillance may be transforming what has been a sojourner farm worker stream into settlers" in rural California.[42] Similarly, unauthorized immigrants in the San Diego area have been staying longer in the United States than they had intended in the face of increasing boundary enforcement.[43]

The length of the U.S. boundaries, and the strength of the various factors that push, pull, and facilitate unauthorized immigration to the United States make boundary enforcement a daunting project under the best of political circumstances. These factors, combined with the multiple domestic and binational (U.S.–Mexico) political constraints that limit the level of boundary militarization that would be needed to have a significant impact on migrants' ability to enter the country extralegally, suggest that enforcement of immigration laws as they relate to employment is really the only way to make a serious dent in unauthorized immigration (assuming this is a desirable goal). Employment of unauthorized immigrants is rife throughout the United States in the low-wage manufacturing and service sectors, in addition to agriculture, and is usually concentrated in specific industries. But there is insufficient political will in Washington to enforce already-existing employer sanctions or to strengthen them.[44]

For such reasons, the actual strategy of the INS puts far greater emphasis on high-profile policing measures along the boundary than on workplace enforcement. As of late 1997, for example, the INS had only twenty-three workplace inspectors in the San Diego area. In the Los Angeles District of the INS (an area comprising a population of more than 20 million people), the INS issued only eighteen "intent to fine" notices to employers for hiring extralegal migrants in FY 1996. Even though the INS issued thirty notices in FY 1997, such numbers are a proverbial "drop in the bucket" given the amount of unauthorized migrants working in the United States. The estimate for San Diego County alone stands at 200,000.[45] For such reasons, Operation Gatekeeper and the larger crackdown on unauthorized immigration appear to have had little effect on immigrant-dependent employers in southern California.[46] Nevertheless, this is not to suggest that Gatekeeper has been of little importance. The creation of an image of control is a highly significant effect of the Clinton administration's boundary buildup.[47]

OPENING AND CLOSING THE DOOR TO SOUTHERN CALIFORNIA

As demonstrated above, there are political and practical contradictions to opening the boundary to the flow of (nonillicit) goods and capital and closing the boundary to activities such as unauthorized entries. For the champions of these seemingly contradictory processes, however, these processes are part and parcel of a unified project of creating a border region where law and order as well as economic prosperity reign. As Alan Bersin, the former U.S. Attorney General's Special Representative for Southwest Border Issues, explained,

> [W]e are moving decisively toward a border that functions effectively; one that is a lawful and orderly gateway; one that manages significantly better the problems of illegal immigration and smuggling; and one that promises and routinely delivers handsome dividends from an investment in regional integration.[48]

In fact, these two processes, Clinton administration officials have argued, are actually inextricably linked.[49]

The buildup of the boundary and its "NAFTAization" are also linked in another, more nefarious, manner. As INS Commissioner Doris Meissner acknowledged during testimony to Congress in November 1993, she foresaw that NAFTA would most likely to lead to an *increase* in unauthorized immigration from Mexico to the United States in the short and medium terms. For this reason she stated that "[r]esponding to the likely short- to medium-term impacts of NAFTA will require strengthening our enforcement efforts along the border, both at and between ports of entry."[50] In other words, NAFTA requires enhanced boundary enforcement not simply to create a border region of law and order to facilitate capital accumulation, but also to stymie the anticipated increase in unauthorized immigration generated by the liberalization of the Mexican economy.[51] Thus, the putative problem of unauthorized immigration is, to a certain degree, of the administration's own making. It is an extricable part of the processes that NAFTA embodies and that, according to some, are supposedly making national boundaries redundant.[52]

Even though the simultaneous liberalization and militarization of the U.S.–Mexico boundary may seem paradoxical, two of the key functions of the modern territorial state are the provision of both security and opportunity. The state provides security in the sense that it defines territory through the construction and maintenance of geographical boundaries.[53] Moreover, the resources mobilized to protect the territory provide a certain stability. And the state provides opportunity in working to maximize the economic benefits realized by domestic interests in a competitive world economy. As the cases of immigration control (security) and Mexican migrant labor (opportunity for U.S. capital) demonstrate, however, these functions are sometimes conflicting. And as such, they help illustrate why U.S. efforts to reduce the illicit movement of people and goods across the California–Mexico divide have fallen far short of their stated goal.

As Operation Gatekeeper demonstrates, the modern territorial state is far from disappearing in an era of globalization and growing transboundary flows.[54] Rather, the state is diversifying and developing.[55] This is not to suggest that globalization (conceived as a process rather than a state of affairs)[56] does not have any weakening effects on the state. Clearly, it does. Transnational processes such as migration have helped to transform the state, while making it increasingly difficult for the state to manage extraterritorial processes and, thus, what (and whom) enters national territory.

But as Gatekeeper illustrates, transboundary integration can actually facilitate an enhancement of state power, at least at the social and geographical margins (i.e., toward international boundaries and unauthorized immigrants). Such integration can also lead to increasing demands upon the state for an intensified nationalization of territory and society. Political attacks against immigration and immigrants in California—and in many parts of the world—are instances of such nationalization. The attacks have come about partly in reaction to growing transboundary socioeconomic integration and rising levels of socioeconomic insecurity,[57] brought about in part by a neoliberal form of globalization that intensifies competition between localities, weakens social safety nets, and generally increases socioeconomic instability.[58] In this regard, we might understand popular support for Operation Gatekeeper partly as an attempt to reclaim a sense of security undermined by some of the same forces of regional integration and liberalization that limit the success of Operation Gatekeeper.

CONCLUSION

On the occasion of a May 1999 visit to California by Mexican President Ernesto Zedillo, a statement by the Pacific Council on International Policy in the form of an opinion piece appeared in the *Los Angeles Times*. Entitled "Strengthen Ties Between California and Mexico," the piece contained a list of high-profile signatories drawn from politics, business, academia, and the nonprofit sector and, as such, represented a consensus view of border among a significant slice of California's establishment.[59]

The statement noted that "Increasingly intimate relations between Mexico and California are an irreversible reality, not an option" and advocated strengthening cooperation between the two political entities "in four key areas: economic and social investment, immigration, border development and education." Its section on immigration called for California to "work actively with Mexico, directly and through federal channels, to develop mutually acceptable ways of managing migration flows so that labor needs are met and the rights both of migrants and of native-born citizens are protected." Subsequent sections championed improving transboundary transportation links, as well as border zone infrastructure and planning, and intensifying efforts aimed at harmonizing institutional cooperation across the boundary and at facilitating greater levels of investment in the border region.[60] One of the most striking aspects of the piece was that at least two of the signatories to the statement, Alan Bersin and former California Democratic Party gubernatorial candidate Kathleen Brown, had actively championed the radical increase in boundary enforcement that resulted in Operation Gatekeeper. Bersin, in fact, was one of its chief architects in his former capacity as the U.S. Attorney General's Special Representative for Southwest Border Issues.

It is hardly a coincidence that we see such individuals working both to increase transboundary ties between California and Mexico as well as to enhance boundary enforcement. Transnational integration emanates from developments and produces outcomes that are simultaneously contradictory and complementary. As the Pacific Council on International Policy acknowledged in its opinion piece published in the *Los Angeles Times*, "as our two societies become more interdependent, frictions may well become more evident, frequent and bothersome."[61] In this regard, increasing transnational integration seems to go hand in hand with the buildup of the immigration enforcement apparatus along national boundaries, at least those between countries with sharply divergent levels of socioeconomic development.[62] In terms of the territorial boundary between the United States and Mexico, these processes are most pronounced along Mexico's boundary with San Diego, an area where the levels of economic integration between the two countries are greatest, but where transboundary sociocultural differences remain significant. These seemingly contradictory developments are an outgrowth of the often-clashing functions of the modern territorial state, functions that are intensified by increasing transboundary flows that embody an age of globalization.

NOTES

1. Peter Andreas, "U.S.–Mexico: Open Markets, Closed Borders," *Foreign Policy*, no. 103, Summer 1996, 51–69. Also see Joseph Nevins, "California Dreaming: Operation Gatekeeper and the Social Geographical Construction of the 'Illegal Alien' along the U.S.–Mexico Boundary" (Ph.D. dissertation, University of California, Los Angeles, Department of Geography, December 1998), chapter 1. NAFTA went into effect on January 1, 1994.

About 2.8 million trucks crossed from Mexico into the United States in 1994; the figure for the previous year was 1.9 million (Andreas 1996: 58). The figure for 1996 was 3.5 million (*Migration News* [online version], various issues, current and back issues available via Internet on the *Migration News* home page: migration.ucdavis.edu).

2. *Migration News*, June 1999.

3. Lawrence A. Herzog, "Urban Planning and Sustainability in the Transfrontier Metropolis: The San Diego–Tijuana Region," in *Sustainable Development in San Diego–Tijuana: Environmental, Social, and Economic Implications of Interdependence*, Mark J. Spalding, ed. (San Diego: Center for U.S.–Mexican Studies, University of California, San Diego, 1999), 5–6. The most significant factor fueling the tremendous economic and demographic growth of Mexico's northern border region has been the rapid growth of *maquiladoras* ("offshore" assembly plants), which have increased from 170 in number in 1970 to 2,400 in 1995. According to Herzog, many experts predicted that NAFTA would lead to a reduction in the concentration of the *maquiladoras* in the border region. Nevertheless, about 80 percent of Mexico's *maquiladoras* were still located along the boundary with the United States as of 1997.

4. *Migration News*, August 1999.

5. John R. Weeks, "Demographic Dynamics of the San Diego–Tijuana Region," in *Sustainable Development in San Diego–Tijuana: Environmental, Social, and Economic Implications of Interdependence*, Mark J. Spalding, ed. (San Diego: Center for U.S.–Mexican Studies, University of California, San Diego, 1999), 18.

6. Alan D. Bersin and Judith S. Feigin, "The Rule of Law at the Margin: Reinventing Prosecution Policy in the Southern District of California," *Georgetown Immigration Law Journal*, vol. 12, no. 2, Winter 1998, 286.

7. *Migration News*, February 1997.

8. Gregory Gross, "San Diego, Tijuana Grow Closer Together," *The San Diego Union-Tribune*, December 5, 1993, A-1+.

9. In this regard, the chapter builds upon work by Peter Andreas, "The Escalation of U.S. Immigration Control in the Post-NAFTA Era," *Political Science Quarterly*, vol. 113, no. 4, 1998–1999, 591–615.

10. See Arjun Appadurai, "Disjuncture and Difference in the Global Cultural Economy," *Theory, Culture & Society*, vol. 7, nos. 2–3, 1990, 295–310.

11. So-called border bandits were usually from Mexico and would attack unauthorized immigrants on the U.S. side of the boundary and then flee back into Tijuana. For a more complete description of issues relating to law enforcement along the U.S.–Mexico boundary in the San Diego region at the beginning of the 1990s, see Nevins 1998, chapter 5.

12. The San Diego Sector of the U.S. Border Patrol is responsible for the sixty-six westernmost miles of the U.S.–Mexico boundary.

13. Sebastian Rotella, *Twilight on the Line: Underworlds and Politics at the U.S.–Mexico Border* (New York: W. W. Norton, 1998), 106.

14. See Ernesto Portillo, "Added Border Agents, Lights Set," *The San Diego Union*, June 21, 1990b: B-1+.

15. Robert A. Jones, "It's Quiet—Too Quiet," *Los Angeles Times*, Sunday, March 22, 1998, B7.

16. *Migration News*, November 1997.

17. *Migration News*, May 1999 and August 1999.

18. Timothy J. Dunn, *The Militarization of the U.S.–Mexico Border, 1978–1992: Low-Intensity Conflict Doctrine Comes Home* (Austin: The Center for Mexican American Studies, University of Texas at Austin, 1996), 17–18.

19. See Thomas Muller, "Nativism in the Mid-1990s: Why Now?" in Juan F. Perea, ed., *Immigrants Out! The New Nativism and the Anti-Immigrant Impulse in the United States* (New York: New York University Press, 1997), 105–118.

20. Dunn 1996, 18; Jana Walters, "Illegal Immigration: The Making of Myth" (unpublished paper completed for a graduate seminar in sociology at the University of Texas at Austin, 1990), 10; Celestino Fernandez and Lawrence R. Pedroza, "The Border Patrol and News Media Coverage of Undocumented Mexican Immigration during the 1970s: A Quantitative Content Analysis in the Sociology of Knowledge," *California Sociologist*, vol. 5, no. 2, Summer 1982, 1–26; Gilbert Cardenas, "Critical Issues in Using Government Data Collected Primarily for Non-Research Purposes," in *Quantitative Data and Immigration Research*, Stephen R. Crouch and Roy Simón Bryce-Laporte, eds. (Washington, D.C.: Research Institute on Immigration and Ethnic Studies, Smithsonian Institution, 1979), 83; and Sasha G. Lewis, *Slave Trade Today: American Exploitation of Illegal Aliens* (Boston: Beacon Press, 1979), 137–141.

21. This is not to suggest that the "problem" of unauthorized immigration was a mere mirage. There were certainly a number of "real" events and developments that pro-restrictionist forces were able to draw upon to substantiate their arguments in favor of enhanced boundary and immigration enforcement. But what a society deems as a "problem" or a "crisis" and how that society understands this problem is far from inevitable. Why one particular issue becomes especially salient as opposed to a whole host of other potential "problems" is a matter that requires an explanation that not only contextualizes the putative problem, but also establishes the social actors that construct the popular image of the problem. Here, the role of state actors in producing the "illegal alien" as a threat to the sociopolitical fabric of the United States is particularly important. See Nevins 1998, chapter 6.

22. See Dunn 1996. Dunn refers to the process of boundary buildup begun during the second half of the Carter administration as the "militarization" of the boundary.

23. See Nevins 1998, chapters 5 and 6.

24. But the militarization of boundary enforcement in the San Diego region was already under way. By April of 1986, for example, U.S. Marines were already working along the boundary in San Diego. Although they were not apprehending unauthorized entrants into the United States, the soldiers were engaging in surveillance. See Robert Dietrich, "Marines Manning Border Sites," *The Tribune* (San Diego), April 24, 1986, A-1+.

25. Although we should not assume that such "objective" differences produce social and territorial boundaries (see Peter Sahlins, *Boundaries: The Making of France and Spain in the Pyrenees* [Berkeley: University of California Press, 1989]), such differences matter given the historical development of Mexico and the United States and the social relations between the populations of the two countries in the border region over the last 150 years. See Nevins 1998, chapter 6.

26. San Diego, for example, was 70 percent "Anglo" and neighboring Chula Vista was 68 percent in 1980. By contrast, the Texas border cities of El Paso and Brownsville were only 33 percent and 16 percent Anglo, respectively. By 1990, the figures for the four cities were 59 percent, 50 percent, 26 percent, and 9 percent, respectively. Oscar Martínez, *Border People: Life and Society in the U.S.–Mexico Borderlands* (Tucson: The University of Arizona Press, 1994), 48–49.

27. Anthropologist Leo Chávez characterizes the region as having two distinct socio-economic groupings: affluent whites and working-class Mexican immigrants who provide service to the former. Leo R. Chávez, *Shadowed Lives: Undocumented Immigrants in American Society* (second edition) (New York: Harcourt Brace Jovanovich, 1998).

28. Quoted in Chávez 1998, 17. Quote taken from E. Bailey and H. G. Reza, "An Alien Presence," *Los Angeles Times*, June 5, 1988: 1, 36.

29. See S. L. Walker, "Residents, Migrants, Are Uneasy Neighbors," *The San Diego Union*, December 22, 1988, A-1+.

30. Richard Walker, "California Rages Against the Dying of the Light," *New Left Review*, no. 209, January/February 1995, 42–74; Richard Walker, "California's Collision of Race and Class," *Representations*, no. 55, Summer 1996, 163–183; and Peter Schrag, *Paradise Lost: California's Experience, America's Future* (New York: The New Press, 1998).

31. See Tomás Almaguer, *Racial Fault Lines: The Historical Origins of White Supremacy in California* (Berkeley: University of California Press, 1994); and Cary McWilliams, *North from Mexico: The Spanish-Speaking People of the United States* (New York: Greenwood, 1968; originally published in 1949).

32. See Sara Diamond, "Right-Wing Politics and the Anti-Immigration Cause," *Social Justice*, vol. 23, no. 3, Fall 1996, 154–168; Ruth Conniff, "The War on Aliens," *The Progressive*, October 22, 1993, 22–29; and Fred Barnes, "Crime Scene: Republicans with a Cause," *The New Republic*, September 5, 1994, 30+.

33. In early 1993, a persistent economic recession, the bombing of the World Trade Center by suspected unauthorized immigrants, and the assassination of two Central Intelligence Agency employees in Virginia by an unauthorized immigrant from Pakistan helped to fuel anti-immigration sentiment further. If any single issue helped create the popular image of the United States under invasion from foreign hordes, however, it was the discovery offshore of ships carrying unauthorized Chinese immigrants. See Nevins 1998, chapter 5.

34. The U.S. Border Patrol is responsible only for the boundary in between ports of entry. It is INS inspectors who work the ports and decide who is eligible to enter the United States.

35. U.S. Immigration and Naturalization Service, "Operation Gatekeeper: New Resources, Enhanced Results" (Washington, D.C.: The Office of Public Affairs, U.S. Immigration and Naturalization Service, July 14, 1998).

36. U.S. General Accounting Office, *Illegal Immigration: Status of Southwest Border Strategy Implementation* (Washington, D.C.: U.S. General Accounting Office, May 1999).

37. U.S. Immigration and Naturalization Service, *Operation Gatekeeper: 3 Years of Results* (Washington, D.C.: The Office of Public Affairs, U.S. Immigration and Naturalization Service, October 1997); and Anne-Marie O'Connor, "INS Crackdown Expands into Imperial Valley," *Los Angeles Times*, October 8, 1997, A1+.

38. See Frank D. Bean et al., *Illegal Mexican Migration and the United States/Mexico Border: The Effects of Operation Hold-the-Line on El Paso/Juarez* (Austin: Population Research Center, The University of Texas at Austin [prepared for the U.S. Commission on Immigration Reform], July 15, 1994).

39. See Wayne A. Cornelius, "The Structural Embeddedness of Demand for Mexican Immigrant Labor: New Evidence from California," in *Crossings: Mexican Immigration in Interdisciplinary Perspectives*, Marcelo Suárez-Orozco, ed. (Cambridge: Harvard University Press, for the David Rockefeller Center for Latin American Studies, 1998), 115–144; Audrey Singer and Douglas Massey, "The Social Process of Undocumented Border Crossing Among

Mexican Migrants," *International Migration Review*, vol. 32, no. 3, Fall 1998, 561–592; and Andreas 1998–1999.

40. Quoted in *Migration News*, November 1999.

41. A study of extralegal migrants from western Mexico found that only 23 percent stay in the United States longer than ten years before returning to Mexico. About 50 percent of the migrants return to Mexico after only two years. The data used in the study derive from surveys conducted by Douglas Massey and Jorge Durand between 1982 and 1993 in six states of western Mexico. See Belinda I. Reyes, *Dynamics of Immigration: Return Migration to Western Mexico* (San Francisco: Public Policy Institute of California, 1997).

42. J. Edward Taylor, Philip L. Martin, and Michael Fix, *Poverty amid Prosperity: Immigration and the Changing Face of Rural California* (Washington, D.C.: The Urban Institute Press, 1997), 83–84. Also see Bettina Boxall, "Migrants' New Roots Transform Rural Life," *Los Angeles Times*, April 20, 1999, A-1+.

43. Cornelius 1998, 131–132. Along the same lines, a staff report by the U.S. Commission on Immigration Reform discovered that some unauthorized migrants were responding to Gatekeeper by staying in the United States longer. See U.S. Commission on Immigration Reform, "Staff Report on Border Law Enforcement and Removal Initiatives in San Diego, CA" (Washington, D.C.: U.S. Commission on Immigration Reform, November 1995).

44. See, for example, Marc Cooper, "The Heartland's Raw Deal: How Meatpacking is Creating a New Immigrant Underclass," *The Nation*, vol. 264, no. 4, February 3, 1997, 11–17; Stephen J. Hedges et al., "The New Jungle," *U.S. News & World Report*, vol. 121, no. 12, September 23, 1996, 34–45; Jesse Katz, "1,000 Miles of Hope, Heartache," *Los Angeles Times*, November 10, 1996, A1+; Marcus Stern, "The Border Fences are Stronger and the Number of Guards Has Grown. Yet Undocumented Immigrants Find Their Way into the United States. They Come for Jobs. And They're Getting Them," *The San Diego Union-Tribune*, November 2, 1997; Marcus Stern, "Labor Contractors Contribute to Illegal Immigration's Spread throughout U.S.," *The San Diego Union-Tribune*, November 2, 1997; Marcus Stern, "Low-Skill Labor Markets Full of Illegal Workers, but Employers Are Seldom Fined," *The San Diego Union-Tribune*, November 2, 1997; Marcus Stern, "Legislators Put Focus on Fences, Not Jobs," *The San Diego Union-Tribune*, November 3, 1997; and Marcus Stern, "A Semi-Tough Policy on Illegal Workers" (op-ed), *The Washington Post*, July 5, 1998, C2.

45. Robert Kahn, "Operation Gatekeeper," *Z Magazine*, vol. 10, no. 12, December 1997, 14–15.

46. See Cornelius, "The Structural Embeddedness of Demand for Mexican Immigrant Labor."

47. Peter Andreas, "The U.S. Immigration Control Offensive: Constructing an Image of Order on the Southwest Border," in *Crossings: Mexican Immigration in Interdisciplinary Perspectives*, Marcelo Suárez-Orozco, ed. (Cambridge, Mass.: Harvard University Press, for the David Rockefeller Center for Latin American Studies, 1998), 343–356. We cannot reduce enforcement efforts, however, to such symbolic outcomes (or intentions for that matter). Gatekeeper has also had some important material outcomes. See Nevins 1998, chapter 7.

48. Alan D. Bersin, "Reinventing the U.S./Mexico Border" (op-ed), *The San Diego Union-Tribune*, August 25, 1996.

49. According to Robert Bach, Executive Associate Commissioner for Policy and Planning for the INS, the policy of the Clinton administration perceives the U.S–Mexico border re-

gion as an opportunity, a place, and an anchor. The border is an opportunity in that its proper organization allows regional integration and NAFTA to occur and allows for economic progress on both sides of the boundary. The border is a place in the sense that its sociocultural patterns are geographically unique—an important factor that the administration takes into consideration so that federal policy works for families, workers, and employers on both sides of the international divide. And, although border policy is only one piece of a much larger strategy of immigration enforcement, the border is an anchor, primarily for the purposes of law enforcement. To realize its vision, the Clinton administration has sought to build an institutional framework within and upon which "the market" can flourish. As a set of institutional relationships based on the law, this market is taken to be one in which everyone can participate and from which people on both sides of the boundary will benefit. Bach refers to this policy as the "Meissner doctrine"—named after INS Commissioner Doris Meissner and her late husband Charles Meissner (who died in 1996), the former head of international commerce at the Department of Commerce. Robert Bach, unpublished talk at Immigration Control Panel at workshop entitled "Perspectives on U.S.–Mexico Border Policy" (Center for U.S.–Mexican Studies, University of California, San Diego, October 17, 1997), tape recording of talk on file with author.

50. U.S. Congress, Subcommittee on International Law, Immigration, and Refugees of the Committee on the Judiciary, House of Representatives, 103rd Congress, "Immigration-Related Issues in the North American Free Trade Agreement" (November 3, 1993) (Washington, D.C.: U.S. Government Printing Office, 1994), 36.

51. Increasing liberalization of the national economy, for example, has facilitated a significant exodus from Mexico's countryside: from 1980 to 1990, for example, the amount of the country's population living in rural areas declined from 36 percent to 28 percent. John Warnock, *The Other Mexico: The North American Triangle Completed* (Montreal: Black Rose Books, 1995), 197. Numerous studies suggested that the implementation of NAFTA and the related liberalization of the Mexican economy would lead to an increase in migration from Mexico to the United States (see Andreas 1998–1999).

52. See Kenichi Ohmae, *The End of the Nation State: The Rise of Regional Economies* (New York: The Free Press, 1995).

53. Peter J. Taylor, *Political Geography: World-Economy, Nation-State and Locality* (New York: John Wiley & Sons, 1993).

54. Anthony Giddens describes globalization "as the intensification of worldwide social relations which link distant localities in such a way that local happenings are shaped by events occurring many miles away and vice versa." *The Consequences of Modernity* (Stanford: Stanford University Press, 1990), 94.

55. Michael Mann, "Nation-States in Europe and Other Continents: Diversifying, Developing, Not Dying," *Daedalus*, vol. 122, no. 3, Summer 1993, 115–140.

56. Giddens 1990, and David Harvey, "Globalization in Question," *Rethinking Marxism*, vol. 8, no. 4, Winter 1995, 1–17.

57. Saskia Sassen, *Globalization and Its Discontents: Essays on the New Mobility of People and Money* (New York: The New Press, 1998).

58. See Jamie Peck and Adam Tickell, "A Jungle Law Breaks Out: Neoliberalism and Global-Local Disorder," *Area*, vol. 26, no. 4, 1994, 317–326.

59. Pacific Council on International Policy, "Strengthen Ties Between California and Mexico" (op-ed), *Los Angeles Times*, May 18, 1999, B7. Signatories to the piece included: Alan Bersin, the former United States Attorney General's Special Representative for

Southwest Border Issues; Kathleen Brown, the California Democratic Party's gubernatorial nominee in 1994 and current president of Private Bank West, Bank of America; Susan Golding, Mayor of San Diego; Antonia Hernandez, president, Mexican-American Legal Defense Fund (MALDEF); and Julie Meier Wright, CEO, San Diego Development Corporation.

60. Pacific Council on International Policy, 1999.

61. Pacific Council on International Policy, 1999.

62. Thus, we find intensified policing efforts along a variety of international boundaries throughout the world dividing the relatively wealthy from the poor, including the boundaries between South Africa and Mozambique, Spain (Ceuta and Melilla) and Morocco, and Germany and Poland. See Bob Drogin, "Post-Apartheid S. Africa Targets Illegal Migrants," *Los Angeles Times*, October 7, 1996, A1+; Matthew Carr, "Policing the Frontier: Ceuta and Melilla," *Race & Class*, vol. 39, no. 1, July–September 1997, 61–66; and Neil King, "A New Era for European Immigrants: Coping with Europe's Immigration Wave Is Nearly on a Par with Common Currency," *The Wall Street Journal*, May 4, 1998. Also see Andreas 1998–1999.

7

The Logic and Contradictions of Intensified Border Enforcement in Texas

David Spener[1]

The U.S. government has committed itself to a substantial fortification of its southern border with Mexico in recent years. The goal has been to curtail the unauthorized overland movement of persons and contraband into its national territory. While much attention has been paid to the apparent success of the Immigration and Naturalization Service (INS) in gaining control of the border along its most heavily transgressed segment between San Diego and Tijuana, it remains to be seen whether this achievement can be replicated elsewhere. In this chapter, I discuss the difficulties the INS faces in exerting control over the border in Texas through an examination of its two principal efforts to do so: Operation Hold the Line in the El Paso sector and Operation Rio Grande in the McAllen, Laredo, and Del Rio sectors. In doing so, I review the logic and evaluate the effectiveness of the attempt by the U.S. Border Patrol/U.S. Department of Justice to deter unauthorized border crossing through the development of a new strategy consisting of forward deployment of a greatly increased number of agents and the intensified application of criminal sanctions against recidivist illegal entrants and "alien smugglers." Subsequently, I argue that as this strategy is more fully implemented in the Texas border region, it gives rise to a series of contradictions that work against its success in achieving meaningful deterrence.

In undertaking my analysis of the logic and effectiveness of deterrence along the Texas–Mexico border, I explore the empirical space that lies between the U.S. government's assertion of its sovereign right to "monopolize the legitimate means of movement" across its borders and its actual exercise of control over movement that it labels as illegitimate (see Torpey, this volume, for a more thorough discussion of the state's prerogatives and abilities in this regard). As such, this will be mainly an "on-the-ground" account of developments in the region. In my approach, I recognize that the Texas–Mexico border has historically been open to illegitimate as well as legitimate movement. Contemporary attempts to curtail unauthorized movement across it run counter not only to the traditional sociocultural integration of the Rio Grande Valley, but also to more than a century of accumulated Mexican social capital that propels undocumented migration to and through Texas in order to meet U.S. employers' demand for manual labor. These and other "preexisting conditions" have led some analysts to conclude that "border crackdowns" are incapable of significantly arresting the flow of undocumented migrants into the United States.[2] Other authors have suggested that the current "battle for the border" has less to do with the *actual* exercise of physical control over cross-border movement and much more to do with the *symbolic* assertion of the ability and will to exercise control.[3]

Nevertheless, I concur with Torpey (this volume), who argues that modern nation–states have generally been quite successful in implementing restrictions on the transborder movement of persons. In the case of the United States, the fact that it has not effectively barred illegitimate movement across its border with Mexico is not because it has lacked the coercive means to do so, but because it has not yet decisively directed those means to that end. In addition, recent research suggests the personnel and equipment resources needed to greatly curtail unauthorized border crossing may be much less than one might expect for a 2,000-mile-long border.[4] Moreover, although they are ever mindful of the symbolic aspects of their mission, the agencies of the U.S. government that dedicate themselves wholly or in part to border control appear to be diligently attempting to reach their objective of preventing unauthorized entry of sovereign territory. In the 1990s, they were under strong political pressure to reach this objective, both from the Clinton administration and from most of Texas's Congressional delegation, which included several members who are particularly influential with regard to border policy. Thus, we are obligated to contemplate the possibility that the new round of efforts to significantly curtail illegitimate movement may ultimately—and perhaps soon—prove successful. It is to that empirical question that I now turn.

THE LOGIC OF DETERRENCE

There have been three central objectives guiding the U.S. government's Southwest border immigration control efforts since 1993. First, the government seeks to physically prevent unauthorized crossings of the international boundary. Second, it seeks to quickly apprehend foreign nationals who cross the international boundary illegally in order to prevent them from establishing residence, gaining employment, or committing criminal acts on U.S. territory. The third objective is to discourage repeated attempts to enter illegally by effectively applying criminal sanctions against foreign nationals who enter the United States illegally as well as to foreigners or U.S. nationals who assist them in doing so. None of these objectives is new, but each has been pursued with dramatically increased energy and resources since the launching of Operation Blockade in El Paso, Texas, in September 1993. The pursuit of these objectives is consistent with deterrence theory in criminology, which rests on the notion that criminal behavior will be curbed insofar as law-breakers face a high probability of apprehension by the authorities and are swiftly and severely punished for their transgressions.[5]

Research has shown that Mexican undocumented migration to the United States is a phenomenon that has been greatly facilitated by dense social networks linking migrants, their friends, and their kin residing in communities in the Mexican interior, in the United States, and at the border itself.[6] These networks provide their members with reliable information relevant to their migration plans. Thus, to the extent that changes in U.S. law enforcement strategies actually increase the "severity, certainty, and celerity" of punishment for those who violate immigration laws, news of this fact can be counted on to be carried via migrant networks to potential violators.

The role of Mexican migrant networks in conveying the deterrence message is vital, because these same networks have accumulated several generations' worth of wisdom about the process of unauthorized border crossing. This wisdom includes not only information about how and where to stage a crossing, routes to follow once a crossing has been made, and dangers to avoid along the way, but also how to avoid apprehension by the border patrol and what to expect and how to behave if apprehended. As noted by several authors, at the outset of the 1990s, migrants "knew" that there was a good chance they would not be caught at all by the border patrol. If they were caught, there was no advantage to resistance. Most of the time agents would not abuse them and they would not be jailed for any extended period. The only thing that would typically happen is that they would be taken back across the border into Mexico and released. Then they would be able to cross again. After a few tries, they would get past the border patrol's defenses and head on to their final destinations.[7] Heyman described the relationship between U.S. authorities and undocumented migrants as one that was characterized by a variety of ritualized behaviors he referred to as the "voluntary departure complex," where all involved understood that they were playing an elaborate game whose outcome was a forgone conclusion.[8] With its new enforcement strategies, the U.S. government sought to break up this complex and thereby transform the received wisdom about border crossing that was transmitted to migrants.

DETERRENCE EFFORTS IN TEXAS: OPERATIONS HOLD THE LINE AND RIO GRANDE

By 1996, around 7 million Mexican immigrants resided in the United States,[9] most of whom had originally entered the country illegally.[10] According to INS estimates, the vast majority of undocumented Mexicans residing in the United States had "entered without inspection," meaning that they had crossed the border surreptitiously away from official ports of entry.[11] Indeed, in spite of the fact that the U.S. Border Patrol was making upwards of 1 million apprehensions of unauthorized border crossers each year by the mid-1980s, it seemed that it had neither the ability nor the will to substantially reduce the flow of unauthorized Mexicans entering the country.

Operation Hold the Line

Nowhere was the ineffectiveness of the border patrol more apparent than in El Paso in the early 1990s. In this Texas city abutting sprawling Ciudad Juárez, Chihuahua, the Río Grande/Río Bravo del Norte was shallow and narrow enough so as not to constitute a substantial barrier to most persons wishing to cross. Nearly any *juarense* who wished to enter El Paso without authorization could do so, and many commuted to jobs as domestic and construction workers on a daily basis. In addition, El Paso was favored as a crossing point by more undocumented long-distance migrants than any other place along the border except San Diego. Although the 600 or so border patrol agents in El Paso did little to deter illegal border crossing, they did keep busy chasing down suspected unauthorized Mexicans after they entered the sector, making 250,000 apprehensions in fiscal year (FY) 1992.[12] These apprehensions were the fruit of a "cat and mouse" game that all too frequently exposed migrants, members of the community, and agents themselves to considerable risk of injury. In addition, in a community where around three-quarters of the population was of Mexican ancestry and a fifth of the population had been born in Mexico, agents were prone to mistakenly identify citizens and legal U.S. residents as the suspected "illegals" they were pursuing, leading to human rights complaints from the local community.[13]

On the morning of September 19, 1993, the El Paso sector of the U.S. Border Patrol launched "Operation Blockade" under the direction of its new chief, Silvestre Reyes. Reyes redeployed 400 of his sector's 650 agents "forward" to the banks of the Río Grande itself, stringing them out in their vehicles within easy sight of one another along a twenty-mile stretch of the border running from Ysleta in the east to Monument One in the west. In addition, Reyes's agents repaired holes in border fences downtown and had the INS provide additional personnel to work the legal ports of entry on the international bridges connecting El Paso and Juárez.[14] The purpose of Operation Blockade (later renamed "Operation Hold the Line" after objections from Mexican officials and local residents) was to make it impossible for migrants to enter the city of El Paso from neighboring Juárez except through legal ports of entry where they would be required to present valid documents to INS officials.

Operation Hold the Line (OHTL) produced a number of outcomes that are relevant to understanding enforcement initiatives undertaken by U.S. authorities border-wide in its aftermath:[15]

1. OHTL dramatically reduced the number of unauthorized crossings made from Juárez into the urbanized portions of the El Paso metropolitan area. This was indicated by the steep decline in apprehensions made in the El Paso sector, from 286,000 in FY 1993 to just 80,000 in FY 1994.[16]

2. OHTL helped restore the credibility of the Border Patrol in El Paso and was widely supported by the U.S. citizen population there. Silvestre Reyes became a folk hero to many and was subsequently elected to represent the El Paso area in the U.S. House of Representatives.

3. The operation led unauthorized migrants who remained committed to entering the United States to stage their crossings at other, less well-defended points along the border. This was indicated by sharply increased apprehensions of migrants elsewhere along the border following OHTL, including the Tucson, Del Rio, McAllen, and Laredo sectors. Undocumented migrants whose destination was El Paso simply made an "end-run" around the line of agents stationed between Ysleta and Monument One.

4. OHTL had a proportionally bigger impact on the number of unauthorized border crossings being made than on the number of unauthorized border *crossers*. According to the Border Patrol, prior to OHTL, 60 percent of apprehendees in the El Paso sector were residents of Ciudad Juárez. Many *juarenses* responded to OHTL not by giving up on gaining entry into El Paso, but rather by making less frequent crossings, either by reducing their visits or by extending the time they spent in El Paso each time they visited.

5. Making "entry without inspection" more difficult raises the salience of the use of fraudulent immigration documents or the misuse of valid documents. In El Paso, many migrants were found to be in possession of forged or altered documents, attempting to use someone else's valid documents to enter the country, or to be using nonimmigrant visas (such as the commonly held border crossing card) to illegally work and/or establish residence in the United States.[17]

6. The strategy embodied in OHTL would require far greater personnel and equipment to maintain in the long term than were available in the El Paso sector at the time it was unilaterally launched by Silvestre Reyes.[18]

Since 1993, U.S. border control initiatives have been inspired mainly by OHTL lesson numbers 1, 2, 3, and 6, as the El Paso operation was followed by Operation Gatekeeper in the San Diego sector (see Nevins chapter, this volume), Operation Safeguard in the Tucson sector, and Operation Rio Grande in the McAllen and Laredo sectors.[19] The border patrol's budget was raised from around $400 million in FY 1993 to $877 million in FY 1998, and the total number of authorized border patrol agents in the nine sectors along the border with Mexico increased from 3,389 in FY 1993 to 7,231 in FY 1998.[20]

Operation Rio Grande

If the U.S. government is to successfully deter entry without inspection along the entire international boundary with Mexico, it will have to exert a high degree of control over that portion of the boundary that is covered by the McAllen, Laredo, and Del Rio sectors in Texas. Achieving control of this stretch of the border will require considerably greater resources and effort than it has taken thus far to reduce crossings in El Paso and San Diego since it is much longer, has dense vegetation in many areas, features many towns and rural crossings, and is home to a mainly Mexican American/Mexican immigrant population.

The border patrol began its major effort to deter unauthorized border crossing in the Lower Rio Grande Valley in August 1997 when it launched Operation Rio Grande (ORG) in the McAllen sector along the river between Brownsville and Matamoros. In addition to assigning more agents to patrol the Brownsville levee along the river in their vehicles, a substantial technological component was included at the outset, including huge portable floodlights to illuminate both sides of the river at night, low-light television monitors, infrared surveillance trucks, encrypted radios, and six new helicopters. INS Commissioner Doris Meissner announced that unlike previous operations in the valley, the resources being invested in ORG would be permanent, and extended westward up the river to Del Rio over the course of two to three years.[21]

Indeed, from FY 1996 to FY 1998 a net total of 929 agents were added to the force patrolling the McAllen, Laredo, and Del Rio sectors, with the bulk of these (488) going to the McAllen sector.[22] In addition to dramatically increasing the number of agents patrolling these sectors, the border patrol, in conjunction with the Army's Joint Task Force 6, undertook construction of 240 miles of roadway, 12 helicopter launch pads, and 50 high-tech lights in the Laredo sector.[23] By March 1999, border patrol officials in the Laredo sector planned to place stationary video surveillance cameras on the riverbank several miles beyond the end of the line held by agents in the urban portion of the sector. Beyond that, the border patrol began to experiment with the use of "unmanned aerial vehicles" or "drones" to fly above the Laredo sector beaming back images to sector headquarters, these in addition to new high-tech helicopters purchased for the area.[24] And, although the practice had been underway for at least 10 years, it was reported in mid-1999 that the Texas National Guard was engaging in special surveillance operations along the Río Grande in response to requests from state and local law enforcement officials concerned with drug smuggling.[25]

In addition to developing a more extensive and sophisticated infrastructure for apprehending undocumented migrants (as well as smugglers of contraband), Operation Rio Grande incorporated the new IDENT data system, which collected and stored apprehendees' biometric information, including photograph and fingerprints. IDENT would potentially be of great use to the INS/U.S. Border Patrol by making it possible to identify "criminal aliens" (i.e., those who had been charged and/or convicted of other crimes), "recidivists" (i.e., migrants who were apprehended again after being "voluntarily returned" or deported to Mexico), and suspected alien and drug smugglers who were also apprehended on multiple occasions in the same area.

Apprehensions of undocumented migrants had been rising steadily in the Laredo, McAllen, and Del Rio sectors since FY 1994 when Operation Hold the Line was undertaken in the El Paso sector. In the McAllen and Laredo sectors, however, apprehensions peaked in FY 1997 and dropped substantially in FY 1998 as Operation Rio Grande was established in those sectors. This followed the experience in El Paso, though not as dramatically given the greater enforcement challenges facing these sectors as well as the fact that the "hydraulic pressure" on these two sectors had already been increased by the "closing" of San Diego and El Paso to unauthorized crossings by long-distance migrants. Also not surprisingly, apprehensions in the Del Rio sector, which had yet to receive the major increase in resources available to it that the sectors downstream had, rose substantially in FY 1998.[26] This trend of falling apprehensions in the Lower Rio Grande Valley and rising apprehensions in the mid to upper valley appears to have continued in FY 1999, according to preliminary reports.[27]

CRIMINAL SANCTIONS AS A DETERRANT TO UNAUTHORIZED MIGRATION

Increasing the effectiveness of the border patrol in apprehending unauthorized entrants at or near the Texas–Mexico border is a crucial element of the deterrence strategy being pursued by the U.S. government. Nevertheless, in order for the "voluntary departure complex" described by Heyman to be broken up,[28] penetration of border patrol defenses by unauthorized crossers must either be made physically impossible (or at least extremely difficult, hazardous, and expensive) or repeated apprehension by the border patrol must have real negative consequences for apprehendees. Beginning in 1994, the U.S. Department of Justice initiated a policy of more vigorously prosecuting immigration law violations. In addition, the federal immigration reform legislation signed into law in 1996 significantly increased penalties for illegal entry and alien smuggling. Now, with the IDENT system in place, the border patrol is in a better position to identify "recidivist" illegal entrants, those suspected of alien smuggling based upon repeated apprehension and other border patrol intelligence, as well as aliens who are excludable for having committed or being suspected of having committed other crimes.

In Texas, these developments have resulted in a spectacular increase in the number of immigration crime prosecutions and convictions in recent years. According to the Transactional Records Access Clearinghouse (TRAC) database maintained by Syracuse University, the number of federal criminal prosecutions resulting in convictions that was initiated by the INS in the border region of Texas grew more than sixfold, from just 455 in FY 1994 to 3,114 in FY 1998. In addition, the TRAC data show that at the national level, the median prison sentence for immigration and immigration-related crimes rose from just two months in FY 1992 to twelve months in FY 1998.[29] In the press, the TRAC report was taken to show that the INS, federal prosecutors, and the courts had finally decided to get tough on immigration crime in Texas.[30]

More prosecutions and longer sentences are not sufficient to deter immigration crimes, however, since most criminological studies show that it is the certainty of punishment that has the greatest deterrent effect.[31] TRAC data show that nearly all prosecutions brought for immigrant crimes result in convictions. Thus, the likelihood of punishment depends upon a) the likelihood of an unauthorized crosser (including smugglers) being apprehended on any given crossing and b) the number of times s/he must be apprehended before charges are brought.

As is the case with most victimless crimes, the actual number of illegal crossings made of the U.S.–Mexico border in Texas and in other districts is not known. The number of apprehensions following such crossings is known, however, and we may think of these as the number of arrests made for immigration law violations by the border patrol in the Texas border region. Here it is evident that not very many apprehensions result in the filing of criminal charges. Although the number of federal misdemeanor and felony immigration-crime prosecutions in Texas rose from just 4,300 in FY 1993 to 18,065 in FY 1998, the number of prosecutions in the latter year amounted to just 3.2 percent of the border patrol's 563,783 apprehensions on the Texas–Mexico border that year.[32] In other words, more than 90 percent of apprehensions in Texas resulted in voluntary return to Mexico.

Although public defenders assigned to the west Texas district of the federal court system report that a large number of first-time apprehendees have been referred by the border patrol for misdemeanor illegal entry prosecution in the Del Rio sector, it is clear that prosecution of first-time illegal entrants is quite uncommon. Resources are not available in terms of agents, prosecutors, and jail cells in Texas to prosecute a very large proportion of the 500,000+ apprehensions made along the state's border with Mexico. Instead, the border patrol, making effective use of the IDENT system and depending upon the agent-hours and detention space available to it at any given time, focuses its efforts on referring "recidivist" crossers and suspected smugglers for prosecution.

As shown by Heyman's and Massey and Singer's research,[33] apprehension and return to Mexico does not by itself constitute a punishment severe enough to deter many Mexican unauthorized border crossers. Given that misdemeanor illegal entry charges typically result only in the return of apprehendees to Mexico, we may assume that, for deterrence purposes, it is the certainty of the threat of incarceration for *felony* illegal reentry that must be assessed.

The true proportion of unauthorized border crossings resulting in apprehension by the authorities is unknown. In the Laredo sector, border patrol agents I spoke with in 1998 and 1999 reported that about 50 percent of crossings resulted in apprehension, a considerable improvement since the launching of Operation Rio

Grande. In addition, I was told that the sector followed a "three strikes policy," meaning that migrants were charged with misdemeanor illegal entry and deported following their third apprehension within a six-month period. Taking these agents at their word, this would mean that migrants face about a one in eight chance of misdemeanor prosecution and deportation per trip to the United States. The chances of prosecution for felony illegal reentry, which can result in imprisonment for up to five years, fall to just one in sixteen, even if felony charges are brought upon the first apprehension following deportation. This illustration includes an additional assumption, one which flies in the face of what research has shown about the process of undocumented migration: that each unauthorized crossing is an independent event, meaning that crossers cannot learn things on their unsuccessful crossings that improve their chances of avoiding apprehension by the border patrol. In fact, migrants do learn from their mistakes and typically travel with fellow migrants or employ *coyotes* who not only are knowledgeable about the best routes and strategies for crossing, but who may also have "intelligence" on the border patrol's latest deployments and maneuvers.[34]

Another point worth considering is that undocumented Mexican migrants, especially young men, have demonstrated over the course of several generations that they are not particularly risk-averse when it comes to border crossing, with thousands of individuals having swum the Río Grande, trekked across deserts, hopped freight trains, been packed into sweltering tractor-trailer compartments, and been the victim of shakedowns by Mexican police and nighttime assaults on both sides of the border. This, of course, does not take into account the hazardous types of work many migrants engage in once they have made it past the border patrol. Thus, even if the likelihood of incarceration for illegal entry were made relatively high, U.S. border control policy must contemplate the possibility that many, if not most, migrants will continue to attempt unauthorized crossings.

At present, about 2,000 persons each year are being convicted of felonious immigration crimes in Texas (mainly illegal reentry and alien smuggling). Detention space for immigrants apprehended by the border patrol as well as those held over for prosecution is in extremely short supply in the state, leading the Federal Bureau of Prisons to begin to seek private prison operators to provide 10,000 additional beds for prisoners in the border region.[35] The huge increase in federal prosecutions for both immigration and drug-related crimes in the Texas border region has strained the courts and the Federal Marshal's Service well beyond their intended capacity as more people were indicted for felonies in tiny Del Rio, Texas, than in Houston with its 4-million-plus inhabitants.[36] Clearly, if present border patrol apprehension levels in the state continue and if a greater percentage of recidivist illegal entrants are to be prosecuted, the federal government will have to dedicate far greater resources to the courts and prisons in the region than it currently contemplates.

On the other hand, if the border patrol had sufficient resources at its disposal to use its forward deployment strategy in Texas to make it nearly impossible to cross the border illegally and evade apprehension en route to interior U.S. destinations, we presume that, as time went on, very few unauthorized migrants/smugglers would attempt illegal entry. This would greatly reduce pressure on the federal courts and prison system and would also be a far more cost effective strategy than having to prosecute and incarcerate thousands of individuals whose "crime" is the international equivalent of jaywalking/trespassing. And while skeptics may claim that prevention of illegal entry is not a reachable goal of U.S. policy, world history shows that nation–states can quite effectively seal their borders to both immigration and emigration when they have the will to do so—or have we already forgotten the Berlin Wall?

Currently, however, it seems clear that the border patrol, at least in Texas, has nowhere near the resources it would need to successfully minimize illegal border crossings. Conservative estimates made recently by Bean, Capps, and Haynes, suggest that in order for the border patrol to achieve the effectiveness of OHTL along the entire U.S.–Mexico border, there would need to be more than a doubling of agents in the southwest border sectors—from 7,231 authorized for FY 1998 to more than 16,000. In Texas the number would have to nearly triple, from 3,381 in FY 1998 to 9,425, with substantial increases required in all sectors in the state.[37] While such an increase would be quite dramatic in relative terms, in absolute terms it would seem to be achievable. By way of comparison, more than 12,000 U.S. Army troops are already stationed just in Fort Bliss, located on the border in El Paso. The Houston Police Department, with a much smaller area to cover, has 5,100 officers on its force. This point is especially relevant when we realize that the relationship between level of deterrence and resources dedicated to it is neither continuous nor linear; in other words, that the ultimate impact of the border buildup may not be felt incrementally but abruptly when all of its elements are in place border wide.

THE LIMITS AND CONTRADICTIONS OF DETERRENCE IN TEXAS

It remains to be seen whether the buildup of border patrol forces along the Texas–Mexico border will result in substantial deterrence of entry without inspection as the number of agents, backed by appropriate material resources, approaches and, perhaps, surpasses the 9,425 that Bean, Capps, and Haynes estimate are needed. What has become clear, however, is that the border patrol is having such great difficulty in recruiting, training, bringing on-line, and retaining agents that its growth along the Texas border has been retarded to the point that it was unable to reach the authorized number of agents for FY 1999. Part of the reason for this is the concern of the INS's parent agency, the U.S. Department of Justice, that putting too many inexperienced agents into the field at one time could lead not only to ineffective patrolling, but increased risk to agents, migrants, and local residents, including the risk of human rights violations. This concern led Attorney General Janet Reno to announce a moratorium on sending new agents into the field until agents already on-line gained more experience, prompting applause from human rights groups and howls of protest from Texas's congressional delegation.[38] A second reason for the difficulty in reaching on-line agent targets has been the boom economy of the late 1990s and relatively low salaries of border patrol agents. Simply put, the agent's job has not been attractive enough to lure sufficient new recruits nor retain veterans who can find more lucrative opportunities elsewhere.[39]

The difficulty in recruiting, training, and retaining sufficient border patrol agents to sustain a rapid growth in force in Texas is just one of several emerging contradictions in border policy that call its ultimate effectiveness into question. Indeed, it is the only contradiction that appears to be easily resolved in the short term. Let us now turn our attention to other problems that are far less tractable.

Local Crossers in the Río Grande Valley

The majority of the persons apprehended by the border patrol prior to Operations Hold the Line and Rio Grande in the affected sectors were residents of adjacent Mexican border communities.[40] Based on the research of Operation Hold the Line, we should not expect most crossers to give up on visiting Texas border communities. Rather, they are likely to reduce the number of crossings they make, spend more time on the Texas side per crossing, and/or establish more exclusive residence in Texas border communities, giving up their visits "home" to see friends and family on the Mexican side. Local border residents are more likely than long-distance migrants, who are merely "passing through," to be intimately familiar with crossing points, border patrol deployments, and the best times to attempt unauthorized crossings. Furthermore, they are more likely to have social network connections to the Texas border communities across the river, such that they are more able to count on assistance from friends and kin in making their crossings. Thus, in the Texas border region the greatest effect of new efforts to deter entry without inspection may be to slow, but not nearly eliminate, the oscillation of the local Mexican population back and forth across the international line in the immediate border region itself.

Document Fraud

"Entry without inspection" is by no means the only way to gain unauthorized access to the United States. The INS's own research estimates that the majority of people residing illegally in the United States entered the country originally with legal, nonimmigrant visas.[41] Other research has found that the widespread use of fraudulent documents by foreign nationals has thus far made effective enforcement of the prohibitions against the employment of "illegal aliens" in the United States impossible,[42] with major document fraud rings being uncovered in a number of locations in and outside the United States.[43]

Concern about the misuse of border crossing cards to work and establish residence in the United States, and to travel into the U.S. interior, as well as the production of counterfeit cards and use of valid cards by impostors has led to the imposition of a ten-year expiration date on the card and mandated replacement of old cards with expensive new machine-readable "laser visas" featuring holographic images, digital photographs, and electronically encoded biometric data.[44] Similarly, new high-tech "permanent resident cards" are also now being issued to replace expired "green cards."[45]

The issuance of more tamper-resistant, high-tech entry documents may reduce the incidence of document fraud at the border itself, but will not by itself solve the fraud problem. These documents are issued to literally millions of persons following interviews by U.S. consular or immigration officials of Mexicans (and other nationals) that include the inspection of low-tech, forgeable Mexican documents. In addition, due to the sheer number of foreign nationals entering at land ports, it is not clear that INS personnel are able to closely compare the features of the person represented on the high-tech card with the person presenting him/herself for inspection. Despite the issuance of new documents, thousands of old border crossing cards, naturalization cards, and legal permanent resident cards are still valid, remain in circulation and will remain so for a number of years, so that easier possibilities of fraud still exist.[46]

Once unauthorized migrants are past the port of entry itself, the checking of documents to verify legal status becomes much more problematic. Since away from ports it cannot be presumed that a person is a foreign national and civil liberties concerns have precluded the institution of a national identity card for U.S. citizens, any number of easily obtained U.S. documents can be presented to authorities. Furthermore, the capacity to closely check the authenticity of the new high-tech documents by swiping them through a reader and checking them against a central database does not yet exist. As was seen in the summer of 1999, even the IDENT system used at the border, which now collects data on nearly 100 percent of border patrol apprehensions, is not yet adequately linked to other law enforcement databases nationwide: A suspected serial killer who was detained in El Paso by the border patrol and whose data was entered into IDENT was voluntarily returned to Mexico even though he was wanted by the FBI and in several states.[47]

In sum, as entry without inspection becomes more difficult as a consequence of the new border patrol strategy and increased enforcement capacity, we may witness not so much a reduction in the flows and stocks of unauthorized Mexican migrants in Texas and the rest of the United States, but a shift in mode of entry. There is little reason to believe that Mexicans cannot become more like the unauthorized residents from other countries, the majority of whom entered the United States with documents, whether valid or not. And while obtaining false documents or using legal documents improperly may raise the costs of unauthorized entry into the United States, it is not evident that it raises costs prohibitively for a large number of Mexican and other nationals entering the country along the Texas–Mexico border.

Migrant Smugglers

Smuggling has a long tradition along the Texas–Mexico border. In fact after the border patrol was first created in 1924, it largely dedicated its efforts to combating the smuggling of liquor into the United States during Prohibition and many of its first recruits were drawn from the Texas Rangers.[48] Today, a large proportion of the cocaine and heroin that enters the United States does so through Texas. In addition to smugglers of contraband, alien smugglers known as *coyotes* and *pateros* have long helped groups of Mexican and other migrants enter Texas illegally. Already before the recent crackdown on the border, a very large proportion of first-time Mexican border crossers engaged the services of a smuggler to enter the United States illegally and reach their intended destination in the interior.[49] In the aftermath of Operations Hold the Line and Rio Grande, unauthorized migrants entering Texas appear to have become more dependent upon smugglers to get through the border patrol's beefed-up defenses. Smugglers in border towns such as Nuevo Laredo and Matamoros organize groups of migrants and attempt to lead them through or around border patrol defenses on the Texas side. They may also sell or rent immigration documents to aspiring migrants and arrange air travel for them from the Texas border cities. A few have even used semitrucks to take up to 100 migrants at a time through INS checkpoints. Some of these smugglers are "honorable," others are dishonest and little concerned for the welfare of their clients, while others still are violent and abusive.

As I note elsewhere, smuggling enterprises are difficult for U.S. law enforcement authorities to break up since the only members who are likely to be apprehended are the guides leading migrants through the brush on foot or the drivers taking them in vehicles to their next destination, usually San Antonio, Houston, or Dallas.[50] Hence the threat of apprehension and criminal prosecution does not pose much of a deterrent for smuggling enterprises as a whole, even if the risk rises substantially for certain participants within them.

Although prices may have risen somewhat since the launching of Operation Rio Grande in 1997, by mid-1999 Mexican nationals still generally paid no more than $1,000 to be taken to a major Texas city, with the exact amount depending upon the nature/quality of the services provided and most of the payment made upon arrival in the destination city.[51] This amount, while not trivial, is typically worthwhile for migrants to pay insofar as it markedly improves their chances of penetrating border patrol defenses safely and typically can be earned back working in Texas or elsewhere in a matter of weeks.[52] None of the various migrants, smugglers, border patrol agents, federal prosecutors, immigration attorneys, public defenders, and human rights workers whom I have interviewed over the last two years on either side of the border has claimed that Operation Rio Grande has overcome the challenges posed by "alien smuggling" enterprises in the region.

Corruption of U.S. Law Enforcement Officials

Just as the Río Grande Valley in Texas has a long tradition of smuggling, so it also has a long tradition of the corruption of public servants by smugglers. To the extent that prevention of entry without inspection is successful, it is likely that the smugglers of contraband and migrants will use their considerable profits to either engage the services of public servants, pay public servants to turn a blind eye to their unlawful activities, or both. In some cases, law enforcement authorities will be tempted to go into the smuggling business themselves. A recent General Accounting Office (GAO) report to Congress expressed serious concern about the measured and potential extent of such corruption with regard to drug trafficking in particular.[53] Examples of each of these types of cases have occurred in the last several years in the Texas border region. In July 1998, a border patrol agent was arrested at the Sarita checkpoint on U.S. 77 attempting to move fourteen Mexican and Central American migrants to Houston.[54] In September 1999, a twenty-year veteran of the border patrol who was stationed in Harlingen was indicted by a grand jury in Brownsville for selling immigration documents to unauthorized migrants wishing to enter and/or remain in the United States.[55] While the extent of such corruption within federal agencies along the border in Texas is not known, we may expect the temptations facing employees of the INS and the Customs Service to increase along with the intensification of enforcement efforts.

Human Rights Concerns in the Texas Border Region

The imposition of Operation Rio Grande, like Hold the Line before it, has had implications for the respect of human rights in the Texas border region. As already noted above, U.S. Attorney General Janet Reno slowed the growth of the border patrol in the region in part to guarantee that new agents would be properly trained in all law enforcement procedures, including those involving respect for the rights of persons apprehended and/or detained for interrogation. This decision came following reports of widespread human rights violations involving U.S. authorities on the border from a number of monitoring organizations, including Amnesty International, the American Friends Service Committee, and Casa Proyecto Libertad in Harlingen, Texas.[56] The types of violations reported by these organizations are consistent with those predicted by Dunn's prescient analysis of the application of low-intensity conflict doctrine to the border region in an effort to control civilian populations through paramilitary tactics.[57]

If, as I have already suggested, unauthorized migrants increasingly rely upon false documents and *coyotes* or *pateros* in response to tightened physical control of the border, the potential for human rights abuses may increase in the Texas border region. Unless the border patrol is willing to restrict itself to apprehending migrants at the moment of illegal crossing itself, it will find itself having to make difficult judgment calls about who it has "reasonable suspicion" to detain and interrogate in a region where more than 80 percent of the population is of Mexican ancestry and around one-quarter were born in Mexico.

Human rights organizations have already vociferously protested the targeting of Mexicans and Mexican Americans as a suspect population in Texas.[58] In this context, the small town of El Cenizo, Texas, decided to conduct all its municipal business in Spanish and ordered its employees not to cooperate with U.S. immigration authorities so as to encourage residents' participation in local governance.[59] It is not inconceivable that others may follow.

One of the major consequences of the border patrol's new strategy has been to push migrants to make their treks into the United States in more remote areas where they face increased risk of injury and death from drowning and exposure.[60] In the Texas border region, this has been an especially deadly consequence, particularly in the summer months when temperatures in the arid ranchlands can reach well into the hundreds. During the intense heat wave of the summer of 1998, the first complete summer in which Operation Rio Grande was in place, at least fifty-three deaths from heat and dehydration were documented between May 1 and August 25, up from sixteen the year before.[61]

The most celebrated human rights incident in Texas since the buildup of forces along the border has been the shooting death of goatherd Ezequiel Hernández, a U.S. native, by Marines on a drug patrol near Redford, Texas.[62] This incident led to a suspension of such military patrols in the region. Nonetheless, other federal forces such as the border patrol and the Drug Enforcement Administration are taking responsibility for general law enforcement in the Texas border region.[63] As a consequence, we can expect federal agents to become involved in more confrontations with the local population in addition to the "alien" population whose actions they were intended to police. Depending upon the oversight of these forces' operations and the quality of the training they receive, this may lead to increased human rights complaints as well.

Legal Cross-Border Movement and Trade with Mexico[64]

During most of its history, the Texas–Mexico border has been an extremely porous, if not an entirely open border. This has been true with regard to the movement of both people and commodities. The 1990s witnessed changes in the relative porosity of the entire border region as the effects of the North American Free Trade Agreement (NAFTA) led to dramatically increased legal cross-border flows of goods, along with the vehicles and people bearing them, at the same time that U.S. policy made substantial efforts to restrict the unauthorized movement of migrants and drugs.[65] Texas figures especially large in both these developments: 75 percent of U.S.–Mexico trade passes through Texas customs ports and nearly half of the border patrol's agents are stationed in the state at present. As has already been shown in the cases of Operations Hold the Line and Gatekeeper, increases in attempted illegal movement of goods and persons through authorized ports of entry is one of the most significant consequences of making entry without inspection more difficult.[66] To the extent that the border patrol's deployments in Texas are successful in limiting cross-ing away from official ports of entry, it is likely to push both unauthorized migrants and smugglers through legal ports. Larger numbers of migrants are likely to attempt entry using false documents or by stowing away in car trunks or truck trailers. A greater proportion of drugs entering the country are also likely to be moved with other commodities passing through legal ports.

The challenges this development creates for U.S. authorities are significant. His-torically, it has been possible for nation–states to tightly restrict the movement of goods and persons across their borders, but history is largely mute regarding the fea-sibility of a state simultaneously restricting the entry of unwanted persons while promoting cross-border trade and the increased flows of vehicles, commodities, and persons that accompany expanded trade. The dollar value of imports and exports passing through Texas land ports since the creation of the North American Free Trade Agreement has skyrocketed, with imports from Mexico doubling from $29.5 bil-lion in FY 1994 to $59.7 billion in FY 1998. This increase in trade has been ac-companied by a doubling in both truck and rail crossings northbound into the United States since 1993. By 1998, total border crossings in and out of Texas's offi-cial ports made using all modes of transport reached 106 million (or over 290,000 crossings daily), with nearly half (51 million) consisting of crossings into Texas. This heavy traffic has placed great strains on the border infrastructure in Texas, leading to frequent and lengthy delays in vehicle crossings in both directions, producing not only inconveniences to travelers, but economic losses and increased pollution for border communities.[67]

A variety of measures, including the application of x-ray technologies and some automation of inspection of commercial vehicles and routine private-vehicle com-muters, have been taken by the U.S. Customs Service and the INS to smooth and speed the inspection process at the border, but these remain to be implemented at most ports of entry, including those in Texas.[68] If U.S. authorities wish to detect and reduce the increased unauthorized movement of contraband and persons through official ports of entry in Texas that arises as a consequence of the border patrol's new enforcement strategies, inspection of entering vehicles and persons will need to be stepped up as well. Other things being equal, this can only lead to further conges-tion and delays in cities like Laredo and El Paso, arousing the ire of local business elites and voters.

In order to effectively monitor and discourage the misuse of nonimmigrant visas by foreign nationals along the border, the INS will need to inspect the documents not only of those entering the United States at land ports, but those exiting it as well. This is not yet being done in Texas, although the development of such a sys-tem has been mandated by Congress for all U.S. land ports.[69] The implementation of such a system could have a major impact along the Texas border where thousands of Mexican residents enter the country using the border-crossing card, which allows for a stay not to exceed seventy-two hours and precludes U.S. employment.[70] Currently, there is no practical way to check if the seventy-two-hour limit is being obeyed. A federal pilot program that was to test an exit-check system was scotched in Eagle Pass after local officials and businesspeople complained that the ensuing delays would discourage Mexican businesspeople and shoppers from visiting the city. Opposition to the federal exit-check plan is now led by the Border Trade Alliance, a pro-NAFTA business association that is politically influential in the Texas border region.[71] This type of opposition has led Congress to extend the deadline for the implementation of an entry/exit control system from September 30, 1998 to March 31, 2001.[72]

Keeping Migrants Out, Bringing Workers In: The New Labor Shortage

In addition to the growing cross-border flows implied by increased trade with Mexico under NAFTA, a final significant contradiction facing the efforts of U.S. agencies in the region to deterring illegal entry is the labor shortage in key industries brought about by the late 1990s economic boom. The Texas economy has been one of the chief beneficiaries of this boom, with unemployment levels in the major cities of Dallas–Fort Worth, Houston, Austin, and San Antonio hovering between 2 and 4 percent.[73] The population growth and new construction that has accompanied Texas's economic success has created a tremendous demand for low-cost labor, particularly in the areas of personal services, agriculture, and construction. Much of this demand for labor has been met by Mexican immigrants, who entered the state in record numbers in the 1990s. A recent study conducted of the California economy found that the large majority of people holding many types of jobs in agriculture, manufacturing (sewing machine operators and electronics assemblers), construction (drywall installers), and services (maids, nannies, and gardeners) were held by immigrants.[74] While no comparable study has yet been conducted in Texas, it would not be surprising to find similar results. Clearly, the magnet for undocumented Mexican labor to enter the state is very strong as the century draws to a close.

While the Clinton administration's policies sought to prevent illegal migration by controlling the border proceed apace with the backing/pressure from key members of Texas's congressional delegation, there was growing support in the business community and among border-state governors for a new bracero-style guest worker program for Mexicans to meet labor shortages in key areas. At their annual meeting in September 1999, the U.S. and Mexican border-state governors, led by Arizona Governor Jane Hull, endorsed the idea of a new guest worker program.[75] Governor George W. Bush of Texas, who did not attend the governors' meeting, has long been unsympathetic to the sentiments inspiring California's Proposition 187 and has offered his cautious support to the guest worker proposal (though he does not endorse a new amnesty program for undocumented workers). Legislation has also been introduced in Congress to create a new guest worker program for agriculture and chances for passage appear better than they were when previous legislation died last year.

CONCLUSION

The current era of U.S. attempts to enforce its southern border with Mexico began in Texas and will likely end in Texas as well. Gaining control of the border in Texas poses especially large challenges to U.S. authorities not only because more than half the length of the border is claimed by the state, but also because of the Texas border region's tight cultural, social, and economic integration with Mexico. Massive new infusions of personnel and resources will be required before the border patrol and the rest of the INS and U.S. Department of Justice will be able to claim that they are seriously deterring Mexicans and other nationals from attempting unauthorized entry into the United States. Although the government has thus far seemed unusually willing to foot the bill for a border buildup, it seems more likely that at some point in the next few years the border patrol, perhaps having considerably reduced the number of entries without inspection in Texas, will claim to have achieved an effective level of border control. That this control is more apparent than real may not detract from the claims of victory, as the aftermath of Operation Hold the Line has shown.

The real issue at hand now seems to be not border control per se, but rather how border control efforts fit within a wider set of policies that permit the United States to continue to feed its century-long addiction to cheap Mexican labor. At this writing, federal legislation has been proposed to create a new guest worker program to import Mexicans legally into the country to plant and harvest crops and perhaps fill labor shortages in other industries as well. It is possible that we will soon witness a return to the situation prevailing in the 1950s when the U.S. government was engaged simultaneously in the massive importation and deportation of Mexicans. Historically, the Texas–Mexico border, like the U.S.–Mexico border as a whole, has been open to Mexicans intent upon crossing it. Never, including today, has the United States placed a credible deterrent in their path. Instead, it has chosen to allow entry, albeit with considerable difficulty, while limiting the types of claims Mexicans may make on the state once they have entered. A key element to limiting those claims has been to criminalize Mexicans' very presence in the country, making them "outlaws in the promised land" who are subject to the constant threat of removal should they emerge from the underground.[76] The 1990s buildup of force at the border and in other areas of heavy immigrant population around the country can be seen as the state's attempt to intensify the policing of a workforce that is at once economically vital but culturally and politically threatening. If this indeed were the objective of current policy, we might say that it has been achieved or is on the way to being achieved. If, on the other hand, the objective is to deter Mexicans and other nationals from coming into the country without an official invitation, it most certainly has not.

NOTES

1. Portions of the research conducted for this chapter were supported by the Tom and Mary Turner Faculty Fellowship of Trinity University. The author thanks Peter Andreas and Randy Capps for helpful comments on an earlier draft.

2. See, for example, Douglas S. Massey, "March of Folly: U.S. Immigration Policy After NAFTA," *American Prospect*, no. 37, March–April 1998.

3. Peter Andreas, "The Escalation of U.S. Immigrant Control in the Post-NAFTA Era," *Political Science Quarterly*, no. 113, 1998; Néstor Rodríguez, "The Battle for the Border: Notes on Autonomous Migration, Transnational Communities, and the State," *Social Justice*, vol. 23, no. 3, 1996.

4. Frank D. Bean, Randy Capps, and Charles W. Haynes, "An Estimate of Border Patrol Personnel Needed at the Southwest Border to Achieve the Level of Effectiveness of Operation Hold-the-Line," written testimony presented to the Subcommittee on Immigration and Claims, Committee on the Judiciary, U.S. House of Representatives, Washington, D.C., February 25, 1999.

5. Ronald L. Akers, *Criminological Theories: Introduction and Evaluation* (Los Angeles: Roxbury, 1994); Allen E. Liska, *Perspectives on Deviance: Second Edition* (Englewood Cliffs, N.J.: Prentice Hall, 1987).

6. Douglas S. Massey, Rafael Alarcón, Jorge Durand, and Humberto González, *Return to Aztlan: The Social Process of International Migration from Western Mexico* (Berkeley: University of California Press, 1987); Douglas S. Massey and Felipe García España, "The Social Process of International Migration," *Science*, no. 237, 1987; Roger Rouse, "Mexican Migration and the Social Space of Postmodernism," *Diaspora*, vol. 1, no. 1, 1991; Audrey Singer and Douglas S. Massey, "The Social Process of Undocumented Border Crossing Among Mexican Migrants," *International Migration Review*, vol. 32, no. 3, 1998.

7. Josiah Heyman, "Putting Power in the Anthropology of Bureaucracy: The Immigration and Naturalization Service at the Mexico–United States Border," *Current Anthropology*, no. 36, 1995; Sherrie A. Kossoudji, "Playing Cat and Mouse at the U.S.–Mexico Border," *Demography*, vol. 29, no. 2, 1992; Douglas S. Massey, and Audrey Singer, "New Estimates of Undocumented Mexican Migration and the Probability of Apprehension," *Demography*, vol. 32, no. 2, 1995.

8. Heyman, "Putting Power in the Anthropology of Bureaucracy."

9. Binational Study on Migration, *Migration between Mexico and the United States* (Washington, D.C.: U.S. Commission on Immigration Reform, 1997).

10. Gelbard and Carter report that only 760,000 Mexican-born persons were recorded by the U.S. Census. Between 1970 and 1995, less than 2 million Mexicans were legally admitted to the United States, indicating that around 4 million of the more than 6 million net growth in the Mexican population was due to undocumented immigration. Alene H. Gelbard and Marion Carter, "Mexican Immigration and the U.S. Population," in *At the Crossroads: Mexico and U.S. Immigration Policy*, Frank D. Bean et al., eds. (Lanham, Md.: Rowman & Littlefield, 1997).

11. Robert Warren, *Estimates of the Undocumented Immigrant Population Residing in the United States, by Country of Origin and State of Residence: October 1992* (Washington, D.C.: INS, Statistics Division, 1994).

12. INS, "Southwest Border Apprehensions by Sector: Fiscal Years 1960 through January 1999," mimeo, 1999.

13. Frank D. Bean et al., *Illegal Mexican Migration & the United States/Mexico Border: The Effects of Operation Hold the Line on El Paso/Juárez* (Washington, D.C.: U.S. Commission on Immigration Reform, 1994).

14. Bean et al., *Illegal Mexican Migration & the United States/Mexico Border.*

15. For a more extensive discussion of these, see Bean et al., *Illegal Mexican Migration & the United States/Mexico Border* and David Spener, "Controlling the Border in El Paso del Norte: Operation Blockade or Operation Charade?" in *Border Ethnographies. The Limits of Border Theory*, Pablo Vila, ed. (Minneapolis: University of Minnesota Press, forthcoming).

16. INS, "Southwest Border Apprehensions."

17. I have argued elsewhere that the misuse by Mexican nationals of nonimmigrant visas and the use of fraudulent documents to enter the United States to seek employment and/or establish residence may be far more widespread than has generally been presumed. See "The Mexican Border Crossing Card and U.S. Border Control Policy: A Neglected Topic in the Immigration Debate," paper presented on August 22, 1999 in Washington, D.C., at the annual meeting of the American Sociological Association. In his now classic work *Los Mojados*, Julian Samora noted the common use by Mexican border residents of the border-crossing card to enter the United States in order to subsequently gain employment and/or establish residence. See his *Los Mojados: The Wetback Story* (Notre Dame, Ind.: University of Notre Dame Press, 1971).

18. In fact, additional research on the El Paso sector conducted by Bean, Capps, and Haynes conservatively estimated that in order to successfully maintain deterrence of unauthorized crossings in the sector, the border patrol would need a minimum of 2,052 agents, or more than *three times* the number of agents stationed in the sector in September 1993 when Operation Hold the Line was launched.

19. Bean, Capps, and Haynes, "An Estimate of Border Patrol Personnel"; GAO, *Illegal Aliens: Fraudulent Documents Undermining the Effectiveness of the Employment Verification System* (Washington, D.C.: GAO, 1999).

20. GAO, *Illegal Aliens.*

21. *San Antonio Express-News,* "Patrols Beefed up on Texas Border," August 26, 1997.

22. GAO, *Illegal Immigration: Status of Southwest Border Strategy Implementation* (Washington, D.C.: GAO, 1999), 32.

23. *San Antonio Express-News,* "Judge Gives OK to Army Border Work," February 14, 1998.

24. *San Antonio Express-News,* "Drones Tested for Spotting Smugglers," June 9, 1999.

25. *San Antonio Express-News,* "Bush Defends Texas Guard Use at Border," June 24, 1999; "Guard Keeps Border Watch," June 9, 1999.

26. In FY 1993, apprehensions in Laredo, McAllen, and Del Rio stood at 70,000, 110,000, and 55,000, respectively. By FY 1997, apprehensions in Laredo and McAllen reached 145,000 and 245,000, respectively, falling to around 100,000 and 200,000 in FY 1998. By FY 1998, apprehensions in Del Rio had reached nearly 150,000. See INS, "Southwest Border Apprehensions by Sector: Fiscal Years 1960 through January 1999."

27. *San Antonio Express-News,* "Change Seen in Crossings," October 5, 1999.

28. Heyman, "Putting Power in the Anthropology of Bureaucracy."

29. Transactional Records Access Clearinghouse, *INS: New Findings*, Retrieved on July 26, 1999, from: www.trac.syr.edu/tracins/findings/aboutINS/newFindings.html.

30. *San Antonio Express-News*, "Immigration Crimes Get Stiffer Terms: INS-Related Convictions See Increase in South Texas," July 26, 1999.

31. Ronald L. Akers, *Criminological Theories: Introduction and Evaluation* (Los Angeles: Roxbury, 1994); Allen E. Liska, *Perspectives on Deviance: Second Edition* (Englewood Cliffs, N.J.: Prentice Hall, 1987).

32. Data are from the INS and tables faxed to the author by the Statistical Records Division of the U.S. Federal Court System.

33. Heyman "Putting Power in the Anthropology of Bureaucracy"; Massey and Singer, "New Estimates of Undocumented Mexican Migration and the Probability of Apprehension"; Singer and Massey, "The Social Process of Undocumented Border Crossing Among Mexican Migrants."

34. David Spener, "Smuggling Mexican Migrants through South Texas: Challenges Posed by Operation Rio Grande," in *Global Human Trafficking in Comparative Perspective*, David J. Kyle and Rey Koslowski, eds. (Baltimore: Johns Hopkins University Press, 2001).

35. Associated Press, "Need for New Prison Beds Has Operators Looking Toward Border," July 6, 1999.

36. *San Antonio Express-News*, "Border Courts Face Backlog," July 9, 1999.

37. Bean, Capps, and Haynes, "An Estimate of Border Patrol Personnel."

38. GAO, *Illegal Immigration; San Antonio Express-News*, "Reno Calls Border Plan Dangerous: AG Says Influx of New Agents Threatens Patrol's Integrity," March 9, 1999.

39. Associated Press, "Border Patrol Having Trouble Finding New Recruits," June 3, 1999; *San Antonio Express-News*, "Residents Cite Fear Created by Crisis on the Border," June 10, 1999.

40. Bean et al., *Illegal Mexican Migration & the United States/Mexico Border*, "San Diego: A Corridor for Long-Distance, Determined Crossers," retrieved on March 9, 1999 from: www.ins.usdoj.gov/public_affairs/progress_reports/Gatekeeper/ 238.html.

41. Robert Warren, *Estimates of the Undocumented Immigrant Population Residing in the United States*.

42. GAO, *Illegal Aliens*.

43. *San Antonio Express-News*, "Mexico Arrests 12 in Bogus Documents Raid," January 17, 1998; INS, "INS Busts Major Counterfeit Document Ring," news release, May 21, 1998, retrieved from: www.ins.usdoj.gov/public_affairs/news_ releases/bust.htm on March 5, 1999; INS, "INS Cracks National Counterfeit Document Operation," news release, November 13, 1998, retrieved from: www.ins.usdoj.gov/public_affairs/news_ releases/fineprnt.htm on March 5, 1999.

44. *San Antonio Express-News*, "U.S. Responds to Concern about 'Laser Visa' Plan," April 7, 1998; "Envoy to Work on Visa Facility," February 21, 1998; INS, "INS Issues First High-Tech 'Green Cards,'" news release, April 21, 1998, retrieved from: www.ins.usdoj.gov/ graphics/ publicaffairs/newsrels/cards.htm on November 4, 1999; *San Antonio Express-News*, "$20 Non-Immigrant Visa Fee Is Seen Hurting Tourist Trade," June 22, 1996.

45. U.S. Inspector General, *Immigration and Naturalization Service Replacement of Resident Alien Identity Cards, Audit Report 97–06* (Washington, D.C.: U.S. Inspector General, 1997); INS, "INS Issues First High-Tech 'Green Cards.'"

46. INS, "INS Issues First High-Tech 'Green Cards'"; U.S. Inspector General, *Immigration and Naturalization Service Replacement of Resident Alien Identity Cards.*

47. *Houston Chronicle*, "INS Soul-Searching in Wake of Resendez-Ramirez Release: Agency Wants to Get Around Technical Limits That Caused Problem," June 27, 1999.

48. Timothy J. Dunn, *The Militarization of the U.S.–Mexico Border 1978–1992: Low-Intensity Conflict Doctrine Comes Home* (Austin: CMAS Books, Center for Mexican American Studies, University of Texas, 1996).

49. Singer and Massey, "The Social Process of Undocumented Border Crossing Among Mexican Migrants."

50. Spener, "Smuggling Mexican Migrants through South Texas."

51. David Spener, "This Coyote's Life," *NACLA Report on the Americas*, November 1999; Spener, "Smuggling Mexican Migrants through South Texas"; Interviews conducted by author in Monterrey and San Antonio, July 1999.

52. In addition, the bulk of the fee is generally paid upon the migrant's arrival in the U.S. destination by his/her friends or relatives already living and working here. Thus, the increased fee need not be paid out of the migrant's peso-denominated Mexican savings.

53. GAO, *Drug Control: INS and Customs Can Do More to Prevent Drug-Related Employee Corruption* (Washington, D.C.: GAO, 1999).

54. *Valley Morning Star*, "10-Year Border Patrol Vet Arrested," July 16, 1998.

55. *San Antonio Express-News*, "INS Agent, Schoolteacher Face Charges: 2 Accused of Selling Fake Papers to Immigrants," September 3, 1999.

56. Amnesty International, *United States of America: Human Rights Concerns in the Border Region with Mexico* (New York: Amnesty International, 1998); *In Motion Magazine*, "The Militarization of the U.S.–Mexico Border: Part 1: Border Communities Respond to Militarization: Interview with María Jiménez," February 2, 1998, retrieved on July 9, 1999 from: www.inmotion magazine.com/mj1.html; Nate Selzer, "Immigration Law Enforcement and Human Rights Abuses," *Borderlines*, no. 50, November 1998, retrieved October 15, 1999 from: www.zianet.com /irc1/bordline/1998/b150/b150bf.html.

57. Dunn, *The Militarization of the U.S.–Mexico Border 1978–1992.* See Selzer, "Immigration Law Enforcement" for examples of specific types of abuses that have been documented in the region.

58. *In Motion Magazine*, "The Militarization of the U.S.–Mexico Border."

59. *Los Angeles Times*, "Town Speaks the Language of Its People," August 13, 1999. Interviews with town officials and residents of El Cenizo by author in November 1999.

60. Bean et al., *Illegal Mexican Migration & the United States/Mexico Border*; Karl Eschbach, Jacqueline Hagan, Néstor Rodríguez, Rubén Hernández, and Stanley Bailey, "Death at the Border," *International Migration Review*, vol. 33, no. 2, 1999.

61. Associated Press, "Immigrant Heat Deaths Triple '97 Rate in Texas," August 26, 1998.

62. *The New York Times*, "After Marine on Patrol Kills a Teen-Ager, a Texas Border Village Wonders Why," June 29, 1997.

63. See, for example, *San Antonio Express-News*, "Year Later, Agents Mourn 2 Slain Comrades," July 7, 1999

64. Except where otherwise noted, the source for statistical data discussed in this section is the Texas Center for Border Enterprise and Economic Development at Texas A&M International University.

65. Andreas, "The Escalation of U.S. Immigrant Control in the Post-NAFTA Era"; Peter Andreas, "U.S.–Mexico: Open Markets, Closed Border," *Foreign Policy*, vol. 103, 1996.

66. Bean et al., *Illegal Mexican Migration & the United States/Mexico Border*; GAO, *Illegal Immigration*.

67. GAO, *U.S.–Mexico Border: Issues and Challenges Confronting the United States and Mexico* (Washington, D.C.: GAO, 1999); *San Antonio Express-News*, "INS Cutback Jams Traffic at the Border," July 12, 1999; Texas Comptroller of Public Accounts, *Bordering the Future* (Austin: Texas Comptroller of Public Accounts, 1998).

68. GAO, *U.S.–Mexico Border: Issues and Challenges*.

69. GAO, *U.S.–Mexico Border: Issues and Challenges*.

70. In 1997 the U.S. Information Agency estimated that approximately 5.5 million Mexican citizens residing in Mexico possessed a valid border-crossing card. U.S. Information Agency, "Mexican Border Crossing Cards: Briefing Paper B-77-97" (Washington, D.C.: U.S. Information Agency, 1997).

71. *San Antonio Express-News*, "Alliance to Fight New Rules on Border," November 24, 1998.

72. GAO, *U.S.–Mexico Border: Issues and Challenges*.

73. Texas Workforce Commission, *MSA Unemployment Rankings, September 1999*, retrieved on November 6, 1999 from: www.twc.state.tx.us/lmi/lfs/type/unemployment/unemploymentmsarankcurrent.html

74. Wayne Cornelius, *The Role of Immigrant Labor in the U.S. and Japanese Economies: A Comparative Study of San Diego and Hamamatsu, Japan* (San Diego: Center for U.S.–Mexican Studies, University of California, San Diego, 1998).

75. *Christian Science Monitor*, "Guest Workers: A Way to Solve Labor Shortage?" September 20, 1999.

76. James D. Cockcroft, *Outlaws in the Promised Land: Mexican Immigrant Workers and America's Future* (New York: Grove Press, 1986).

8

U.S. Border Controls: A Mexican Perspective

Gustavo Mohar and María-Elena Alcaraz[1]

While much has been written about the enhanced U.S. efforts to control undocumented migration across its southwest border, much less has been said about the Mexican government's response. In this chapter we present our view of Mexico's approach to this issue, the basic philosophy behind its actions, and our account of what has been accomplished by its policies, including their limitations and possibilities. We describe what Mexico has done on its side of the borderline (as well as along its own southern border) and what has been accomplished bilaterally since the new U.S. strategy of containment was initiated at the border.

U.S.–MEXICO RELATIONS IN THE 1990S

Since the mid-1990s, the U.S. and Mexican governments have taken a new approach toward dealing with matters of mutual concern along the border. This new approach involves permanent engagement in constructive and realistic dialogue on a range of issues on the bilateral agenda, making sure that differing viewpoints on certain sensitive subjects do not "contaminate" their dialogue and cooperation on others.

Previously, both governments largely avoided immigration issues in their formal conversations. Today, these issues are in the forefront of this new bilateral approach. Substantive progress has been made in finding the "common ground" to deal with these matters in a constructive manner. The primary goal has been to achieve a better understanding of the nature, complexity, challenges, and opportunities the migration of Mexican nationals to the United States truly represents.[2]

The reality posed by enhanced U.S. border controls in the mid-1990s demanded immediate and concerted actions by the Mexican government to better "manage" the situation. Mexico was well aware that the flow of people crossing the common border without documents would not stop immediately. Insufficient domestic economic growth in the aftermath of the economic crisis of December 1994, the powerful magnet of job opportunities in the United States, and established social networks on both sides would continue to attract many Mexicans to the "North."

With this in mind, in February 1995, the formal dialogue between both governments led to the development of several bilateral agreements and operational mechanisms to accommodate their respective interests,[3] including Mexico's demand of respect for the human and civil rights of its migrants, regardless of their migratory status, and U.S. authorities' right to enforce its immigration laws and border control policy. Formalizing these agreements has proven to be mutually beneficial, both in terms of preventing bilateral conflicts and in terms of protecting the well-being of thousands of people in both countries.

But while recognizing the progress made through constant and open dialogue between these countries, the present challenge still is how to exercise the sovereign right of each nation to control its borders while facilitating the movement of people. While the North American Free Trade Agreement (NAFTA) has promoted an explosive increase in bilateral trade of goods and services, which require expeditious movement at the border, the U.S. controls established to deter and prevent illegal crossings have created what seems to be a contradictory situation. The deployment of a massive number of agents supported by state-of-the-art technology, sensors, nightlights, wiring, walls, fences, and helicopters has created an image of a region at war.[4] This seems incompatible among neighboring countries in a new era of partnership and mutual trust and respect.

THE U.S.–MEXICO COMMON BORDER

The 2,000-mile-long U.S.–Mexico border is one of the world's busiest regions, where over 10 million people live in twelve neighboring cities, bringing together thirty-nine municipalities in Mexico and twenty-five counties in the United States. The border has forty-four ports of entry, where in 1998 more than 300 million persons, 70 million cars, and more than 6 million commercial trucks legally crossed (the trucks carrying 80 percent of the total bilateral trade, which amounts to over $180 billion a year).[5] Also, on the Mexican side of the border there are over 1,675 *maquiladora* plants,[6] which provide some 600,000 jobs to Mexicans.

At the same time, the U.S.–Mexico border is a region laden with a variety of problems derived from immigration, trade, the environment, and drug trafficking. These problems directly impact the quality of life and the ties among the border communities, as well as the region's infrastructure, transboundary resources, water management, and waste disposal. Hence, the border is the geographical enclave where all the issues on the U.S.–Mexico bilateral agenda express themselves in a microcosm.

However, the origins of the shared problems at the border are found many miles away from this relatively thin, 100-kilometer-wide area: the Mexican towns and cities of migrants' origin and in the U.S. fields and cities where migrants find jobs. To assume that the solution to the immigration flows will be found solely through border controls is a partial and shortsighted view. Regardless of the sovereign right of nations to implement border policy, to a migrant who has a job waiting "on the other side," the border is only an obstacle along the way. Therefore, the solution to border problems and its adequate management must be found where they belong: improving labor opportunities in Mexico and recognizing the existence of labor offerings, and the historical networks of family and social relations among Mexicans on both sides of the border who help migrants obtain the jobs.

MEXICO AND THE UNITED STATES UNDER NAFTA

To explore NAFTA's economic, environmental, and labor impacts in the United States and Mexico would go beyond the scope of this work. Suffice it to say that there is a growing consensus that as a whole, the trade accord has had a positive impact in both countries.

The New York–based Council of the Americas correctly points out the positive effects in its NAFTA fifth anniversary report.[7] For the United States, it concluded that the trade pact fostered growth in cross-border investment, improving the competitiveness of American companies, and, contrary to the general expectation of massive exodus of U.S. jobs to Mexico, it enhanced U.S. companies' ability to keep high-skilled, high-wage jobs.[8] With regard to Mexico, it underscored the country's far-reaching political and economic reforms aimed at promoting democracy, economic transparency, and trade liberalization, concluding that Mexico was able to recover faster from its 1994 financial crisis due in good measure to structural changes to its economy derived from NAFTA.[9]

In the Mexican case, however, changes in the labor market need to be explained in the broader context of its economic restructuring, starting in the 1980s, long before NAFTA. Migration pressures and constant flows of people to the United States should be understood as a combination of factors, which include the magnet of U.S. economic growth and the lack of sustained economic growth and development in Mexico.

Notwithstanding the positive effects of NAFTA mentioned above, migration of Mexican nationals to the United States continues at a persistent rate. Labor mobility was explicitly excluded from the NAFTA negotiations under the premise adopted by the governments that sustained economic development would expand and modernize the Mexican economy. This in turn would gradually provide the required well-paid jobs to stimulate potential migrants to stay in their places of origin rather than migrate to the United States.

THE BORDER AND IMMIGRATION CONTROL

Recent studies on the Mexican migration phenomenon, including the Binational Study on Migration between Mexico and the United States,[10] reaffirmed that Mexican migration to the United States is a complex and dynamic phenomenon with long-standing roots. Migration northward has existed since the border between the two countries was established in 1848, in particular since the first sizable labor migration flows in the 1870s. Today, much of the migration remains economically driven by wage differentials that affect labor supply-and-demand conditions, and are sustained by family and social networks that connect the two countries.

There is little empirical evidence to validate the Immigration and Naturalization Service (INS) claim that its Southwest border policy of deterrence has been successful.[11] However, experience and information conveyed by the Mexican consulates along the border confirm that as crossing became more difficult at the San Diego–Tijuana region, migrant flows began to move toward the desert zones of the Arizona–Sonora border region.[12]

In 1994 the Mexican government recognized the emergence of a new cycle of anxiety about the presence of migrants in the United States that usually arises during economic downturns. This sentiment started in California with Proposition 187, and soon developed into a major political theme in that year's gubernatorial campaign. The anti-immigrant sentiment reached its peak when the U.S. Congress passed the Illegal Immigration Reform and Immigrant Responsibility Act of 1996 (IIRIRA), the most comprehensive reform of U.S. immigration legislation in its history.[13] The IIRIRA is a highly restrictive law, and there are many U.S. organizations and groups committed to the effort of having Congress amend some of its harshest provisions.[14]

During the congressional hearings where the immigration legislative changes were debated, it was clear that the general mood included a strong feeling that the "problem of illegal aliens" originated at the U.S. Southwest border, and that the border was "out of control."[15] These perceptions were heightened when the first border control operations were implemented and their apparent initial success gave the impression of regained control of the U.S. Southwest border, and thus, added to the prevailing atmosphere against "illegal aliens." The objective of "Operation Hold the Line" and "Operation Gatekeeper" is to prevent, discourage, or otherwise detain and return migrants trying to cross into the United States without proper documentation.[16]

The new provisions of IIRIRA were accompanied by an unprecedented budget increase to the INS. Since 1994, the agency's budget has more than tripled: from $1.4 billion in fiscal year (FY) 1994 to $2.6 billion allocated for FY 1996, reaching $4.2 billion in FY 1999.[17] The U.S. Congress also mandated an increase of 1,000 border patrol agents and 300 support personnel per year between FY 1997 and FY 2001,[18] thus increasing the numbers from some 4,000 agents in 1994 to more than 8,000 by 1999, with the vast majority of them deployed at the U.S.–Mexico border.

Mexico was therefore confronted with the difficult task of trying to reconcile the principles of respect for the sovereign authority of the United States to adopt and enforce its own laws, with its legitimate concern and responsibility to defend the civil and human rights of Mexicans residing, documented or undocumented, in the United States who were the most negatively affected by the new immigration control provisions. This became an imperative for Mexico since more than 95 percent of its nationals living abroad reside in the United States.[19]

In fact, in FY 1999 the INS removed from the interior of the United States 177,000 aliens, of which 83 percent were Mexican nationals.[20] Most of the Mexicans removed were detained at job sites in U.S. cities, based on the INS interior enforcement operations implemented as part of the agency's overall "strategy of containment." In the border region, detention of Mexicans crossing without authorization reached about 800,000 (according to the Mexican Migration Institute, or more than 1.2 million reported by the INS.)

SAFE AND ORDERLY REPATRIATION OF MEXICAN NATIONALS

Following the presidential commitments of 1997, and in harmony with Mexico's concern for the protection of its nationals when detained by U.S. immigration authorities, both countries agreed that Mexican nationals were to be returned in a safe and orderly manner, fully respecting their dignity and their human and civil rights.

This bilateral effort was an important turning point between the Mexican and U.S. governments because, notwithstanding each country's policies of border control, it proved that through dialogue and cooperation seemingly insurmountable differences could be overcome for the benefit of people on both sides of the border.

Starting in December 1997 in El Paso, Texas, and Ciudad Juárez, Chihuahua, the processes of returning Mexican nationals was carried out with two priorities: ensuring the migrants' safety, while allowing authorities on both sides of the border to work in an orderly manner to send and receive the returned migrants.[21] The completion of these arrangements throughout the common border has been the means to prevent chaotic situations for border communities, stemming from the massive returns of expelled migrants. Prior to the negotiation of the arrangements, several cases of people abandoned during the night in isolated areas were the victims of numerous crimes, including robbery and rape, which became the source for extreme concern to federal, state, and local governments, especially on the Mexican side of the border. The so-called "Local Arrangements for the Safe and Orderly Repatriation of Mexican Nationals"[22] were negotiated and agreed upon by local immigration and consular officials on both sides of the border, with the approval of Mexico's Ministries of Foreign Relations and of the Interior, and the U.S. Department of State and the INS.

U.S. BORDER CONTROL POLICIES: CONSEQUENCES AND RESPONSES

The most dramatic consequence of U.S. border control policies has been the loss of lives. Since 1997, the bodies of more than 600 Mexican young men and woman have been found.[23] They died in their effort to avoid the "migra" by crossing the border through more isolated, dangerous areas, ranging from frozen mountains to infernal deserts. For instance, in a small stretch of the Colorado river on the outskirts of Calexico, California, known as the "All-American Canal," forty-nine bodies were found in 1998 in what looks like smooth, calm waters,[24] but in reality is a deep canal with strong underwater currents.

To confront this situation, the Mexican government has used its limited resources to implement a number of imaginative solutions in its own territory. It also has used the diplomatic arena to find ways to avoid these tragic incidents. In the diplomatic arena, the goal has been to "institutionalize" U.S.–Mexico bilateral mechanisms to manage the many issues on the bilateral border agenda, by establishing in the last five years several binational working groups, committees, and ad-hoc commissions.

Extensive research has been conducted with the purpose of understanding the challenges faced by Mexico as the only U.S. southern neighbor with a common land border. The asymmetry of this relationship is a topic that goes beyond the purpose of this chapter. However, it is not hard to understand the tremendous difficulties that the Mexican government faces in order to "present its case" to the United States in a way that makes the bilateral relationship manageable.

As mentioned earlier, diverse memoranda, agreements, and statements have been negotiated and implemented. Today, migration and border control issues have reached the highest levels of both governments. During President Clinton's visit to Mexico City in May 1997, the *Joint Presidential Statement on Migration* was signed,[25] whereby they publicly addressed the importance these issues had for both countries. While recognizing that these types of documents have limitations, it is important to emphasize that the commitment by the presidents of Mexico and the United States became the framework for actions to be undertaken by both administrations. The presidents' commitment to finding more constructive ways to deal in a bilateral manner with immigration issues,[26] and their reiterated political will to avoid conflicts at their countries' common border through cooperation,[27] has become the benchmark, during the following years, for the U.S.–Mexico bilateral agenda on migration and border affairs.

MIGRANT PROTECTION GROUPS

Another effort undertaken by the Mexican authorities to deal with increasing incidents of abuse and crime against migrants on the Mexican side of the border was the creation in 1991 of the migrant protection groups, better known as "Beta Groups." The National Migration Institute (INM), Mexico's immigration authority, established these elite groups in the Tijuana border region in 1991, with the primary mission of protecting migrants from attacks or abuse by traffickers or criminals along Mexico's border regions, regardless of their nationality or migration status in Mexican territory. The Beta Groups have gained prestige and recognition not only in Mexico, but also by U.S. law enforcement agencies such as the border patrol. They work daily risking their lives from constant violent confrontations with smugglers or criminals. Their honesty and dedication makes them an example to other law enforcement authorities. The Beta Groups have been expanded and reinforced since 1994.[28]

BORDER SAFETY INITIATIVE

Given the increase in deaths of undocumented migrants as they attempt to enter the United States through inhospitable or high-risk areas along the border, both governments agreed to launch a joint effort to prevent these deaths. On July 1, 1998, the "Border Safety Initiative" was implemented.[29] This safety campaign reinforced the measures already undertaken by the Beta Groups to protect migrants found along Mexico's side of the border. Under the joint agreement, border patrol agents would also work to protect migrants. The campaign has been a coordinated and mutually supportive effort that includes actions focused on prevention, and on search and rescue missions for migrants lost or those who, having entered U.S. territory frequently guided by unscrupulous traffickers who use them as prey, abandon them in desert or mountainous areas. It also includes the gruesome task of identifying the remains of those unfortunate migrants who die during the attempt to cross the border.

The preventive phase of the safety initiative consists in the posting of large signs along both sides of the border region by Beta Groups and the INS, warning migrants of the risks they would face at certain crossing areas. Public announcements are also being aired in radio stations throughout Mexico and in the U.S. border region. Mexican consulates along the U.S. border are widely distributing the *"Tarjeta de Orientación Básica al Migrante"* (migrant information card), which contains basic information on migrant rights in U.S. territory and how to contact the nearest consular office.

For the search and rescue missions, Mexican and U.S. authorities have been trained in emergency aid. Mexican consulates help these authorities to locate lost or dead migrants both in Mexico and in the United States. When remains are found without identification, Mexican consular officials also help forensic authorities in the identification of these migrants. The safety campaign is conducted throughout the year.[30] However, during the summer and winter months its activities are intensified because of the extremely high and low temperatures in the border region that increase the danger to the well-being of migrants.

A priority in the daily work of Mexican consular offices is to provide protection and counseling to ensure the respect of the human and civil rights of Mexican nationals in the United States.[31] Through the consultation mechanisms established between the consulates and the local U.S. immigration authorities, they make sure that Mexicans arrested by border patrol, INS, or other law enforcement officials are afforded all the protections provided by the law. Also, many diplomatic notes have been presented to the U.S. Department of State whereby the Government of Mexico expressed its concerns, frustrations, and demands for the due legal process to be followed investigating and prosecuting border agents charged with abusing Mexican migrants.

MEXICO'S SOUTHERN BORDER

To better understand Mexico's position regarding U.S. policy toward its southwest border, it is important to briefly review the migratory situation at Mexico's southern border. In many ways this region is a mirror image of Mexico's border with the United States. To reconcile the legitimate demands presented by Mexico to the United States for a fair and respectful application of U.S. laws, the Mexican government has had to revisit its own position, policies, challenges, and opportunities presented by migrant workers coming from Central America, especially from Guatemala. It has also established procedures to ensure the fair and legal treatment of transmigrants crossing Mexico's territory trying to reach the United States.

Unprecedented steps have been taken to "manage" the migration agenda between Mexico and its southern neighbors, particularly with Guatemala. Similar agreements, statements, and mechanisms as the ones established with the United States have been signed and implemented with Guatemalan immigration authorities for the protection of migrants. Like Mexican workers who migrate to "the North," tens of thousand of undocumented Central American migrants cross the Mexican border every year, most of them with the goal of reaching the United States. In addition, thousands of Guatemalan farm laborers cross the border each year to work temporarily in Mexican coffee and sugar cane plantations; they usually return to their places of origin after the harvest season. The following are some examples of the intense activity at the Mexico–Guatemala border resembling that of the U.S.–Mexico border.

Mexico is a country of transit for thousands of Central and South American undocumented migrants intending to enter the United States. In 1998, more than 111,000 people were detained by the Mexican National Migration Institute and returned to their countries of origin. People from more than twenty-five countries, of which 90 percent were nationals from Guatemala, Honduras, and El Salvador, stated that their goal was to reach the U.S. labor market.[32]

The history of these flows is as old and persistent as the Mexican migration to the United States. Similar abuses are sadly committed against them by Mexican authorities and traffickers. There is a long tradition of Guatemalan peasants crossing each year to harvest the coffee and sugar plantations in Mexico's southeastern states, resembling the traditional exploitation that many Mexican agricultural workers suffer in the fields of California or Texas.

In 1995 Mexico and Guatemala established a binational working group dedicated to analyze and present both governments with proposals for the best way to manage migration in the region. Since then, several agreements have been reached that resemble those signed with U.S. authorities. The "southern" Migrant Protection Groups, known as "Rainbow Groups," were established in 1996, with a mission similar to that of the Beta Groups operating in the northern border. Their mission is also to prevent, advise, and protect migrants coming from the South from acts of abuse or violence, a job that has proven to be extremely positive in the defense of undocumented Central and South American migrants, as well as people of other nationalities who intend to use Mexico as a transit path to the United States.

Also, border-crossing cards are now issued to Guatemalan and Belize nationals living in border cities to facilitate their daily crossings to Mexican territory, and Central American consulates in Mexico are given all kinds of prerogatives to exercise their right to advise and protect their own nationals. A notable difference between Mexico's northern and southern borders is the agreement reached with Guatemalan authorities to issue special temporary working cards to Guatemalan seasonal agricultural workers.

Serious problems and challenges still exist, and Mexico is fostering continued dialogue and cooperation with its southern neighbors to ensure that mutually agreed-on solutions are found and implemented to result in a safe and properly managed border.

CONCLUSION

The policy of intensified border controls established by the U.S. government will have a long-term effect in the border region. Regardless of its merits or efficacy in deterring migrants from crossing, the fact is that this deployment represents a critical change of environment that requires a new imaginative and forceful approach by both governments.

Mexico has to reassess its own position concerning the migration of its nationals to the United States. This is an historical economic and political "pending assignment" that still needs to be addressed. It is necessary that Mexico's recent move toward competitive economic policies and a more democratic political system be used as an opportunity to induce and develop a national debate beyond the constitutional, and at times rather sterile discourse of noninterference with the right of free movement of people.

There have been multiple changes during the last decade to Mexico's political, economic, and social fabric. Today, a much more open discussion is being held in public and private spheres on topics traditionally ignored or disregarded. The role of migrants who leave Mexico for short or long periods of time needs to be reevaluated in its full social, cultural, and economic implications. That discussion should result in a more explicit Mexican policy toward international migration.

For the United States, the "Mexican case" represents a challenge to find policies compatible with its own history as a country of immigration. The question is whether the United States is able to finally accept that its southern neighbor deserves special attention. Solving the migration dilemma with Mexico is a logical and natural step in the unavoidable process of economic integration. The border should be the place to unify instead of divide the two countries. Political will from the leadership in the United States is necessary so that objective analysis can ensue on the role of the Mexican labor force in the U.S. economy, and how it could be integrated in a legitimate manner into the North American labor market.

Much progress has been made in the bilateral migration agenda by engaging in a continuous dialogue between the two governments. Although still at a modest scale, the bilateral mechanisms established have helped prevent numerous conflicts, and have benefited thousands of people on both sides of the border. Clearly, much more needs to be done, but the cooperative foundations have already been built during the past five years for more and better solutions on border control policies and migration issues.

NOTES

1. This chapter reflects the personal views of the authors and not necessarily the official position of the Government of Mexico.

2. Rafael Fernández de Castro, *The Mexican Government's Position on Migration: From Non-Engagement to an Active Search for a New Understanding. Is It Worth It?* (Mexico City: Instituto Tecnologico Autonoma de Mexico, 1998).

3. On February 13 and 14, 1995, high-level government officials from Mexico and the United States responsible for immigration and border affairs held their first formal meeting in Zacatecas, Mexico. A Joint Statement was issued to set the tone and political will of both governments to deal with those issues.

4. The U.S. Congress mandated the INS, through the passage of IIRIRA, a yearly increase of 1,000 border patrol agents from FY 1997 until FY 2001. Up to October 1999, most of the new agents have been deployed at the U.S.–Mexico border.

5. Source: *NAFTA Trends*, a periodical information bulletin prepared by the NAFTA Office at the Embassy of Mexico in Washington. January 1999.

6. *Maquiladoras* are assembly plants established mostly in Mexican cities close to its border with the United States, under a special legal and fiscal agreement that allows for the import of raw materials to be assembled in Mexico and the assembled product be exported back to the country of origin without import or export taxes and duties. Under this framework, only a small percentage (never more than 10 percent) of the finished product may remain for sale in Mexico.

7. *NAFTA at Five Years*. Council of the Americas and the U.S. Council of the Mexico–U.S. Bureau Committee. January 1999.

8. *NAFTA at Five Years.* The report also notes that the U.S. unemployment rate had dropped steadily since 1994. By October 1998 this rate stood at a twenty-eight-year low with the creation of 14.2 million jobs, with 483,000 of those in the manufacturing sector, many of which could be attributed to NAFTA.

9. *NAFTA at Five Years.* It stated that a clear difference in the outcome of Mexico's 1994–1995 financial crisis was that in 1995 Mexico was able to accede international financial markets in six months, rather than the six years it took in the previous crisis of 1983.

10. The *Binational Study of Migration between Mexico and the United States* is the first study of its kind where both governments financed an all-encompassing research on the history and complexities of the migration phenomenon between Mexico and the United States. They designated ten prestigious scholars each to conduct the two-year study. Its Executive Summary was published in Mexico City in October 1997.

11. Peter Andreas, "The U.S. Immigration Control Offensive: Constructing an Image of Order on the Southwest Border," in Marcelo Suarez-Orozco, ed., *Crossings: Mexican Immigration in Interdisciplinary Perspectives* (Cambridge: Harvard University Press, 1998).

12. Based on reports by the Mexican Consulates in San Diego and Calexico, California; and Douglas, Nogales, and Tucson, Arizona (1997–1999).

13. President Clinton signed the new legislation into law on September 20, 1996.

14. This effort is widely known as "Fix 96." Starting in the summer of 1999, several pro-migrant and human and labor rights organizations have organized marches to Capitol Hill in Washington.

15. Assorted Congressional Record reports. *First and Second Sessions of the 104th Congress* (Washington, D.C.: U.S. Congress, 1995–1996).

16. Operation Hold the Line was implemented in El Paso, Texas, in the fall of 1993 and Operation Gatekeeper in the San Diego border region in October 1994.

17. U.S. Department of Justice, Immigration and Naturalization Service. *1995, 1997 and 1998 Annual Reports.*

18. Douglas S. Massey, "March of Folly: U.S. Immigration Policy after NAFTA," *The American Prospect* (March–April 1998).

19. *Instituto Federal Electoral, Informe Final que presenta la Comisión de Especialistas que estudia las modalidades del voto de los mexicanos residents en el Extranjero* (IFE: México, D.F., 1998). Although this experts' report to the Mexican Congress on Mexican nationals living abroad was on the feasibility of Mexicans' vote outside of Mexico, it reflects the latest data on Mexican nationals living outside Mexican territory.

20. *Reforma,* "Expulsa EU a más de 147 mil mexicanos este año" (Mexico City: November 13, 1999), 8-A. Based on preliminary figures issued by the INS for FY 1999.

21. The "local arrangements" included mutually agreed-on hours and land ports where specific repatriations were to take place, taking into account specific characteristics of each region and the importance of avoiding the separation of family units. Special procedures were established for U.S. authorities to repatriate Mexican women who are traveling alone, pregnant, or with children; for old, ill, or disabled people; and for children and juveniles who had to be received by Mexican authorities for proper care. Special procedures were also incorporated to handle the return of ex-convicts who had served sentences in the United States for serious criminal offenses.

22. Six local arrangements were signed between December 1997 and February 1999, covering the entire U.S.–Mexico border from San Diego–Tijuana to Brownsville–Matamoros.

23. According to official numbers compiled by the Secretaría de Relaciones Exteriores

in Mexico, from reports by Mexico's ten consulates at the U.S.–Mexico border, 131 persons died in 1997; 290 in 1998; 346 in 1999; and from January to March 2000, 98 have perished.

24. Specific data provided by the Consulate of Mexico in Calexico, California.

25. The *Presidential Statement on Migration* was signed by U.S. President William J. Clinton and Mexican President Ernesto Zedillo in Mexico City on May 6, 1997, on the occasion of Clinton's official visit to Mexico.

26. *The Presidential Statement.* In their statement, the presidents recognized that "the issue of migration of Mexican nationals to the United States is a priority in our bilateral relation. We, the Presidents of Mexico and the United States hereby politically commit our respective governments to strive to ensure a proper and respectful management of this complex phenomenon, taking into consideration its diverse causes and economic and social consequences in both countries."

27. *The Presidential Statement.* The presidents also affirmed their political will to better the conditions at their common border by stating that they "affirm[ed] our governments political will to strive to fulfill a vision of our shared border in the twenty first century as a place that supports and depends on building communities of cooperation rather than of conflict."

28. At present, there are six Beta Groups working along the U.S.–Mexico border from Tijuana to Matamoros. The largest is based in Tijuana and has forty-five elements. The total corps of the Beta Groups is 123 agents, operating with very limited resources.

29. The "Border Safety Initiative" was announced by Mexican Ambassador Jesús Reyes-Heroles and INS Commissioner Doris Meissner at a press conference in Washington, D.C., on June 16, 1998.

30. In 1998, 550 migrants were rescued on both sides of the border. In 1999, preliminary numbers from the Beta Groups and the border patrol place the number of rescues at more than 1,500.

31. Mexico has forty-two consulates throughout the United States.

32. Instituto Nacional de Migración, *Informe Anual de Actividades 1998* (México, D.F.: Enero 1999.)

Part Three

European Border Controls

9

Eastern Europe as Gatekeeper: The Immigration and Asylum Policies of an Enlarging European Union

Milada Anna Vachudová

The construction of a common external border around the member states of the European Union (EU) and the creation of a common visa policy had significant implications for east central and southeastern European states in the 1990s. The reinforcement of the external border, in conjunction with increasingly restrictive asylum policies in west European states and readmission agreements, forced the EU's eastern and southern neighbors to cope with the EU's unwanted migrants. This turned parts of east central and southeastern Europe into a potentially tense migration buffer zone. Because the EU's postcommunist neighbors were serious applicants for EU membership, they had no choice but to be vigilant in guarding their borders to the west, and compliant with requests to take back illegal immigrants in order to stay in the good graces of EU governments. Demonstrating that they could control their borders became a way for Poland, Hungary, Slovakia, Slovenia, and the Czech Republic to prove their "Western" character. Meanwhile, the common visa list isolated the citizens and elites of most southeastern European states from western Europe by requiring them to get visas to travel to the Schengen area. These states did generate substantial numbers of refugees, asylum seekers, and economic migrants who entered western Europe during the 1990s. However, democratization and economic revitalization—the only long-term solutions to the migration problem of the region—were sometimes ill-served by the EU's visa and trade policies.

In order to earn EU membership, east central and southeastern European states were also required to begin very thoroughly adopting the EU "acquis" in the field of justice and home affairs.[1] The Tampere European Council in October 1999 reaffirmed that as a consequence of the integration of the Schengen *acquis* into the EU, the candidates must accept it in full. Fortifying their eastern and southern borders while abiding by the common visa list will, however, impose substantial costs on the acceding states: for Hungary in the closing of its borders to visa-free travel for ethnic Hungarians in neighboring states; for Poland in the loss of economic activity along its eastern border; and for the Czech Republic in the likely elimination of its customs union with Slovakia.[2] Again, this risks stunting the democratization, Europeanization, and economic revitalization of the states left beyond the Schengen wall as, for example, visa requirements cut Ukraine and Belarus off from Poland, or Romania and the Federal Republic of Yugoslavia off from Hungary.[3]

This chapter will proceed in six stages. It will first take stock of levels of immigration from east central and southeastern Europe in the 1990s.[4] Second, it will describe the west European backlash against foreign residents that formed the context for changes in national asylum and immigration policies after 1989. Third, it will chronicle the ongoing transfer of decision-making power from national governments to the EU, sparked by the creation of the common external border as well as the rising salience of immigration in the domestic politics of EU member states. Fourth, it will examine the uncomfortable situation of the east central European states who are expected to guard the gates to the west while adopting EU border control and visa practices in anticipation of accession. Fifth, it will suggest ways in which the EU can mitigate the migration problems it has helped create in order to keep them from destabilizing its eastern and southern neighbors. Finally, it will show how some of the EU's policies undermine not only the over-arching goal of stabilizing southeastern Europe, but also the more concrete goals of limiting the flow of refugees, asylum seekers, and economic migrants from the southeast.

MIGRATION INTO WESTERN EUROPE AFTER 1989

After 1989, east European states formed two distinct groups: southeastern European states generated substantial numbers of refugees and economic migrants traveling northward and westward, while east central European states became reluctant gatekeepers for the EU, harboring unwanted immigrants or sending them back eastward and southward.

Analysts predicted in the early 1990s that western Europe would be forced to endure a tide of migration from east central Europe, for two reasons. First, the newfound freedom of movement and the economic hardships associated with marketizing reforms were expected to precipitate an overwhelming influx of economic migrants.[5] In fact, despite the persistent economic divide between East and West, only manageable numbers of east central Europeans left their countries after 1989 in search of a higher standard of living. Second, some observers feared that large waves of immigrants would enter western Europe to escape conflict in east central Europe. Forced migration, after all, accounts for much of the history of population movements in the region. This fear increased after the onset of war in Yugoslavia. East central Europe, however, was a peaceful region during the 1990s and the anticipated flood of refugees never materialized.[6]

Still, western Europe, especially Germany, did experience a substantial increase in immigration from the east after 1989.[7] Much of this increase was attributable to three discrete groups of migrants: ethnic Germans "returning" to Germany, Roma (Gypsies) escaping discrimination and poverty, and Yugoslav refugees fleeing war.

Aussiedlers

From 1989 to 1994, nearly two million ethnic Germans, or "Aussiedlers," profited from Germany's ethnic definition of citizenship to move to Germany.[8] Most came from Poland, the former Soviet Union, or Romania. Some Aussiedlers were spurred to emigrate by discrimination; many others, however, had at best a nominal German cultural identity and emigrated to benefit from Germany's prosperity. Aussiedlers therefore blurred the distinction between "ethnic migration" (return to an ethnic homeland) and "economic migration."

Roma

Roma came to western Europe from Romania, Bulgaria, and other states in the hundreds of thousands after 1989. Their exodus was motivated by ethnic intolerance and dire economic conditions, and facilitated by nomadic traditions. The Roma have low educational standards, very high rates of unemployment, little political power, and no ethnic homeland to shelter them or to champion their rights. They face pervasive racism and discrimination throughout east central Europe.[9] In Romania they were subject to political trials, violence organized by state authorities, spontaneous pogroms, and forced resettlements in the 1980s and early 1990s.[10] Many Roma from Romania sought refuge in Germany where, along with other migrants who crossed perceived cultural and racial divides, they became the target of racism.[11] From 1997 onward, hundreds of Roma from the Czech Republic and Slovakia sought asylum in Canada and the United Kingdom due to growing intolerance at home. A fraction were granted asylum; Canada and the United Kingdom responded by periodically reinstating visas for Czech and Slovak citizens.[12]

Refugees from the Yugoslav Wars

Refugees from the wars in Bosnia–Herzegovina and Croatia were given temporary refugee protection in west European states: 700,000 were outside of the borders of the former Yugoslavia by 1993 and some 2 million by 1995.[13] By the end of 1998, three years after the signing of the Dayton Peace Agreement, only about 40 percent of the refugees in western Europe had returned to Bosnia.[14] Germany, Austria, Hungary, and Switzerland—attractive by virtue of proximity, prosperity, and/ or existing Yugoslav communities—sheltered a great majority of these refugees. For example, it is estimated that in 1995 there were 350,000 Bosnians in Germany; by mid-1998 190,000 had returned and 2,000 had been deported.[15] Beginning in 1998, Serb repression in Kosovo sparked a steady exodus of ethnic Albanians to western Europe.[16] The exodus swelled to some 700,000 refugees during the air strikes in 1999, but many remained in neighboring Macedonia or Albania and returned immediately after the end of the air strikes.

The Roma and the Yugoslav refugees, however, were not alone in entering western Europe in the 1990s. From the east and south, from the former Soviet Union and the Balkans, increasing numbers of east European migrants did embark on difficult journeys westward, to escape poverty and conflict, and to seek economic advancement in western Europe. Others came from the Middle East, Asia, and Africa, but transited through east central or southeastern Europe. Many crossed the border into Germany from Poland or the Czech Republic; others crossed into Austria from Hungary or Slovakia. As there exist no legal channels of immigration to western Europe for persons fleeing poverty or generalized violence, migrants entered illegally, or claimed political asylum regardless of their background.

THE CHANGING ASYLUM AND IMMIGRATION POLICIES OF WEST EUROPEAN STATES

A backlash by west European electorates against foreign residents, especially the rising numbers of asylum seekers, prompted all west European governments to implement increasingly efficient and summary national policies.[17] The popularity of extreme right-wing parties, who blamed foreigners for rising unemployment, violent crime, and other forms of social malaise, rose sharply in the early 1990s.[18] Leaders of mainstream parties, anxious to neutralize the extreme right, took on board many of its slogans and preoccupations. In essence, they coopted the extreme right's diagnosis of what was ailing society (foreigners) as well as its prescribed cure (the removal of foreigners). This was based on the logic that, while retaining power, they would deal with the crisis of xenophobia more correctly and without undermining democracy. Others argued that when mainstream parties adopted some of the rhetoric of the extreme right, they legitimized xenophobic political discourse. Meanwhile, a long-standing debate on immigration intensified: To what extent should immigrants be expected to conform to the local culture? Are governments fueling xenophobia by purposefully hampering the integration of immigrants into society, for example, in Germany by denying them citizenship?

A milestone in the transformation of Europe's immigration regime occurred in the summer of 1993, when Bonn tightened Germany's hitherto liberal asylum laws in response to a domestic surge of extreme nationalism leveled against foreigners. This surge had prompted German Foreign Minister Klaus Kinkel to warn that immigration was threatening the stability of German democracy.[19] In addition to asylum seekers, the antiforeigner sentiment was sparked by two groups which Germany had invited onto German soil: ethnic German Aussiedlers (discussed above) and non-German guest workers.[20] From the 1950s to the 1970s, Germany and neighboring Austria recruited hundreds of thousands of guest workers from Turkey and Yugoslavia. (Indeed, from the perspective of east Europeans who might seek employment in western Europe, the revolutions of 1989 should have come two decades earlier.[21]) During the economic contractions of the early 1970s, the guest worker programs ended, but ongoing family reunification created high levels of "regular" immigration.[22]

Germany was the destination of over half of all east Europeans applying for asylum in western Europe. From 1989 to the peak year of 1992, about 1 million applications for asylum were filed in Germany, of which some 560,000 came from eastern Europe (including the former Soviet Union). Of these eastern applicants, 43 percent were Yugoslavs and 33 percent were Romanian citizens.[23] Under the 1951 Geneva convention, only refugees—defined as discrete targets of persecution—qualify for asylum. Only a small percentage of applicants were granted asylum (for example, only 4 percent in Germany in 1992), but the subsequent failure to expel refused asylum seekers allowed a form of covert migration. The United Nations High Commissioner for Refugees (UNHCR) estimated in 1997 that Germany was harboring about 1.3 million refugees, as much as 10 percent of the world's total.[24] Still, overall, in 1997 and 1998, more foreigners left Germany than tried to settle there.

Most west European states responded to the sharp increase of applications for asylum in the early 1990s with tough new immigration policies, discussed below. Though the new policies were designed to curb the misuse of asylum channels, it was feared that they increased the number of immigrants illegally entering western Europe. They did successfully reduce the number of asylum seekers: the number of applications which had peaked at almost 700,000 in 1992 dropped to some 240,000 in 1995.[25] Numbers rose once more in the late 1990s, chiefly due to the war in Kosovo.

At the turn of the century, most west European states continued to have substantial backlogs of applications amidst ongoing controversies about how to care for asylum applicants while their applications were being processed. The established procedures were widely considered overwhelmed and inefficient. National politicians and populations bristled at the presence of asylum seekers as well as illegal workers, while transnational organizations feared that more restrictive policies were endangering Europe's tradition as a place of refuge for targets of political persecution. As the EU put in place a "common external border," more and more decisions on how to fight the influx of illegal immigrants were made at the EU level by agreement among national governments in the European Council. All the while, immigration lost none of its salience in the domestic politics of member states, and the perception of an unmanageable, illegal of flow of migrants into western Europe persisted even as declining birth rates and shortages in computer specialists created powerful incentives to encourage immigration.

THE SCHENGEN AGREEMENT AND PLANS FOR EU ASYLUM AND IMMIGRATION POLICIES

Over the course of the 1990s, the EU member states were cooperating within the intergovernmental justice and home affairs "third pillar" of the EU to tighten the common external border in order to fight illegal immigration and international crime. In addition to sorting out just what the existing justice and home affairs "acquis" comprised, they were at work in 1999 on proposals to share the burden of temporary refugee protection and to harmonize the treatment of asylum seekers.[26] They were even contemplating the eventual alignment of national policies for the naturalization of long-term third-country residents.

The Schengen Agreement among the Benelux countries, France and Germany, signed in 1985 outside of the framework of the EU, laid the foundation for cooperation in the area of border controls. By 1997, the Schengen Agreement had been incorporated into the EU framework by the Treaty of Amsterdam, and all EU member states except Ireland and Britain had become members.[27] The agreement gradually eliminated controls for persons crossing the internal national borders of the Schengen area. This necessarily led to the reinforcement and standardization of the newly created common external border, as each Schengen member would have to accept the persons allowed to cross the borders of other member states. New rules sought to compensate for the "security deficit" caused by the abolition of internal border controls. The most visible manifestation of the common external border became the common visa list: to prevent "visa shopping," all participating states agreed to impose visa requirements on citizens of the same countries.

In general, the policies generated by the harmonization of border controls and visa requirements were more restrictive than the national policies they replaced. Harmonization at the EU level was dictated by the domestic politics of (certain) member states that insisted that the states of southeastern Europe, even those negotiating for membership, remain on the mandatory visa list. As will be explored in this chapter, this exclusion was at cross-purposes with the EU's long-term goal of stabilizing and democratizing southeastern Europe.

The harmonization of asylum policies at the EU level, in contrast, seemed to promise the liberalization of (certain) national policies by reinforcing the principles of the 1951 Geneva Convention. The first high-profile report, however, did not bode well: During the Austrian presidency of the EU in July 1998, the Austrian government drafted a "Strategy paper on immigration and asylum policy," which called for giant steps toward a unified EU approach to border controls and asylum seekers. The paper observed that, "the EU States have thus far not achieved any real success in combating the abuse of the right of asylum." The first version, and to a lesser extent the second, were sharply criticized by the UNHCR and by nongovernmental organizations (NGOs) for seeking to undermine existing refugee protection standards, in particular the 1951 Convention.[28]

The tenor changed during the Finnish presidency of the EU. The Tampere Special European Council (meeting of Heads of State and Government) of October 1999 expanded on a European Commission action plan published in July 1998 entitled "Towards an Area of Freedom, Security and Justice." The European Council produced a document entitled the "Presidency Conclusions," which proposed forging common policies in the areas of temporary refugee protection, asylum, and immigration.[29] Unlike the Austrian strategy paper, this document was met with approbation by the UNHCR and by NGOs defending the right of asylum.[30]

The European Council proposed a "Common EU Asylum and Migration Policy" to standardize the way asylum seekers are treated and how their applications are processed. This may prevent the imposition of overly restrictive asylum procedures by some states, while also preventing "asylum shopping" by migrants for the least restrictive procedures. The Council called for legislation that provides for "a clear and workable determination of the State responsible for the examination of asylum applications, common standards for a fair and efficient asylum procedure, common minimum conditions of reception of asylum seekers, and the approximation of rules on the recognition and content of refugee status" (Par. 14). The Schengen Information System (SIS) already lists the names of individuals who apply for asylum in more than one EU member state, but the European Council urged the creation of a database of fingerprints solely for the identification of asylum seekers (Eurodac) (Par. 17).

With respect to immigration policies, the conclusions did not address national rules for naturalization of third-country nationals, but did call for "a set of uniform rights" for third-country nationals resident in the EU which are "near as possible to those enjoyed by EU citizens" (Par. 21). The European Council also called on the Commission to study how to create a financial reserve that would be available to help member states cope with a mass influx of refugees (Par. 16). To this end an emergency fund of $268 million was proposed. The states that received a very large proportion of the refugees entering the EU had called for years for some kind of "burden sharing" to help spread the cost of caring for refugees awarded temporary protection.

THE EU'S UNWANTED MIGRANTS: TRANSIT MIGRANTS, ASYLUM SEEKERS, AND REFUGEES IN EASTERN EUROPE

The creation of the EU's external border in conjunction with more restrictive asylum policies in west European states based on the "safe country principle" and re-admission agreements forced the EU's eastern and southern neighbors to cope with the EU's unwanted migrants. Citizens of the EU's immediate eastern and southeastern neighbors—the Czech lands, Slovakia, Hungary, Poland, and Slovenia—emigrated westward only in small numbers as demonstrated above. Meanwhile, their countries formed a "territorial buffer" between the EU and those countries whose citizens have demonstrated a greater propensity to migrate: Romania, Bulgaria, the former Yugoslavia, and the former Soviet Union (with the exception of the Baltic states). Meanwhile, the governments of the EU's immediate neighbors made a substantial effort to guard their western borders and adopt the EU's border policies in order to qualify for EU membership. When four of five of these states (all but Slovakia) began EU accession negotiations in 1998, the pressure to conform and to cooperate rose substantially.[31]

"Transit migration," defined as "migration to a country with the intention of seeking the possibility there to emigrate to another country as the country of final destination," became a significant problem for the Czech Republic, Hungary, Poland, Slovakia, and Slovenia. In addition to the social costs of hosting large numbers of illegal immigrants, this sort of migration presented a special challenge. "Transit migrants" *ex definitio* have no desire to settle where they are, and yet east central European states must keep them from moving west in order to preserve good relations with the EU. Moreover, after the EU tightened its borders in 1993, these states confronted the expanding activity of the ever more sophisticated criminal gangs who traffic in humans attempting to reach the West.[32] The 1998 Austrian strategy paper observed dimly that "cooperation with the transit States has not succeeded in stopping the influx of illegal migrants, but has influenced the volumes concerned; it has not been possible to force back on a lasting basis the international criminal organizations trafficking in human beings. Only in visa policy and practice is it possible to identify clear progress."[33]

As increasingly prosperous democracies, east central European states also became a destination for immigration in their own right. Roma from Romania and Bulgaria flooded into all four states.[34] Some 200,000 Roma from Romania cross the Polish border each year, many of them temporary labor migrants.[35] Poland also experienced a great influx of citizens of republics of the former Soviet Union, hundreds of thousands of whom worked illegally.[36] To the extent that the Czech Republic, Poland, Hungary, and Slovenia became more attractive by virtue of their growing prosperity and secured greater control over their borders, they in turn began to create transit migration problems for their eastern and southern neighbors.

But in the main, east central and southeastern European states were poorly equipped to turn back or absorb migrants from the former Soviet Union, the Balkans, or the Third World.[37] They had to cope with small but increasing numbers of illegal migrants from Asia, Africa, and the Middle East—migrants who crossed cultural/racial divides and who were therefore more difficult to absorb. Meanwhile, the postcommunist governments did not inherit from their communist predecessors any viable state policies or institutional infrastructure for processing asylum applications or caring for different categories of migrants. In exchange for taking back transit migrants, some financial, organizational, and technical assistance with reinforcing borders and accommodating migrants was provided bilaterally by west European states (especially Germany) and through the EU's Phare program.

Poland and the Czech Republic also provided an "asylum buffer" for the EU after July 1993, when Germany changed its Basic Law such that asylum seekers entering from a "safe country" could be refused entry at the German border. The "safe country principle" was subsequently adopted by all EU member states. All states bordering the EU were designated as "safe": no asylum applicant can travel to the EU by land. Meanwhile, the EU's neighbors were compelled to sign readmission agreements with west European states to take back all illegal immigrants, including asylum seekers. When Austria joined the EU in 1995, its neighbors Hungary and Slovakia joined the EU's immigration *cordon sanitaire*. For its part, Slovenia provided a barrier between the other post-Yugoslav states and two EU member states, Italy and Austria. In 1997 the competence to conclude readmission agreements was transferred to the Community by the Amsterdam Treaty. The 1999 Tampere European Council reaffirmed that the EU would make maximum use of readmission agreements with states of transit and of origin.

The fear of being saddled with tens of thousands of asylum seekers rejected by Germany and Austria caused a chain reaction eastward of tighter border controls, dubbed Europe's "new iron curtains." Various visa, hard currency, and invitation requirements were imposed on citizens of Bosnia–Herzegovina, the former Soviet Union, and the Third World in the early 1990s. Most east central European states also adopted the "safe country principle" and declared all neighboring states to be "safe." This triggered a web of readmission agreements that provided for the deportation of asylum seekers and illegal immigrants to the state from which they had entered. In 1998, for example, some 10,000 persons were returned to Poland under readmission agreements, and Poland in its turn returned 6,500 people to neighboring countries. Germany returned roughly 5,000 people to Poland in 1998, down from 6,200 people in 1997.[38] Poland attributed the reduction to new rules requiring Russians and Belarusians to obtain visas, and Ukrainians to present proof of financial means, in order to enter Poland.

Beyond straining the abilities of states neighboring the EU, the web of readmission agreements reaching ever further east and south of the EU posed two problems. First, for states for whom EU membership is not a prospect, there was no obvious reason to cooperate with west European officials attempting to send back illegal migrants.[39] Second, the human rights and the right of nonrefoulement of asylum seekers bounced backward by way of the chain of readmission agreements were endangered. When the EU declared all of its neighbors to the east and south as "safe countries," Poland, the Czech Republic, Slovakia, Hungary, and Slovenia mostly deserved such an appellation (even though their procedures for caring for asylum seekers and processing their asylum applications were skeletal at best). But as the number of asylum seekers rose, they declared their neighbors such as Romania, Bulgaria, and Ukraine to be safe countries. Yet their neighbors were sometimes unsafe or simply unable to cope with asylum seekers.[40] In other words, states with the ability to implement readmission agreements pushed asylum seekers toward states that had yet to develop humane and fair policies for dealing with them. Admission was easier, but the economy poorer and the society more prone to mistreat asylum seekers. For its part, the government was often unable to afford to deport them to their home country or to the previous "safe" country they had visited.

East central European states, especially Hungary, also had to cope with refugees from the wars in the former Yugoslavia, with the help of only small financial and knowledge transfers from western Europe. Refugees from Bosnia–Herzegovina entered Hungary in the tens of thousands in the early 1990s. Given its size and modest economy, Hungary arguably shouldered the greatest burden of sheltering Bosnian refugees.[41] Meanwhile, from the late 1980s onward Hungary had to provide refuge to tens of thousands of ethnic Hungarians from neighboring states. By 1990 some 40,000 ethnic Hungarians fleeing Ceausescu's Romania had sought refuge in Hungary. In 1991 a second wave of ethnic Hungarians arrived, these fleeing Serb aggression and forced conscription in Vojvodina. As in the case of ethnic German immigrants to Germany, ethnic Hungarian immigrants suffered from and contributed to growing intolerance of foreigners in Hungary. Though Hungary extended preferential treatment to immigrants who were ethnic Hungarians, it did not encourage the Diaspora to leave their homes in Slovakia, Romania, or Vojvodina.[42]

In 1999, NATO's air strikes against the Federal Republic of Yugoslavia (FRY) prompted fears that Serb retaliation against Vojvodina's ethnic Hungarian minority would spark another exodus to Hungary. A NATO member, Hungary sought to uphold its commitments to the alliance while limiting its participation in the bombing campaign. Some 30,000 Vojvodina Hungarians reportedly came to Hungary as tourists during the air strikes between March and June 1999 along with thousands of other FRY citizens. Of those who applied for refugee status, most received only a temporary right of residence, which excluded a work permit.[43]

HELPING EASTERN EUROPE COPE WITH RISING NUMBERS OF MIGRANTS

The EU has appointed east central European states as its immigration gatekeepers at a time when they are undergoing very difficult political and economic changes. Rising levels of immigration hold certain dangers for domestic politics in postcommunist Europe. Given the strains of economic change, especially the high level of unemployment (which was virtually nonexistent under communism), there is little reason to expect that marginalized segments of society in east European states should prove more tolerant of rising immigration than their counterparts in western Europe. That racist violence has so far been minimal is impressive, since political actors in the states in question have been in a much weaker position than Germany or Austria to prevent it. Thus far, the extreme right has been less popular in eastern than in western Europe. There is as yet no trend corresponding to the popularity of the National Front in France and the Freedom Party in Austria.

Rising levels of immigration, however, could increase the popularity of the far right in eastern Europe, which tends to simultaneously oppose EU membership, immigration, and liberal reform. This could be compounded by double standards regarding the number and the integration of immigrants within candidates for EU membership. Future EU leaders may argue that EU membership is inappropriate for, say, Romania or Slovakia, because it has too many third-country migrants that might move westward, or because these migrants have triggered racist violence. Given that the EU's policies are designed to divert immigration to neighboring states, and given the levels of racist violence in some EU member states, such a position would be hypocritical. Shunting immigrants onto east European countries and applying double standards on the critical issue of immigration could harm the cause of reform in eastern Europe, and thus undermine the EU's own interest in the stability of the region.

Since obtaining EU membership remains the foremost goal throughout the region, however, the EU should pressure governments to improve their treatment of migrants as a condition of continued progress toward EU membership.[44] The EU should also provide more substantial financial and technical assistance for these states to reinforce their borders, apprehend illegal migrants, shelter asylum seekers, and absorb refugees.[45] Burden sharing should extend to states beyond the EU's border, for whom the EU's policies have helped to create a cumbersome transit migration problem and a potential refugee problem. But effective burden sharing may require accepting people as well as giving money. The policy of paying poorer neighbors to deal with migrants will prove counterproductive if the numbers become overwhelming.

Meanwhile, immigration from the east should not be understood by the EU in monolithic terms. The opportunities for national economies afforded by migration have been highlighted by many economic studies.[46] In particular, the influx of young and educated east Europeans may play a role in the future economic growth of a western Europe where fertility has fallen below replacement levels. The Portuguese presidency of the European Union proposed that declining birth rates and aging populations mean that the EU needs to develop a strategy for legal immigration. A controversial United Nations report pointed to the need for many European states to accept substantial numbers of immigrants annually (in the case of Germany, 500,000) in order to keep the population steady.[47]

CONCLUSION: THE POWER OF INCLUSION AND EXCLUSION IN EUROPE—MAKING THE STABILITY PACT FOR SOUTHEASTERN EUROPE A SUCCESS

This chapter has distinguished between states of east central Europe and states of southeastern Europe. Whereas the main concern with respect to east central Europe must be that issues connected to the EU external border do not derail a generally successful reform process, the main concern with respect to southeastern Europe must be the provision of stability to prevent future waves of migration. Whereas citizens of east central Europe generally stayed put, southeastern Europe (the former Yugoslavia, Albania, Romania, and Bulgaria) accounted for a high proportion of the asylum seekers, refugees, and economic migrants that entered western Europe in the 1990s.

In southeastern Europe, the stakes are higher, and the dilemmas sharper. Policies designed to combat the influx of people from southeastern Europe reveal the tension between the short-term electoral interests of west European governments and the long-term foreign policy goals articulated by the EU.[48] The EU's trade and visa policies, which have immediate repercussions for domestic politics in member states, are at cross purposes with its fledgling foreign policy, which has yet to impose clear costs and benefits on domestic groups. (Many have argued, of course, that the *absence* of a coherent EU foreign policy in the 1990s, particularly toward the former Yugoslavia, has been very costly for member states.) Only in 1998 and 1999 did the EU's Common Foreign and Security Policy begin to evolve toward assuming some of the foreign policy competencies of a state. The success of the Common Foreign and Security Policy will be measured by its ability to apply the instruments available to the EU—trade agreements, visa requirements, and the incentives of EU membership—to fulfilling its declared foreign policy goals, even if this entails overruling the short-term interests of some member states and incurring substantial economic costs. The rhetoric of creating a Common Asylum Policy is so far encouraging in this regard, as it privileges long-term goals and principles to these kinds of short-term interests.

The EU's foreign policy after the Kosovo crisis seemed for the first time to be based on the grudging realization that EU enlargement itself may be the best way to promote peace, democracy, and economic growth in the whole of Europe. The prospect of EU membership as a motor for political and economic change was explicitly set out in the EU-led Stability Pact for southeastern Europe adopted at Sarajevo in July 1999. In order for the flow of asylum seekers, refugees, and economic migrants from southeastern Europe to be curbed decisively, the region's moderate elites must hold power, put an end to violent conflict, and revitalize the economy. All the while, these elites must fend off extremist forces by convincing voters that difficult reforms of the economy and the state will lead to greater prosperity and to membership in the EU. If extreme governments who do not seek EU membership remain in (or return to) power in southeastern European states, these states will likely continue to generate migrants. Moreover, these sorts of governments will be much less willing to serve as migration buffers for the EU.

There are two pressure points at which the EU should use its resources and leverage to find long-term solutions to the migration problems of southeastern Europe. First, it should work for continued economic recovery in the region. Second, it should help support moderate politicians. Thus far, the perceived interests of member governments in protecting EU markets from foreign competition and EU territory from foreigners have led to policies which are counterproductive to the overarching goal of securing economic recovery and democracy in the Balkans. These policies are therefore also counterproductive to a comprehensive solution to the problem of illegal migration from southeastern Europe.

EU member states should allow unrestricted market access to southeastern European producers in all sectors in the new Stabilization and Association Agreements to be signed with Macedonia, Bosnia–Herzegovina, Albania, Croatia, and the FRY once they meet basic democracy requirements. Existing association agreements with Bulgaria and Romania should be revised to allow market access for agricultural goods. Economists agree that market access is the single most important tool in preventing the economic deterioration which might spark a wave of migrants seeking entry into the EU labor market.[49] By strengthening economies, market access for eastern goods will encourage workers to stay where they are: free trade is thus "the best single migration policy that could be put in place."[50] At the same time, growth from free trade will help states shelter refugees and secure their borders against illegal migrants, as well as dampen racial tensions associated with rising immigration. In the long run, a Europe-wide free-trade area may be the most effective means of minimizing East–West migratory pressures.[51]

The trade agreements signed with east central European states in the early 1990s imposed restrictions and long transition periods on those sectors (steel, textiles, and agriculture) in which eastern producers were the most competitive.[52] This catered to the interests of powerful producers within the EU, although studies showed that the impact of immediate and complete market access for east central European goods on these producers would have been minimal. In the case of the Stabilization and Association Agreements, the EU should resist protecting its markets from the goods these poor and fragile states are most able to export. Access to the EU market would also prove very instrumental in attracting much-needed foreign investment to the region.

Meanwhile, the EU should consider how visa requirements undermine the creation and the power of moderate elites in southeastern European states. By 1999, of the citizens of the EU's ten states associated, only Bulgarians and Romanians had to obtain visas before entering the Schengen area. This was also the case for citizens of Macedonia, Bosnia–Herzegovina, Albania, Croatia, and the FRY. European leaders seemed indifferent to the negative consequences of restrictive visa policies for democracy in the Balkans. West Europeans count on business, academic, civic, and policy leaders to Europeanize their countries. But these very people are discouraged from traveling to professional meetings in western Europe because obtaining a visa requires many documents, queuing at the embassy, and then a long wait, sometimes measured in months. Only those with sufficient connections to get a multiple-entry Schengen visa are spared the frustration. The inconvenience and humiliation is felt most acutely by precisely those elites who are expected to Westernize their countries.

The visa requirements have fueled anti-EU sentiment in southeastern European states. Elites as well as ordinary citizens are frustrated and resentful and feel like third-class Europeans. This decreases the willingness of politicians and other public figures to portray themselves as pro-European, undermines the popularity of those who do, and feeds a sense of futility about ever being allowed into the European club. The sense of isolation will only mount as first-wave candidates to the EU such as Hungary and the Czech Republic implement Schengen visa policies in order to make good on their bids for membership. This will make it necessary to obtain a visa to travel to Budapest, Prague, or Warsaw as well as Paris, Berlin, or Brussels.

The visa requirements for citizens of Bulgaria, Romania, and the FRY traveling to the Schengen area stem from the fear and the reality of illegal immigration from the Balkans into the EU, discussed earlier. Still, given the disproportionate role a relatively small number of political, cultural, and economic elites play in setting policy and influencing political culture, it would be wise to consider expedited visa procedures for professional meetings and family visits. Moreover, the removal of reforming countries from the EU's common visa list should be on the agenda as part of a strategy to strengthen the hand of pro-Western elites in the Balkans, while integrating the region into Europe. In early 2000, the Commission did propose that Bulgaria and Romania be removed from the list, but it was not expected the EU member states would agree to the change that year.

During the long wait for full integration, the EU should do what it can to strengthen the economies and moderate elites of southeastern Europe. This will serve the narrow political interest of EU governments in controlling illegal migration: these states will cease to create refugees, cope better with all categories of migrants on their own soil, and generate fewer economic migrants of their own. Meanwhile, it will serve the EU's ambitious, long-term goal of stabilizing and democratizing the whole of southeastern Europe.

NOTES

1. The European Council in June 1998 set up an expert group composed of representatives of the member states and the European Commission, which is responsible for preparing collective evaluations of the situation in the candidate countries on the enactment, application, and effective implementation of the *acquis* in the field of justice and home affairs. The preliminary reports on Estonia and Poland were completed in October 1999. The 2203rd Council meeting, Justice and Home Affairs, Luxembourg, October 4, 1999, 11281/99 (Presse 288). On the impact of the conditionality of EU membership on the domestic policymaking of east European candidates, see Milada Anna Vachudová, *Revolution, Democracy and Integration* (Oxford: Oxford University Press, forthcoming).

2. Under pressure from the German government, the free movement of persons across the Czech–Slovak border had already been eliminated by the Czech government. Accords

signed before the Czech–Slovak split had envisaged minimal border formalities to allow the virtual free movement of people within a free-trade zone. In 2000, the Czech government also agreed to give up its customs union with Slovakia if the Czech Republic enters the EU before Slovakia. "Cesko slíbilo Bruselu, ze zrusí celní unii se Slovenskem," *Lidové Noviny*, April 12, 2000, 1.

3. Timothy Snyder, "W poszukiwaniu wschodniego interesu," *Unia-Polska* 1, no. 1 (October 1998), electronic edition at: www.unia-polska.pl. See also Freudenstein, this volume.

4. For the purposes of this chapter, east central Europe refers to Poland, Hungary, the Czech Republic, Slovakia, and Slovenia. Romania, Bulgaria, Albania, Macedonia, Croatia, Bosnia–Herzegovina, and the Federal Republic of Yugoslavia comprise southeastern Europe.

5. Surveys did reveal that a high percentage of the region's population respond in the affirmative when asked if they would like to emigrate. For example, Robert J. Brym, "The Emigration Potential of Czechoslovakia, Hungary, Lithuania, Poland and Russia: Recent Survey Results," *International Sociology* 7, no. 4 (December 1992): 387–395.

6. There were no large-scale, violent conflicts in east central Europe that might have created refugee flows akin to the conflicts in the FRY. The treatment of the Turkish minority in Bulgaria and the Hungarian minorities in Romania and Slovakia warranted concern in the early and mid-1990s while nationalist governments held power. However, in all three cases the prospects for violent conflict were always very small, and most refugees would have fled to their ethnic homelands (Hungary and Turkey), not to western Europe. The possibility of an exodus from the former Soviet Union sparked by violence and economic deprivation made west Europeans even more apprehensive. Despite the collapse of the empire and of the centrally planned economy, an unmanageable movement of people westward likewise did not occur.

7. There was also an increasing flow of people crossing into western Europe from the south, chiefly from North Africa and the Middle East.

8. Ethnic Germans from eastern Europe (excluding the GDR) moving to Germany numbered 377,000 in 1989; 397,000 in 1990; 220,000 in 1991; 220,000 in 1992; 231,000 in 1993; and 223,000 in 1994 (totaling nearly 1.7 million over six years). To control the influx, Germany's "right of return" law was modified to restrict Aussiedler immigration to 220,000 per year, and the German government offered financial incentives to ethnic Germans willing to stay put. Some three to four million ethnic Germans remain in the East. See Jurgen Fijalkowski, "Aggressive Nationalism, Immigration Pressure and Asylum Policy Disputes in Contemporary Germany," *International Migration Review* 27, no. 4 (Winter 1993): 858–859; and UN Economic Commission for Europe, *Economic Survey of Europe 1994–95* (New York: United Nations, 1995), 232.

9. There are some 30,000 Roma of Polish citizenship, 300,000 of Czech citizenship, 400,000 of Slovak citizenship, 800,000 of Hungarian citizenship, 800,000 of Bulgarian citizenship, and at least 2,000,000 of Romanian citizenship. Zoltan Barany, "Grim Realities in Eastern Europe," *Transition*, 1, no. 4 (March 29, 1995).

10. Max van der Stoel, CSCE High Commissioner on National Minorities, speech at CSCE Human Dimension Seminar on "Roma in the CSCE Region," Warsaw, September 20, 1994; Alain Reyniers, "En Roumanie, de l'esclavage à la démocratie," *Hommes et Migrations*, June–July 1995, 60–61; "Limalo szuka prawdziwych Cyganów," *Gazeta Magazyn*, 187 (October 4, 1996), 7.

11. Some 300,000 Romanian citizens, mostly Roma, entered Germany from 1991 to 1993; 180,000 subsequently left voluntarily or were deported on the basis of Germany's new asylum laws and the readmission agreement contained in the German–Romanian convention of 1992. UN Economic Commission, *Economic Survey,* 231.

12. "Diskriminace Romu delá CR v zahranicí nejvetsí problémy," *Lidové Noviny,* July 7, 1998, 3.

13. "Borderline cases," *The Financial Times,* October 16, 1999, 16; and Kathleen Newland, "Involuntary Migration: Refugees in the New Europe," in *Migration and the New Europe,* Kimberly A. Hamilton, ed. (Washington, D.C.: Center for Strategic and International Studies, 1994), 58.

14. "Migration in Central and Eastern Europe: 1999 Review," International Organization for Migration (IOM) and International Centre for Migration Policy Development (ICMPD) (Geneva: United Nations, 1999) at: www.iom.int.

15. "Germany: CSU Takes Hard Line," *Migration News* 5, no. 8 (August 1998) at: migration.ucdavis.edu.

16. On the refugee crisis sparked by the war in Kosovo, see Koslowski in this volume.

17. Even at their peak in 1992, asylum seekers were far from overwhelming western Europe: the proportions of applicants to population were 0.56 percent in Germany, 0.94 percent in Sweden, and less than 0.05 percent in France and Britain. In 1998, the number of inhabitants per asylum seeker in the EU ranged from 340 in the Netherlands to 830 in Germany to 29,740 in Portugal. Newland, "Involuntary Migration: Refugees in the New Europe," 62; and "Borderline Cases," 16.

18. Tom J. Farer argues that "the swelling number of people crossing [perceived cultural/racial divides] has substantially contributed to a crescendoing demand among European electorates for sharp limits on all cross-cultural immigration, regardless of the immigrant's motives and needs." Farer, "How the International System Copes with Involuntary Migration: Norms, Institutions and State Practice," *Human Rights Quarterly* 17, no. 1 (1995): 83.

19. "Refugees: Keep Out," *The Economist,* September 19, 1992, 64.

20. A survey conducted in 1990 of sympathizers of the Republicans (the extreme right wing party in Germany) found that 61 percent believed that guest workers were a great burden on Germany; 68 percent and 92 percent felt the same way about ethnic German Aussiedlers and asylum seekers, respectively. Mihalka, "German and Western Response," 45–47.

21. The association agreements signed between the EU and east central European states did not even contain a nondiscrimination clause with respect to unemployment and social benefits for the small number of legal east central European workers allowed by the agreements, although such clauses are to be found in previous agreements between the EU and Tunisia, Algeria, and Morocco.

22. In 1989, of the foreign (non-EC) population of Germany, 65 percent were Yugoslavs and Turks (totaling some 2.3 million persons). The Turkish population in Germany, which was 429,000 in 1970, had quadrupled to 1.7 million persons by 1990. In 1999, an estimated 7.3 million foreigners lived in Germany, of which 2.1 million were Turks. During the course of the 1990s, Germany substantially revised its citizenship laws to allow for the naturalization of legally resident third-country nationals, especially those born in Germany. "Europe's Immigrants: Strangers Inside the Gates," *The Economist,* February 15, 1992, 22; and "Europe: Full Up? Immigration Jangling German Nerves," *The Economist,* March 25, 2000.

23. The numbers of all applications for asylum in Germany in the years 1989 through 1992 were 121,000; 193,000; 256,000; and 450,000; respectively (totaling 1 million, of which some 24 percent were Yugoslavs and 18 percent were Romanians). The peak was 513,000 applications in 1993. The numbers for 1998 and 1999 were 147,000 and 136,000, respectively. From the *Deutsches Statistisches Jahrbuch,* cited in Michael Mihalka, "German and Western Response to Immigration from the East," *RFE/RL Research Report* 3, no. 23 (June 10, 1994), 41; and "Europe: Full Up?"

24. United Nations High Commissioner for Refugees, *The State of the World's Refugees: A Humanitarian Agenda* (New York: Oxford University Press, 1997).

25. Philip Martin and Jonas Widgren, "International Migration: A Global Challenge," *Population Bulletin* 51, no. 1 (April 1996), 26.

26. On the EU's mysterious Schengen *acquis,* see Monica den Boer, "Steamy Windows: The Transparency and Openness in Justice and Home Affairs," *Openness and Transparency in the European Union,* Veerle Deckmyn and Ian Thomson, eds. (Maastricht: European Institute of Public Administration, 1998), 91–105; Brendan PG Smith, "Implementing the Amsterdam Treaty: The Incorporation of the Schengen Acquis into the European Union," unpublished manuscript; and Monica den Boer and William Wallace, "JHA Cooperation in the Amsterdam Era: Programme for Integration or Intergovernmental Drift?" in *Policy-Making in the European Union,* Helen Wallace and William Wallace, eds. (Oxford: Oxford University Press, fourth edition, forthcoming).

27. The United Kingdom applied in the autumn of 1999 to "opt into" provisions to help combat illegal immigration and international crime, giving it access to the SIS and Eurodac. On the British debate, "Blair Plans U-Turn on Border Controls," *The Independent,* March 27, 2000. On the origin and character of the Schengen Agreement, see Anderson, this volume.

28. The first version was published in July 1998 as Council document 9809/98, and the second in September 1998. See: ue.eu.int/jai/. The strategy paper is criticized for painting all asylum seekers as illegal immigrants in disguise, discounting that they may in fact be fleeing from persecution, and dismissing the reality that they may have to enter the country illegally in order to seek asylum.

29. The "Presidency Conclusions" are at: presidency.finland.fi. See also Ulf Haussler, "Tampere Summit," *Migration News* 6, no. 12 (December 1999) at: migration.ucdavis.edu.

30. The European Council on Refugees and Exiles (ECRE), for example, welcomes that a Common European Asylum System will be based on a "full and inclusive application of the Geneva Convention, thus ensuring that nobody is sent back to persecution." According to ECRE, this means that the Council would require member states that apply an overly restrictive interpretation of the Geneva Convention to change that interpretation. "Observations by ECRE on The Presidency Conclusions of the Tampere European Council," October 1999 at: www.ecre.org.

31. On the impact of the accession negotiations, see Jesien, this volume.

32. "The New Trade in Humans," *The Economist,* August 5, 1995, 45–46; "Przed skokiem na Zachód," *Rzeczpospolita,* April 22, 1996, 8; "Jak zatrzymac uchodców," *Rzeczpospolita,* October 8, 1996, 8. See also Koslowski, this volume.

33. "Strategy Paper," Austrian Presidency, 3.

34. Of the 43,000 persons detained at the Czech borders in 1993, more than half were Yugoslavs, 12 percent were Bulgarians, and 10 percent were Romanians. Of the 16,000 per-

sons detained on the Polish borders in the first nine months of 1993, more than 40 percent were Romanians, 10 percent were Bulgarians, 7 percent were Ukrainians, and 5 percent were Russians. "International Migration in the ECE Region," *Migration: Bulletin of the Population Activities Unit of the United Nations Economic Commission for Europe,* nos. 21–22 (1994): 173.

35. "Limalo szuka prawdziwych Cyganów," 9.

36. In the early 1990s, Soviet workers earning U.S. $60–$80 per month in Poland received one-third of the average Polish wage, but twelve times the average wage in the Soviet Union. Adam Bernatowicz, "Polish Migration Policies," *Migration World* 20, no. 3 (1992): 14.

37. To stem the flow of migrants, they had to rely on "negative" incentives: Unlike the West, they were economically unable to offer "positive" incentives to discourage immigration by improving economic conditions at home. Michael Shafir, "Immigrants, Refugees, and Postcommunism," *RFE/RL Research Report* 3, no. 23 (June 10, 1994), 35.

38. "Miliony na przejsciach" *Rzeczpospolita,* January 2, 1999.

39. The 1998 Austrian strategy paper observed gloomily that the wide network of readmission agreements had proved "strikingly unsuccessful" as states of origin refused to take back their own nationals from the country they had entered illegally: "Not until it proves possible to ensure that the principle whereby the State of previous residence immediately and unconditionally takes back every single illegal border-crosser who is not protected by the ban on refoulement is put seamlessly into effect, will the overall migration-slowing effect come into play." "Strategy Paper," Austrian presidency, 4, 17.

40. Also of concern were impoverished states further east who received substantial flows of transit migrants: example, a substantial flow from the former Soviet Union and Romania crossed through Bulgaria to reach Greece. "Joint NGO Statement," in Rachel Brett and Elaine Eddison, *Migration, Refugees and Displaced Persons: Report on the CSCE Human Dimension Seminar* (Colchester: Human Rights Centre, University of Essex, 1993), 20. See also "Asylum Policy in Western Europe, The Role of the European Union," *World Report 1999,* Human Rights Watch at: www.igc.org/hrw.

41. Hungarian refugee camps suddenly overflowed when Austria closed its borders to Bosnian refugees in the summer of 1992. The conditions in these camps demonstrate the consequences of the presence of large numbers of refugees in an east European state which is ill-prepared to receive them. Hungary—already taxed by the recent arrival of tens of thousands of refugees from Romania, struggling with economic reform, and inexperienced in sheltering war refugees—did not always treat Yugoslav refugees appropriately or with compassion. Conditions did improve with time and western assistance. See Maxine Marcus, "Aiding Bosnian Refugees," *Migration World* 23, no. 5 (1995): 18–21; and Judith Pataki, "The Recent History of the Hungarian Refugee Problem," *RFE/RL Research Report* 3, no. 24 (June 17, 1994): 34–38.

42. László Szoke, "Hungarian Perspectives on Emigration and Immigration in the New European Architecture," *International Migration Review* 26, no. 2 (Summer 1992): 308, 311, 315.

43. "Risks of a Decision IV," Budapest *Nepszabadsag,* March 31, 1999, 3, FBIS-EEU-1999-0331; "Security Guarantees and Frightening Challenges," Budapest *Magyar Nemzet,* March 27, 1999, 4, FBIS-EEU-1999-0329; and "Number of FRY Refugees to Hungary Decreasing," Budapest *MTI,* July 1, 1999, 1620 GMT, FBIS-EEU-1999-0701.

44. For recommendations on improving the treatment of asylum seekers in aspiring EU member states, see "Position on the Enlargement of the European Union in Relation to Asylum," ECRE at: www.ecre.org/archive.

45. For details of existing programs, see the Jesien and Freudenstein chapters in this volume.

46. On the benefits of less restrictive immigration policies, see David Henderson, "International Migration: Appraising Current Policies," *International Affairs* 70, no. 1 (1994): 105–108.

47. Italy, for example, would need to accept 2.2 million migrants a year to maintain the ratio of four working people for every person drawing a pension. "The Asylum Debate: EU Struggles to Find Common Approach to Control Influx," *The Guardian,* March 27, 2000.

48. Milada Anna Vachudová, "The European Union Needs to Change Its Spots," *International Herald Tribune,* August 12, 1999, 8. See also Michael Emerson and Daniel Gros, eds., *The CEPS Plan for the Balkans* (Brussels: Centre for European Policy Studies, 1999).

49. However, "the case for trade liberalization by the OECD group does not rest on its possible effects on migration flows: the main argument in its favour is that it would benefit directly the OECD countries themselves." Henderson, "International Migration," 110.

50. Richard Layard, Olivier Blanchard, Rudiger Dornbusch, and Paul Krugman, *East–West Migration: The Alternatives* (Cambridge: MIT Press, 1992), 51. See also Nicholas Hopkinson, "Responses to Western Europe's Immigration Crisis," Wilton Park Paper no. 84, London 1994, 19–21.

51. Among those advocating an all-Europe free-trade area are: Alice Enders and Ronald J. Wonnacott, "The Liberalisation of East–West European Trade: Hubs, Spokes and Further Complications," *The World Economy* 19, no. 3 (May 1996): 253–272.

52. Trade between the EU and east central European states was liberalized through the bilateral Europe Agreements (EAs): these agreements limited market access for east central European goods, especially in so-called "sensitive sectors." The agreements included provisions for "contingent protection" for industrial goods (antidumping measures and a general safeguard clause which may be invoked at any time) and substantial restrictions on market access for agricultural goods. See Riccardo Faini and Richard Portes, "Opportunities Outweigh Adjustment: The Political Economy of Trade with Central and Eastern Europe," in *E.U. Trade with Eastern Europe: Adjustment and Opportunities*, Faini and Portes, eds. (London: CEPR, 1995), 1–18.

10

Río Odra, Río Buh:
Poland, Germany, and the Borders
of Twenty-First-Century Europe

Roland Freudenstein

There is hardly a single event that better highlights the importance of borders in Europe than that fateful day in June 1989, somewhere along the border between Austria and Hungary. The two foreign ministers, Gyula Horn and Alois Mock, met in a sleepy border town in order to present a disbelieving world with a piece of barbed wire they had personally removed from what was then still the Iron Curtain. Hungary seriously began to dismantle all fortifications and obstacles on its border with Austria. What followed is a chain of events that seemed unrelated at first, but that makes a very coherent piece of history, seen from today: The flow of East Germans into Hungary; the election victory of Solidarity in Poland; the West German embassies in Prague and Budapest packed with East Germans; the collapse of communist rule in the German Democratic Republic (GDR); the reunification of Germany; the end of the Soviet Union, of the Cold War, of communism writ large. Some would even claim it was also the end of the twentieth century (assuming it had really begun in 1917, with the Russian Revolution). And it had all begun by making the impenetrable border between two antagonistic systems more penetrable.

Today, a fictitious car trip from Brussels to L'viv takes you across three very different borders. The one between Belgium and Germany is about to disappear completely. You can pass the former highway control post at Aachen (now deserted) at a reduced speed of fifty miles per hour. No one checks your documents, or searches your car. Spot checks are still possible, but only rarely applied. You may be checked before or after the border by mobile patrols, but that, too, is unlikely if you do not happen to drive a stolen car. This is a Schengen border. The border from Germany to Poland in Slubice, fifty miles east of Berlin, is already quite different: You may have to queue up for one or two hours. Every document is looked at; some cars are searched. The border is quite visible. The road quality changes (for the worse)—people just look less affluent. A frontier of poverty, in a way. While westerners go

173

east to buy cheaper gas, or get a haircut at a lower price, German border police are on the prowl to fend off illegal migrants. But the gap here seems minimal compared to the difference between Poland and Ukraine: At Rava Rus'ka, 150 miles southeast of Warsaw, things become eerie. Without diplomatic registration plates, you may have to wait for anything ranging from four hours to an entire day. No Poles are going east, only Ukrainians coming back. The vast majority of the numerous Ukrainian border guards are taking breaks, most of the time. And behind the border, you feel like you landed in a movie on nineteenth-century peasant culture that has somehow taken a wrong turn, because olive green Soviet-looking army trucks are perched on a nearby hill, surveying the area with impressive radar bowls.

We have encountered four kinds of border so far: a "systemic border" (the Hungaro–Austrian one), which has completely changed; a "virtual border" between Belgium and Germany (becoming less and less relevant every day); a "frontier of poverty" between Poland and Germany, which has a good chance of diminishing and becoming "virtual" within ten to twenty years; and, finally, what I would call a "Huntington border" between Poland and Ukraine, one that bears the risk of marking a break between civilizations in the twenty-first century.[1]

That is the situation today, and it reveals a good deal of the dilemmas Europe will face in the next century. They will be explored in the following sections. The first part of this chapter deals with the question of whether the Schengen border works at all. Preliminary experience indicates that it does, provided there are "compensation measures" on the external borders. The second section asks how the border on the Odra River can be modernized, before and after Poland's accession to the European Union (EU). The decisive mechanisms are cooperation and assistance for Poland from its future partners in the European integration process. The third section outlines the political implications to be expected from the transfer of the EU external border to the Buh River. It will be of paramount importance to minimize the negative effects on Poland's relations with Ukraine while recognizing that they cannot be completely avoided if the EU is to be expanded eastward at all in a responsible manner.

SCHENGENLAND: THE VIRTUAL BORDER

Ever since the continental countries of western Europe began to link their fates in the process of European integration in the early 1950s, the definition of what our nation–states mean to each other, and to us, the citizens, has begun to change fundamentally. And since borders are one of the constituent elements of modern nation–states, they, too, have been subject to progressive but persistent change.

Schengen

In 1985, France, Germany, Belgium, the Netherlands, and Luxembourg (five of the member states of the European Communities, or EC, as it was then) signed a treaty in the village of Schengen, Luxembourg. Almost all remaining members in the integration process joined later. The treaty should lead to the eventual abolition of border controls among the participating countries. The signatories were driven by the two following motives.

First, the completely free movement of people, goods, capital, and services, which was at the center of the Single European Act in preparation in 1985, would be taken to its logical end by removing border controls. Second, in a phase of the integration process that was largely characterized by a feeling of stagnation ("Eurosclerosis"), an example of visible progress, especially one that would be so relevant to the individual citizens, was thought to bring back some of the lost sparkle of the integration process in the eye of public opinion.

The treaty was followed by a more concrete execution agreement in 1990, which entered into force on March 26, 1995. From that day onward, border checks were eliminated. Except for Great Britain and Ireland (which are still opting out), all EU member states (plus Iceland and Norway as associated Schengen countries) now make part of "Schengenland," and the treaty, which started out as a purely intergovernmental one, was incorporated into EU law at the Amsterdam conference of June 1997.

Compensation Measures

But the abolition of border controls between the participating countries had an obvious downside, too, in the eyes of public opinion as well as experts. It deprived law enforcement of one of its instruments to fight organized crime and prevent illegal migration. One argument to allay those fears was that for both crime and migration, the classic type of border controls are hardly obstacles anymore. But nevertheless, an impressive package of compensation measures was introduced to complement the introduction of the "virtual border"—and in many respects, up the ante on cooperative law enforcement.

First, external border controls were to be stepped up by all participating countries. Second, the Schengen Information System (SIS) was set up—a computerized service that gives police and immigration officials a "multinational database of undesirables and people suspected of having committed a crime, stolen vehicles or forged money."[2] Its central computer, situated in Strasbourg, contains about 10 million files that can be accessed by any law enforcement unit in the participating countries within a matter of seconds. Third, a European police office, EUROPOL, was created as a result of a German initiative at the Conference of Maastricht in 1991. Having its headquarters in The Hague, EUROPOL supports national police forces in fighting drug-related crime, money-laundering, and international terrorism. The first 160 police officers from the member states have begun working after the EUROPOL Convention went into force in 1998. For the moment, they are mainly involved in data compilation and networking between national authorities. Around 2004, they will also begin initiating their own investigations. Fourth and last, a common visa and asylum policy was considered indispensable. It was progressively put in place, and even complemented by bilateral agreements on the reacceptance of migrants from each of the participating EU member states with 127 third countries, among them the future member states of central and eastern Europe (see below).

Taken together, the elimination of border controls in the EU plus the compensation measures and accompanying policies represent a substantial change in statehood in Europe, with consequences for the entire continent. Schengenland has become a cornerstone of the idea of integration itself—keeping in mind that European integration is still the boldest effort worldwide to redefine the very meaning of the nation–state, in fact implying a decisive departure from the nineteenth-century model of state sovereignty. Germany has, with regard to its own public opinion and the "federalist" tendencies of its political elite,[3] played a dynamic role, generally favoring the transfer of competences to supranational institutions while insisting on tough and efficient compensation policies.

This is the aspect of Schengen that concerns the member states of the EU. But what about their relations with third countries—both with those that are candidates for EU accession in the first decade after 2000, and those which are unlikely to join in the foreseeable future?

RÍO ODRA: SCHENGENLAND'S TEMPORARY EXTERNAL BORDER

The two eminent problems concerning borders and internal security in Europe are migration (encompassing the two issues of illegal work and misuse of political asylum) and organized crime. Both have become more serious problems, in the statistics kept by governments and in the eye of public opinion, since the end of the Cold War. Both are intimately linked to the problem of EU external borders.[4]

Repercussions of Schengenland

Two of the compensation policies discussed above had a direct effect on the countries of central and eastern Europe—the enhancement of external border controls and the bilateral agreements in the wake of Schengen. In Germany's case, this concerned only the borders with Poland and the Czech Republic (and Austria, temporarily). But more specifically, this had one effect on the populations of the two eastern neighbors that gave the word Schengen an ominous ring—at all border crossings, as well as airports, a two-class system was introduced—non-EU citizens are visibly separated from EU ones, and checked more thoroughly in general. The immediate psychological repercussions were understandably strong. But this was a mild reaction when compared to the angry reaction of parts of the Polish political scene at the negotiations for the bilateral readmission agreement concluded between the Polish and German governments on May 7, 1993 (entering into force on July 1 of the same year), in which Poland committed itself to "reaccept" all illegal migrants from third countries who were sent back after having tried to cross the Polish–German border. The negotiations took place in late 1992 and early 1993; what was perceived as undue German pressure were two facts.

First, Germany had made the continuation of Poles' visa-free travel to Germany dependent upon Poland's signature—visa-free travel to Germany had become, since April 1991, a touchstone of the improved bilateral relationship and was held dearly by a great number of Polish citizens. Consequently, the threat of withdrawal was considered brutish. Second, Poland had to change numerous laws and regulations (for example, on asylum) itself in order to adapt to the rising number of migrants.[5]

The agreement stipulated that asylum applicants entering Germany illegally from Poland (acting as a transit country) would be sent back within six months after their arrival or presence had been noticed by the German authorities. However, no asylum seeker present on German territory before entry into force of the agreement could be returned. The upper limit for deportations to Poland for 1993 would be 10,000 persons; later there would be no limitation. Besides that, two clauses actually made Polish acceptance easier. In the case of a sudden or massive influx of immigrants into Poland, Germany agreed to share the burden of temporarily housing some of them. And, more importantly, Germany agreed to provide direct financial assistance of about $80 million (at the exchange rate of 1993) for the first two years after the entry into force. The money was meant to be used for the improvement of Polish infrastructure for refugees and asylum seekers, the strengthening of border protections, and general buildup of police forces.[6]

The wider political significance of the 1993 readmission agreement between Poland and Germany was considerable. Poland thus became the first "safe third country" in central and eastern Europe—the rule of law was considered sufficiently safe in order to make it acceptable to deport illegals to Poland even if they were not Polish residents but had only entered via Poland. Poland itself, in consequence, quickly negotiated readmission agreements with the Czech Republic, Ukraine, Slovakia, Romania, and Bulgaria within only three months of the signing of the agreement with Germany.

Hence the accusations of some that the EU countries, and particularly Germany, "reexport" instability to their eastern neighbors, and force them to do the same, until the weakest—the countries of origin like, say, Romania or Ukraine, are confronted by the problem (see Vachudová, this volume). This argument presupposes, however, that there is a realistic and domestically defendable alternative to readmission agreements, whereas in reality, perhaps the amount of the accompanying assistance can be discussed, but hardly the agreements themselves. They are a logical and necessary step after the creation of Schengenland.

The German–Polish crisis of early 1993 blew over quickly, and Germany began a process of closer consultation, cooperation, and assistance in justice and home affairs, in order to help Poland deal with the problems that were arising partly from Schengen, but also from the general development of the socioeconomic situation in southeastern Europe (Sinti and Roma from Bulgaria and Romania) and the former Soviet Union.

EU and German Assistance Programs

Besides intensified consultations (frequent meetings of interior ministers and ministerial officials, among others) both on the bilateral and on the European levels (in the framework of the EU's structural dialogue with the associated countries), several specific bodies were set up:[7] an "East–West Security Council" working group on security encompassing the eastern L@nder as well as the federal government on the German side, and law enforcement authorities from Poland and six other central and east European countries. Germany initiated it. Its function is strategic coordination and to build up an early warning system concerning smuggling, grand-scale vehicle theft, and gangs helping illegal migrants.

A bilateral Polish–German agreement of November 1991 deals with cooperation in fighting organized crime, and one of May 1993 (as part of the readmission agreement) deals with preventing illegal migration. Since April 1995, there is a concrete agreement on the cooperation of police forces—giving the already existing police contacts a legal basis. Transborder investigation and observation will soon be a part of life. This is the first agreement of its kind between an EU member and a third country. Finally, numerous training schemes—from language courses to joint seminars on white-collar crime and vehicle theft—have been started between German and Polish law enforcement.

Experience with this cooperation is largely positive. Initial distrust on the German side, regarding the reliability and efficiency of law enforcement in the eastern neighboring countries, has been somewhat mollified. But the development of real cooperation is still in an early stage, and will only reach full intensity with the accession of Poland and its central European neighbors to the EU. By that time, assistance for Polish law enforcement and border protection will have to reach entirely different dimensions from current levels.

As a general conclusion to this section, one could say that the compensation measures required by Schengenland, as far as they concern third countries, in themselves make compensation policies toward those countries necessary. Without additional cooperation and assistance, the political and psychological costs for neighboring third countries would be too high.

RÍO BUH: POLAND'S STRATEGIC DILEMMA

Whether in 2003, 2004, or 2005, Poland is earmarked to become an EU member in the near future. Its eastern neighbors are not (with the exception of Lithuania, which may join later and which has enjoyed visa-free access to Schengenland since March 1999). Whatever the Odra border with Germany signifies today, this may shift to the Buh River along Poland's eastern border: and the latter may be even more impenetrable than the former for a very long time. In this context, it has to be said that free movement across its eastern borders has, for Poland, an economic, a cultural, and a deeply political dimension.

In specific sectors of the Polish economy (e.g., agriculture), and especially in the infrastructurally weak areas along the eastern border, small and medium enterprises are still largely dependent on trade with the former U.S.S.R, despite the overall western swing in Poland's external trade since 1989. Besides that, the sheer scale of the movement of persons indicates the significance of the eastern border question for Poland and its relations with Ukraine. Whether migrant workers or small-scale traders, Ukrainians travel to Poland in large numbers, In 1996 alone, around 2.6 million Ukrainians crossed the border to Poland.[8] This also has an aspect relating to the past—with half of pre-1945 Poland east of today's border, the need for a sizeable (though diminishing) part of the Polish population to be able to travel east freely should not be discounted. Even though Poland, lacking a pluralist political system between 1944 and 1989, could not develop refugee lobbies of the political virulence like Germany, the personal and emotional ties of many Poles born east of the River Buh, in the so-called "kresy," are a relevant societal factor.[9]

But perhaps the most important argument is of a more strategic nature. That only an independent Ukraine can prevent a resurgence of Russian hegemony in central Europe has become a credo of Polish foreign policy accepted by the vast majority of the political spectrum. Good relations with Kyiv (despite problems in developing a common perspective on an often painful past) are now part and parcel of a strong bipartisan consensus.

Merging with Schengenland

In the foreseeable future, Río Buh will become a Schengen external border. But even before that, Poland sees itself compelled to tighten the border control regime toward the east. The specific situations with respect to Poland's four eastern neighbors are the following. Lithuania, Poland's neighbor to the northeast, may be excluded, since it is already a candidate country and might even move up to the first group of countries to accede (with Poland).

With Russia, Poland introduced an invitation/voucher scheme in January 1998 that did not create too much of a crisis. Citizens of the Russian Federation have to show a formal invitation by a Polish resident or organization, or prove a hotel reservation. The question remains what the reaction will be when Russians have to get visas in Polish consulates. In fact, it may be expected that in this case Russian public reaction will be far more negative than in the case of Poland's NATO accession (which was really an elite problem without broad significance to the people).

In Belarus, the same situation applies as for Russians. But it should be added that here, the border regime has an important effect on Belarus's internal situation. The hub of Belarusian democratic opposition activity is in Poland. Toughening up the border would inevitably weaken the opposition to the Lukashenka dictatorship.

Ukraine is the exception to the rule along Poland's eastern border. Ukrainians today only have to prove they dispose of a certain sum of money. No visas, invitations, or vouchers are required. Polish politicians are today saying they will introduce visa travel for Ukrainians at the latest possible moment. But even the "proof of possession" was very unpopular among Ukrainian travelers and has allegedly reduced the number of legal border crossings significantly.

In all four cases, the current situation will soon become untenable, probably long before Poland joins the EU. Brussels and the member states are already today emphasizing the necessity of introducing visa regimes, and completely ruling out exceptions for Poland.

The EU and Poland's Eastern Policy

What can be done to limit the foreseeable damage to Poland's eastern relations, which are, of course, also EU eastern relations, keeping in mind that the cardinal problem is Ukraine? The EU will have to develop an overall eastern strategy, encompassing political dialogue, trade, assistance, and crisis management in respect to those former U.S.S.R. countries without the possibility of membership in the foreseeable future. The EU is starting with Russia, and Ukraine and Belarus should follow. This strategy should take future Polish EU membership into account. So far, most EU strategic planning toward Ukraine and other former U.S.S.R. countries is concerned with political and economic developments inside these countries, and disregards the question of what to do about the future border between them and the EU.[10] This represents a serious gap in future-oriented thinking in Brussels and the EU national capitals.

The ultimate chance to prevent the Buh River from becoming a new dividing line in Europe after EU enlargement will lie with Poland, with active assistance from EU institutions. One can imagine a whole array of Polish initiatives across the border, especially with Ukraine. A useful initiative would be agreements on exemptions or simplified processing for inhabitants of border areas. A Polish–Ukrainian university, analogous to the very successful "Viadrina" in Frankfurt/Oder between Poland and Germany was being planned as of this writing. The dialogue about the painful common past has to be continued—here, too, the German–Polish example shows that progress is possible. Such a dialogue may increase mutual interest in difficult times. Other cultural joint ventures are imaginable. And generally, any efforts to strengthen infrastructure and civil society in Poland's underprivileged and underdeveloped east, will help to step up contacts across the Buh River. The Euroregion Buh, created in 1995 as a Polish–Ukrainian venture with blessing and support from the EU, may serve to intensify cross-border cooperation and development.[11] Ultimately, Poland will have to start planning its Ukrainian policy already as a future EU member, and the EU itself must take into account the Polish factor in its efforts to develop a Ukraine strategy.[12]

Yet no one should harbor the illusion that countries like Ukraine can or even must be "reimbursed" for damages incurred through the extension of Schengenland to their western borders. First of all, the most important reason for their unlikeliness to join the EU in the foreseeable future is to be found in these countries themselves, in Kyiv, Moscow, and Minsk, but not in Brussels. It is the unwillingness of political and economic elites to seriously reform their countries that is at the root of the West's relative lack of attention (and assistance) for them. Where assistance cannot responsibly and fruitfully be absorbed, it does not make sense. It is this unwillingness, or inability, which has created the growing gap between the former Soviet republics (minus the Baltic states) and the central European EU accession candidates. No "new Marshall plan" could change that. On the other hand, keeping borders as open as they are now between Poland and its eastern neighbors would jeopardize the eastern enlargement as such, by arousing the ire of public opinion in EU members such as Germany. Hence mitigating effects may be expected, and should be discussed more intensively. But it should be taken into account that Poland's EU accession will have direct positive results on its eastern neighbors, too. They will obviously profit from a stable and prosperous country to the West—no matter what visa regime is in place for travel to Poland.

CONCLUSION

Border controls in the classical sense can be abolished if the following conditions are met. First, a minimal degree of compatibility in standards of living between the participating countries must exist, as well as the political will between populations. The second condition is that compensation measures in crime prevention and migration control have to be put in place. Both conditions exist within the group of EU member states participating in Schengenland. Considering the visible increase in comfort for citizens and the efficiency of compensation measures, Schengen is a success.

Schengen has, however, increased difficulties for EU candidate countries. Their citizens are, today, faced with relatively tighter controls upon entering Schengenland. Being defined as "safe third countries," they had to simultaneously sign readmission agreements with the EU, and in turn with their own neighbors, as part of an enlargement preparation strategy that has no alternative. Moreover, with a view to future EU membership, and while profiting from visa-free travel into Schengenland, they have to tighten controls at their eastern/southeastern borders. In this, they are helped by various programs of assistance and information from the EU.

In a few years, the EU's external border will shift from the Odra River to the Buh River. It will remain there for the foreseeable future. Poland will have to make its

eastern border less penetrable for organized crime and illegal migration, and introduce the same tightening of its non-EU borders as apply today on the outside of
Schengenland. This will have implications for Poland's eastern policy in general. In
times of growing disparities between western and central Europe on the one hand,
and the former U.S.S.R. on the other, an accompanying political strategy will have
to be worked out, in order to minimize the destabilizing effects of the River Buh.
That entails working out an overall EU strategy toward the East, as well as a number of bilateral cross-border cooperation measures between Poland and Ukraine,
especially.

What will remain of our four kinds of borders? There are no more systemic borders in Europe. The chances are that we will, in the not-too-distant future, have only
two kinds: the "virtual" type in Schengenland, and the "frontier of poverty," identi-
cal in this case to a "Huntingtonian" civilizational frontier. It will take considerable
efforts to keep Europe stable along that line. Academics, politicians, and administrators are called upon to start debating these questions now.

NOTES

1. See Samuel P. Huntington, *The Clash of Civilizations and the Remaking of World Order*
(New York: Simon and Schuster, 1996). Page 159 contains the famous "Huntington line"
representing the border between western and eastern Christendom around A.D. 1500.

2. See "Schengen Treaty fully implemented," at: europa.eu/en/agenda/schengen.html.

3. The term "federalist" in the context of the debate on the future of the EU denotes a
tendency first put forward by the "founding fathers"—Adenauer, Schuman, and deGasperi—
which emphasizes supranational elements and the joint exercise of sovereignty in the European institutional framework, thus competing with the so-called "intergovernmental" tendency recently most radically represented by former British Prime Minister Margaret
Thatcher and viewing European integration as a process of more ad-hoc cooperation of sovereign states. Former German Chancellor Helmut Kohl, on the other hand, may well be
considered the embodiment of "Euro-federalist" thinking in the 1990s.

4. In order to assess the politico-psychological pitfalls involved in the question of foreign criminals, compare the effort spent by the German authorities in the official report on
crime statistics, to explain that the higher rate of criminality among "non-Germans" than
Germans is *not* due to stronger criminal tendencies among foreigners per se, but i.a. to the
fact that resident/transient foreigners are, more than the German average, composed of high-
risk groups (such as young urban males). See Presse- und Informationsamt der Bundes-
regierung, "Die Kriminalität in der Bundesrepublik Deutschland," *Bulletin*, no. 29, 289–
290 (Bonn, May 25, 1999).

5. See, for example, the excellent presentation of the entire Polish–German and Polish–
Ukrainian problem in: Klaus Bachmann, *Polska kaczka - europejski staw* (Warsaw 1999), 113–
130.

6. See Wlodek Aniol, *Poland's Migration and Ethnic Policies: European and German
Influences* (Warsaw: Friedrich Ebert Stiftung, 1996), 39.

7. See Wolfram Hils, "Deutschland und seine Nachbarn Polen und Tschechien: Regionale Kooperation im Umweltbereich und bei der Inneren Sicherheit," in *Aus Politik und Zeitgeschichte* (January 15, 1999): 43–54.

8. See Bachmann, *Polska kaczka - europejski staw.*

9. In fact, Hungary (with its large minority in Romania) and the Czech Republic (with its special ties to Slovakia) are even worse off in this light.

10. For a recent example of German strategic thinking on EU enlargement and countries without a concrete membership perspective, see Michael Dauderstädt and Barbara Lippert, *Die deutsche Ratspräsidentschaft: Doppelstrategie zur Vertiefung und Erweiterung der EU* (Bonn: Friedrich Ebert Stiftung, 1998), 47–48. The River Buh problem is not mentioned at all.

11. See Maciej Baltowski and Andrzej Miszczuk, "Granica polsko-ukrainska w perspektywie nowego europejskiego porzadku geopolitycznego," *Przeglad Zachodni,* no. 3 (1999): 29–40.

12. As much as the EU may be criticized for not yet having thought about the Schengen border moving to the Buh River, Poland's political class is also at the very beginning of a thinking and debating process, at best. In the most comprehensive presentation to date of center-right thinking on European integration and Poland's future EU membership, the entire Polish–Ukrainian problem in connection with joining Schengen is not once mentioned: See Jacek Czaputowicz, ed., *Integracja europejska: implikacje dla Polski,* Cracow 1999. However, in some recent press articles, the problem has begun to be raised. See, for example, Tadeusz M. Pluzanski, "Nie bedzie podzialu," *Tygodnik Solidarnosc,* April 21, 2000.

11

Border Controls and the Politics of EU Enlargement

Leszek Jesien[1]

When I first worked in the prime minister's office in 1993, old rules of procedure were still in place. There was strict security upon entering the building. However, those who passed into its corridors all looked alike. The civil servants and the politicians were indistinguishable from the guests, the "aliens." Occasionally there were demonstrations in front of the main entrance, just past the security. Such manifestations were rare enough in those days. But when they took place, all the employees inside were painfully aware of the large numbers of people outside. The outsiders shouted their anger at a power they still found alien. Democracy was taking root in Poland. The European Union (EU) was established that year (on the basis of the European Communities), and hardly accepted the prospect that new democracies such as Poland would join the "club."

My second period of employment at the prime minister's office began five years later. By then, demonstrations had become routine. Almost every other day, good weather permitting of course, the crowds gathered to give voice to their interests. The number of people participating varied from a handful to 10,000: angry workers, inhabitants of small towns, tillers of the soil. Polish farmers, embracing the militancy of their west European fellows, spilled around badly smelling substances of organic origins. At this point, special passes were introduced for the employees. Photos and names were on display hanging on their neck chains. Guests became instantly noticeable with their distinct badges. Interest groups, lobbyists, and even—paradoxically—the other civil servants became "aliens." The standard difference between "us" and "them" became instantly visible. Symbolically, the difference was reduced to a mere fact of displaying a particular kind of metal ID chain. This was the moment when negotiations of the conditions of Poland's accession to the EU got under way. Aside and apart from the countless issues of policy and law, one of the main problems for Polish negotiators was how to convince the EU that they were (so to speak) no longer "them," but also "us." What is this trick that allows one to only pull the right kind of pass from one's front pocket and be permitted to enter? Just as an EU national crosses the EU border casually displaying his or her distinctly red passport.

From the very beginning of European integration one of its fundamental elements was an effort to create an area of free movement of people, without internal border identity checks. This was achieved, however, in 1995 only after some forty years and within the scope of the Schengen Agreement. When the Amsterdam Treaty came into force on May 1, 1999, work began to move this arrangement into the EU.[2] In this project of removing internal borders, it seems that trust among all players in the field is the pivotal issue. If they are to collectively protect their internal security, the integrating nations need to overcome the long-lasting heritage of history, cultural differences, and stereotypes. They need a "critical mass" of mutual trust.

This chapter will deal with the central issue of trust between the EU and its eastern neighbors. It will assess the way trust is being built over the time since opening up of the new democracies in 1989. The first part of this chapter briefly puts the current border situation of Poland into a short historic perspective. It will categorize the Polish borders into three different types: those to disappear at the day of accession, those to remain and be enforced, and those of an intermediate kind that will have to be first strengthened and then dismantled. It will also show some complications inherent in the EU enlargement that will affect border management. Next, we will examine the contemporary functions of the borders, differentiating between traditional linear borders in the region and the new buffer type of today. This part will also look at the challenge of cooperation between the candidates and the EU in the realm of border issues. The third part elaborates the dilemmas posed to the candidates during the membership negotiations. It will show that the question of migration controls is not the only one (and perhaps not the most important one) that will affect the ultimate outcome of negotiations. Even though the proper protection of the EU external border is a necessary precondition for enlargement, the quality of the future enlarged EU will most probably be judged by effective dismantling of internal borders. In both instances, the issue of trust between the EU member states and the EU candidates will prove essential.

TIMING, POLITICS, AND GEOGRAPHY

It is perhaps banal to stress that the configuration of borders changes with time, and that these changes, which reflect the course of politics of the day, force cartographers to amend their previous work. The borders usually change as an effect of war.[3] Let us take the case of Poland in the first half of the twentieth century. World War I (1914–1918) resulted in the rebirth of the Polish State. The war of 1919–1920 with Soviet Russia delineated the eastern boundaries of this renewed Poland. World War

II (1939–1945), however, significantly shrank Poland's territory and pushed it westward by some 300 kilometers. Subsequently, the border situation was frozen in this part of the world for some forty-five years until the collapse of the Iron Curtain (1989). The end of communism—the end of the postwar era—brought new opportunities to the countries of the region. In 1991, the Baltic states of Lithuania, Latvia, and Estonia gained independence. Ukraine and Belarus followed shortly thereafter. In 1993, Czechoslovakia split into the Czech Republic and Slovakia. From that point forward, Poland, having bordered on three states in the recent past (East Germany, Czechoslovakia, and the Soviet Union), had seven new countries as its neighbors (a unified Federal Republic of Germany, the Czech Republic, Slovakia, Ukraine, Belarus, Lithuania, and the Russian Federation).

With this border picture, in 1994 Poland put forward its application for EU membership. Today there are altogether ten central and eastern European countries waiting to accede to the EU (Bulgaria, Czech Republic, Estonia, Hungary, Latvia, Lithuania, Poland, Romania, Slovakia, and Slovenia). The future EU enlargement will further change the nature of borders in the region. These changes will be peaceful, and will involve the quality rather than the placement of borders. The EU has embarked on the road to accession negotiations with the clear idea that (1) the *acquis communautaire* [4] will be sacrosanct—the new member states will have to take on all existing and future obligations—and that (2) there will be only a very limited number of short transition periods for adaptation after accession. In particular, the Amsterdam Treaty in its "Protocol Integrating the Schengen *acquis* into the Framework of the European Union" annexed to the Treaty on European Union and the treaty establishing the European Community states quite explicitly that the new members will have to take on the Schengen *acquis* in full before accession.[5] This relatively rigid stance can be understood in the light of a generally perceived threat to the internal security of the EU.

The Amsterdam Treaty is supposed *inter alia* to address ostensible threats to public order associated with the prospect of an eastern enlargement of the EU. Its first section is entitled "Freedom, Security and Justice," the second chapter of which is to progressively establish an "area" of freedom, security, and justice. Here the Schengen *acquis* and the process of its transposition into the EU *acquis* are to play an essential part. The treaty contains a special declaration stating that the level of security provided by the EU must be at least not lower than that provided by the previously existing intergovernmental Schengen arrangements.[6] The EU wanted to definitively secure the otherwise uncertain future of peaceful living for its citizens. Poland's opening statement, which describes its general approach to negotiations and accession, also stressed the need for full participation in all the EU policies, including a fully functioning enlarged single market. This approach should result in Poland demanding only few transition periods and only where they prove to be absolutely indispensable. Particularly, transitional arrangements should be avoided where their existence may undermine the full operability of the single market.[7]

Interestingly enough, the EU, being in the period of self-creation and self-definition as a political entity, is not at all keen to determine its future boundaries in terms of who (which lands and territories) does belong to it and who does not. It has accepted the new democracies' bid for EU membership only reluctantly, on the basis of a historical opportunity and political necessity, but has never singled out the future members. The so-called "enlargement process" as sketched out by the Luxembourg European Council in December 1997, cautiously followed the formula proposed by the European Commission that the six countries should start the negotiations (Czech Republic, Cyprus, Estonia, Hungary, Poland, and Slovenia) on the grounds of their preparedness to fulfill the famous Copenhagen criteria (functioning democracy, ability to take on the *acquis*, and fully operational free market economy).[8] The Commission decisively rejected claims that the choice was taken on political grounds. However, the inclusion of Estonia in the first wave may still be considered a political signal indicating where the European integration ends for the time being. Two years later the Helsinki European Council of December 1999 opened the way to start the accession negotiations with all remaining candidates: Bulgaria, Latvia, Lithuania, Romania, Slovakia, and Malta. Turkey is now a nonnegotiating candidate for EU membership. The key part in this border puzzle is that no one knows which country will join when, thereby introducing an element of uncertainty that looms over the question of external border protection and management.

There is a significant difference between the traditional way the EU treats its external borders—as lines separating "us" from "them," wherever those happen to be now—and the way it stresses the utmost need for consolidation of everything that finds itself inside this somewhat contingently defined entity. Both factors—a certain vagueness of linear definition and the positive stress given to the consolidation of everything inside the lines—pose conceptual difficulties for the self-definition of the EU, and technical problems for both members and candidates during the accession negotiations. Given the need for proper protection of the external borders of the EU (in view of troubles in fighting organized international crime, drugs and persons trafficking, money laundering, and para-mafia activities), the uncertainty of what actual parts of the borders are to be strengthened does not make life easier for the negotiators. Let us review the case of the Polish borders in this light. There are three different kinds of borders: (1) western—to disappear; (2) eastern—to be strengthened; and (3) intermediate cases—first to be strengthened, then to be dismantled.

On one extreme is the western border—that one between Poland and Germany—which is to vanish at the moment Poland joins the EU.[9] Even this may not be so certain. Keeping in mind the readiness of both sides to limit the eventual transition periods in numbers, scope, and duration, there are nevertheless a few areas where even a single transitional arrangement would have to result in maintaining the border and all of its functions.[10] The three key negotiating chapters in question are "Free Movement of Goods," "Free Movement of People," and "Agriculture." One may imagine a kind of "phasing-out" of the border, which would be needed to keep the checks on goods and people during a transitional period. This, politically, is not at all a good solution either. It may render questionable the very effect of EU enlargement on public opinion on both sides.[11] This means that very important personal effects of enlargement will be felt only after the transitional arrangements would have ended. Thus, in such a case, the enlargement would not happen socially, emotionally, and politically at the date of accession, but later on—at the end of transitions in general.

On the other extreme is the eastern border. In the Polish case it comprises the northern line with Russia (Kaliningrad region) and its parts to the east—with Belarus and Ukraine. Those—for the foreseeable future after Polish accession—will be the external borders of the EU. The security of these borders will be very important for an enlarged union; and in the meantime they will serve as a litmus test for the ability of Poland to implement the Schengen *acquis*. This perspective already raises major concerns of certain EU member states, notably Germany, Austria, Sweden, and Finland. They would like to have the new EU members as a buffer zone filtering all unwanted elements of the flux of people and goods between East and West. They reasonably want to increase their sense of internal, domestic security. Here is where an enlarged EU area of "freedom, security, and justice" will be tested. Here is where freedom might weigh less than security. Here is where the Polish authorities will have to bear their responsibility to bring justice as well.

Between the two extremes of disappearing national borders (western) within the EU and well-defined external border (eastern) of the EU there are the intermediate cases. From today's perspective, those are most likely the Polish–Lithuanian and the Polish–Slovak borders. The essential problem is that they will have to disappear at some point as well, but would have to stay for some time, until Lithuania and Slovakia join the EU. In all their similarities, those borders bring different consequences for the operation of the common EU border system. For example, if Poland is in the EU and Lithuania is still out, it significantly shortens the common Schengen border in comparison with the situation when both countries are in. The Polish–Lithuanian part of an external EU border would account for only 91 kilometers, in comparison with Lithuanian borders with Russia and Belarus, which together amount to 729 kilometers.[12]

Slovakia is an interesting case in this consideration. If Slovakia does not join the EU together with Poland, the Czech Republic, and Hungary, the common EU external border would extend by 1,265 kilometers. But if it does join with the other candidate neighbors, the EU external border would actually shorten by 1 kilometer! It would do so because the Slovak border with Ukraine is 90 kilometers, while its border with Austria accounts for 91 kilometers. Another interesting case in this respect is Hungary, undoubtedly one of the most advanced countries on the way to EU membership. Its membership, in a likely scenario together with Slovenia as the only one of its neighbors to join together, will extend EU borders by 1,540 kilometers. The general effects of EU enlargement on its eastern external borders were

calculated in the annexes. If we assume that the six countries that started the negotiations first (the "Luxembourg group") join the EU together as the first wave, this
would add 4,254 kilometers of new eastern borders. When we look at the picture
after all ten central and east European countries have joined, the total length of new
eastern borders does not change very much: it would reach 4,787 kilometers.

The examples presented here are to illustrate the magnitude of problems if border considerations are taken together with the question of which countries join the
EU at the same time. This is of course also exacerbated by the overall uncertainty
in the EU enlargement calendar. Nobody knows today the order in which countries
will join. In this sense, the annexes simplify the picture, as other patterns of
enlargement are certainly possible. The lives of border management planners will
not be easy.

LINE VERSUS DEPTH

Over time, international borders seem to lose their linear character. Before the contemporary era of the globalization of economic activities, before the arrival of extensive transnational organized crime and massive trafficking of drugs, before the
qualitative increase in international travel, mostly by air, the borders looked more
like lines to be protected and to give protection (see Anderson, and Lahav and
Guiraudon, this volume). It was very often sufficient to seal off a territory from another by physically securing a line. Perhaps the most striking example of a rigid frontier in Europe was the Berlin Wall. The border as a dividing line necessitated the
overall territory of at least one bordering country to be in fact a homogenous entity, strictly policed. People of the "prison" countries of the former Soviet bloc were
restrained not only in their movements across the frontiers, but often also in their
ability to travel within the country. Internal passports were required for travel within
the Soviet Union. In fact, travel from some countries of the former Soviet block (like
Poland, Hungary, and Yugoslavia) to the West was at times easier than between them.
In a very practical sense, the linear borders of police states enclosed their entire territories: just as a prison wall encloses the unlucky one who happens to spend some
time there. A person who crossed a border like this, in his or her travel around the
country, was subsequently controlled at each and every point of the journey. At each
stop he or she needed to register with local police and was frequently stopped on
the roads, not to mention constant attention given by the secret police to the foreigners if they were unfortunate enough to attract its attention.[13]

Today's borders between liberal democratic states are less of the line character, less
clear thresholds than flexible buffer zones serving particular needs of the countries
in question. The geographical lines dividing the territories may be easier to cross,
but there are several mechanisms and institutions that are able to perform control
functions inside the territories. Border guards do their jobs on the border crossing
points, while the local police may assist them in doing the same within the strip of

land adjacent to the borderline. Border guards may themselves have investigative, police-like prerogatives. Attention given by institutions and officers involved may differ according to particular needs. Thus, between states showing significant discrepancies in their economic development, the focus of checks will be put on trafficking of goods and people. In these cases, the control functions will concentrate on a singular issue. They involve cooperation among several institutions (border guards, police, customs, intelligence, and specialized agencies), and stretch across the entire national territories. A modern borderline is more like a buffering cushion—changing its size and firmness according to the actual policies, priorities, and needs of the countries concerned and the nature of various perceived threats to societal security.

If we look at the functions of modern borders, the main purpose they serve is to filter "unwanted elements" rather than to rigidly divide territories. These unwanted elements are often mentioned when talking about borders: organized crime (mafia), smuggled people, drugs and arms, and stolen goods (especially cars and art objects). The particular functions of borders today are:

- Control of identity of people moving across (symbolizing the sense of belonging or exclusion).
- Collection of customs and duties on goods crossing (a state industrial and trade policy).
- Fitosanitary and veterinary control.
- Prevention of trade in illicit goods, particularly drugs, arms, and fossil materials.
- Prevention of people trafficking (illegal migration).

The functions mentioned indicate that today borders serve a mixture of traditional, modern, and contemporary purposes. The traditional ones are identity control and collection of customs and duties. The modern ones are those symbolizing the sense of belonging or exclusion (as a part of the development of the modern nation–state). The new ones are prevention of illegal migration, dangerous goods trafficking, and fitosanitary and veterinary controls. This is not to say that sometimes the new purposes were not fulfilled by the old-time frontiers. However, the stress today is on different issues than in the past. Nevertheless, it remains true that modern borders serve political purposes of establishing and confirming "membership" or "nationality" (see Torpey, this volume). When a person crosses a state border, the experience emphasizes either the sense of belonging or the sense of exclusion (depending whether a person is warmly welcomed, just welcomed, accepted only, or openly refused entry to the territory).

An interesting case in this regard is the effect of abolition of internal frontiers for free movement of people within the EU (as a result of the Schengen Agreement) on the perception of European citizenship. Certainly those who frequently travel in today's Europe do admire and profit from the absence of border controls, particularly when passing through small states by train or car. The illuminated signposts at the airports dividing a flow of people into two groups, "EU nationals" and "Non-EU nationals," do contribute to the European citizenry's growing awareness of their common belonging. In Brussels, one may hear the stories about high-ranking officials traveling to Tallinn, Estonia, for an official visit and having forgotten that they need an Estonian visa—or of other officials having forgotten their passports entirely. Well into the accession negotiations of Estonia, there is still a mutual visa requirement between Estonia and some of the EU member states. It is so normal and usual to cross today's EU internal borders without being checked at all that it seems quite normal and usual to forget about the essentials of international travel. Traveling in Europe slowly becomes a noninternational reality.[14]

There is a significant difference in cross-border activity in the central European region as compared to the rest of the EU. A survey on 1998 Polish border crossings reveals that of 272 million people who entered or left the state, an estimated 75 percent were traveling for commercial purposes to buy goods cheaper in a neighboring country. This kind of "tourism" flourishes in all directions: the Germans come to Poland to buy things cheaper than in Germany, Poles go to Germany to buy the other things. The same applies all along the border, especially in the East. Neighboring foreigners contributed an estimated $4 billion to the Polish economy, while Poles spent almost $1 billion in neighboring countries. Altogether, however, the turnover on the Polish eastern/northern border fell in 1998 by almost 43 percent compared to the figure from 1997.[15] This is attributed not only to the effect of new controls introduced by Poland on the border. The first and most important reason was the acute crisis of the Russian economy and its deteriorating effect on the Belarusian and Ukrainian economies. In addition, the introduction of higher custom tariffs by Russia and Belarus to protect their failing markets played a role.

On their way to the EU, the candidate countries have been offered few helpful mechanisms. The core of the EU relationship with central and east European candidates is still legally based on the Europe Agreements, which are basically of trade nature (striving to achieve a free-trade area) with some elements of legal approximation added. Over time more political elements were introduced, namely the preaccession strategy, the structural dialogue, and the reinforced preaccession strategy. The last part of this development is the Accession Partnerships, which are semilegally binding. They list a set of priorities for the candidates to achieve. They provide financial resources to sustain the efforts of legal and institutional adaptation as well as the implementation of those changes into the economic and administrative reality. There is a strong conditionality link between priorities and finances, and the latter may be refused if progress is not shown. Among priorities listed, the strengthening of border control capacity figures high on the agenda for all the candidates.

On the other hand, the candidates tried without success for several years to enter into cooperation with the Schengen arrangements. This proved difficult because of a certain reluctance of the Schengen member states to share their achievements with the countries perceived as being far from EU membership. Borders in general, and the creation of the common external border in particular, raise the question of "them" or "us" with particular sharpness. Applicants who wish to demonstrate their trustworthiness by cooperating within the Schengen regime meet the resistance of west Europeans fearful of jeopardizing previous achievements by cooperating with unproven partners. This dilemma, along with a slow development of a political dimension in EU-applicant relationships, has added a particular flavor to the EU demand, and applicants' efforts, to put in proper order presumed future EU external borders. Some EU member states, Germany in particular, have nevertheless contributed substantially (on a bilateral basis) to improving Poland's eastern borders. Also, police cooperation in fighting organized crime, drug trafficking, illegal migration, and car theft between the candidates on one side and some EU member states such as Germany and the Netherlands in particular on the other side, provided excellent results.[16]

Only in 1998 did the EU and the candidates enter into a "Preaccession Pact on Organized Crime." The principal aim was, apart from helping the applicant countries to adopt the *acquis* in the justice and home affairs area, to establish joint projects against crime with technical or financial assistance from the EU. The candidates committed themselves to adopting the key international conventions in the area, notably the 1957 European Convention on extradition, the UN Convention on drug trafficking, and the 1977 European Convention on terrorism. An agreement with Europol is planned. But there are still important EU programs and initiatives aimed at improving border protection to which the candidates have only limited access (by invitation from a EU member state).[17] Needless to say, the candidates, not being associated with Europol, do not have access to the Europol Drugs Unit that is responsible for combating drug trafficking. Consequently they cannot cooperate with an intelligence unit within the Drugs Unit, which was set up to improve police and customs cooperation.

In sum, the challenge of dismantling, strengthening, and strengthening-then-dismantling of borders is enormous for all of the east and central European applicants. The EU can do a great deal to help. In fact, it is doing a great deal, but not without equivocation. The cooperation within the third pillar, difficult as it is for the current EU member states themselves, could have been more efficient in preparation for the EU future external borders.

SPLITTING BORDERS FOR NEGOTIATIONS

The multiple functions of modern borders are very clearly seen at the negotiating table. Questions that might appear at first to have only a very tenuous relationship to borders can, if unresolved, became practical reasons to maintain existing border regimes. Functionally, borders are dealt with in various negotiating chapters. Both the abolition of EU internal borders and strengthening of its external frontiers become highly complicated. Let us review them in turn.

The relevance of the areas of "Agriculture" and "Fisheries" to the question of future internal frontiers is relatively straightforward. If, for example, Poland does not fulfill the EU fitosanitary and veterinary standards for agricultural products (for example, milk or meat) the EU may wish to keep the checks on the borders (to be internal borders). The same applies for the fish imported into the Polish market. However, in the view of the Polish government, the local markets solution (goods produced and labeled only for local consumption) should prevent both sides from keeping the internal border. The negotiating chapter on the "Free Movement of Goods," on the other hand, is composed of many traps. One of them may be an implicit linkage between this area and "Company Law" where patent protection finds its negotiating place. Because the patent laws were generally introduced in the east and central European countries later than in the EU countries, it may happen that the patent protection—for pharmaceuticals in particular—is not equal after enlargement. This situation in turn can eventually lead to a temptation to introduce a transition period on behalf of the EU in parallel imports of pharmaceuticals produced in east and central Europe into the EU market.[18] The general principle of free movement of goods can in such cases give way to the interests of one specific sector. In other words, technical issues can take on considerable economic and political importance. It is therefore also important to keep them as they are—technical. Otherwise the border will remain for some time, and the overall political and economic effects of EU enlargement will be undermined.

Another interesting example is the negotiations concerning the "Free Movement of Persons." Some of the EU current member countries (Germany and Austria, in particular) show their concerns about the possibility of an influx of people from new member states seeking jobs on their labor markets. However legitimate this concern may seem, it is based on a current and static perception of a general discrepancy of income that exists today between the EU and central and east European candidates. The economic incentives—high as they might be—do not actually provoke any massive migrations today, at least not within Europe. Thanks to a bilateral agreement between Poland and Germany, there is a yearly quota for the legal employment of Polish workers in Germany. Every year it is not fully exploited. Rapid economic progress by today's candidates, together with labor market, social, and language rigidities in Europe, would argue for a more reasonable approach. Although it is hard to predict the actual outcome of negotiations in this area, public debates have already begun in Austria and Germany, and it seems that with time their temperature lowers. This gives some hope for a more reasonable final outcome. Otherwise, the border would have to remain.

With respect to future external borders, the EU is paying great attention to the way preparations are made to improve the performance of the services that are to work there. In 1998 the EU Council established a special Collective Evaluation Working Group. Its aim is to watch "the enactment, application and effective implementation by applicant countries of the *acquis* of the European Union in the field of Justice and Home Affairs."[19] The group has divided its work into seven thematic groups: asylum, migration, border control, police cooperation, and judicial cooperation in criminal and civil matters. The attention is therefore very much on everything that has to do with common external borders in a larger sense. The assumption is that the findings of the group will be of high relevance to the progress of the negotiations in the area of justice and home affairs. This includes problems of taking over the Schengen *acquis*, and hence directly concerns the issue of the control of the external border.

Poland is fully aware of the importance of the matter. The quality of border control operations, particularly at its eastern border, has in fact improved. The necessary legislation concerning, among others, border protection, aliens, criminal prosecution, drug trafficking, illegal immigration, and judicial administrators has been largely adopted. Reforms of central and local administration helped to give the border-controlling segments of the state new and efficient structures. The fight against organized crime and corruption—particularly at the customs posts—was made a priority. The EU has noted the progress.[20] For its part, the Polish Customs Office is constantly improving its activities as well. The new strategy for achieving the full conformity with the EU requirements was prepared in 1999, with the objective of getting the Customs Office fully operational along the EU rules one year before planned accession, hence on January 1, 2002. This is necessary because the customs union is one of the fundamentals of the EU economic regime. The collection of value-added tax on the external border will constitute a part of Poland's contribution to the EU budget. Therefore, a year of customs operations as in the EU is necessary for anticipatory correction of any possible shortcomings. Since border control issues are intertwined, in April 2000 the Polish government elaborated the Integrated Strategy of the Management of the External Border, the first of its kind among the candidate countries. It linked all the institutions involved in border protection and communicates with other documents, namely the customs strategy. A specific interinstitutional coordinating body was set up in order to implement the strategy efficiently, swiftly, and coherently.

By the sole fact of incorporating the EU *acquis*, the state becomes also a part of a larger political system, that of the EU. The EU—while not a state—has nevertheless acquired a few state-like competencies, as well as the capacity to influence nation–(EU member)–states. In some cases, national officers work on behalf of their nation–states and the EU simultaneously. EU membership confers upon them new or additional duties, standards, and procedures. They perform their controls for both political entities. As national officers, they are also supranational functionaries.

CONCLUSION: SOURCES OF TRUST

A necessary quantum of trust needs to be built between the EU and member states' officials and institutions on the one hand, and the candidates' representatives on the other. The matter of trust can be felt all along the way, as the applicants approach EU membership.

Much has been achieved in this respect since 1993 (during my first employment in the prime minister's office) when a simple mention of EU enlargement provoked stiff responses. Trust, as we know, is built, among other things, upon material foundations. By 1998, when I returned to work in the prime minister's office, a change in Poland's economic image had begun to render it a more credible partner. In the intervening period, Poland's economy had grown very quickly. As a result, even the German notion of *polnische Wirtschaft*, a synonym for low-quality production and poor organization, is now turning to a growing awareness of *polnische Wirtschaftswunder*—the Polish economic miracle.

Economic success supports a partner's belief that one's house is in order, and that one might be able to contribute something to the neighborhood. Trust involves a willingness to share future costs, such as those involved in joining the EU. Some of these costs would have to be borne by Poland in any event—they are simply the costs of transforming Poland into a modern, developed state. Some, however, are simply the costs of accession. The EU external border protection is one of the latter. Poland is ready to bear its share of costs in this case, with some help from the EU. Trust is also about doing things together. We are in fact doing it together—we are raising the standards of the future EU external border, of Poland's border.

In the context of trust, economics and common experience mixes with respect for institutional capacity, effectiveness of rule of law, and even culture and education. With time, practical respect becomes the habit of trust. Indeed time, traditions, and trust are the most precious treasures of the process of integration. And we know that trust, even in sensitive questions such as borders, can arise between EU members and nonmembers. Consider Norway and Iceland, not members of the EU, but included in the Schengen regime as it developed in the Amsterdam Treaty.[21] Thanks to the treaty, those countries, already linked with other Scandinavian EU member states within a free travel area, have gained access to the development of Schengen *acquis*. They may now participate in the EU decision-making process every time their interests (within the Schengen context) are involved. This is a tremendously important relaxation of EU rigidity.

This is what trust means in international affairs. And this is how one can be let in to a well-protected building, just by showing the "border" guards a familiar sign that induces confidence. This may suffice one day to allow a Polish citizen to cross this border. We hope it shall be soon.

NOTES

1. The views expressed in this text are solely personal.

2. It will be either in its first pillar (the European Community) or the third pillar (justice and home affairs cooperation).

3. Sometimes they become different because of other reasons: purchase of land or province, voluntary merger of states or state-like entities, royal marriages, or others. In the history of Poland we witnessed one successful voluntary and significant change of borders. First, the marriage between a Lithuanian prince and a Polish princess allowed for a Jagiellonian dynasty to rule both countries together for some 200 years. Later, the formal union of the two states gave place for the *Rzeczpospolita* (Commonwealth) to emerge and last for another 200 years until the partition of this entity at the end of the eighteenth century.

4. There is no good English equivalent of the French word *acquis,* so widely used in EU jargon. It embraces the letter and the spirit of the treaties, the subsequent legislation, the judgments of the European Court of Justice, and a method of doing things together among the member states. Hence, the *acquis communautaire* refers to the *acquis* of the European Community. The EU *acquis* is composed of three elements: the *acquis communautaire,* the *acquis* in the field of common foreign and security policy, and the *acquis* of justice and home affairs cooperation. The Schengen *acquis* refers to the achievement and the process of establishing of an area without borders for the people of the Schengen Agreement member states.

5. Article 8 of the Protocol states that: "For the purposes of the negotiations for the admission of new Member States into the European Union, the Schengen *acquis* and further measures taken by the institutions within its scope shall be regarded as an *acquis* which must be accepted in full by all States candidates for admission," Conference of the Representatives of the Governments of the Member States, *Treaty of Amsterdam* (Brussels, CONF 4005/ 97, September 23, 1997), TA/P/en 10.

6. Declaration 15 "on the preservation of the level of protection and security provided by the Schengen *acquis"* states simply that: "The Conference agrees that measures to be adopted by the Council, which will have the effect of replacing provisions on the abolition of checks at common borders contained in the 1990 Schengen Convention, should provide at least the same level of protection and security as under the aforementioned provisions of the Schengen Convention," Conference of the Representatives of the Governments of the Member States, *Treaty of Amsterdam,* AF/TA/en 27.

7. The immediate participation in the new EU single currency (euro) was excluded from the very beginning as a precondition for the new members' accession.

8. Conclusions of the European Council in Copenhagen, *Bulletin EC,* 6-1993 (June 1993), I.13, 13.

9. Also the Czech–Polish border is to disappear if both countries join together. Otherwise, this border falls into the third category of intermediate cases.

10. This may apply to the Polish–German border, but also—in a pessimistic scenario— to the Polish–Czech border, if the Czech Republic enters the EU on different terms than Poland does.

11. It is also not a perfect solution for those who would work at the border, for their sense of work, for their ethics, for their stability, for their knowledge of the local particularities and the local people.

12. Data on the length of borders are from the *CIA World Factbook 1998,* Internet version: www.odci.gov/cia/publications/factbook/index.html.

For length of land borders of all the candidate countries from central and eastern Europe and development of the EU external border in two scenarios, see Annex 1.

13. A good collection of stories from traveling across the borders of the former Soviet

bloc countries in the constant "company" of the secret police can be found in: Timothy Garton Ash, *The File. A Personal History* (New York: Vintage, 1998).

14. A British Foreign Office report noted that some 34 million British travel abroad every year. Some 71 percent go to Europe's mainland, of which a high 81 percent go for vacation and tourist purposes. This gives an impressive number of about 20 million British that spend some time on the "continent" every year. Although Britain is a relatively frequently traveling nation in Europe, this seems to be an interesting figure.

15. Central Statistical Office of the Republic of Poland (G.U.S.), *Ruch graniczny i wydatki cudzoziemców w Polsce oraz Polaków za granica w 1998 r. (Border crossings and expenditures of foreigners in Poland and of Poles abroad in 1998)* (Warsaw: G.U.S., 1999), 16.

16. Substantive improvements of the operation of the Polish western border with Germany are also supported by the cross-border and regional cooperation within the EU/CEEC framework. Ironically, from the Polish side it was relatively easy to improve operation of the Polish–German border for historic reasons. Until 1989 this border was the one best protected by the communist regime. For the Poles it was the shortest way to the West, especially to West Berlin. The regime did not pay that much attention to the eastern border: all the regime needed to sufficiently control it was to deny passports to its citizens.

17. Those are: *Odysseus*: training, exchange, and cooperation in asylum, immigration, and the crossing of external borders (including training on identification of false documents); *Oisin*: for police, customs, and other law enforcement officers; *Stop*: for officials dealing with trafficking of persons; *Falcone*: to deal with organized crime.

18. This was also an issue in the case of accession of Spain and Portugal and resulted in several European Court of Justice cases. See Joseph Weiler, *Trading In and With Europe: The Law of the European Union* (Internet version, Fall 1997), http://www.law.wyu.edu/weilerj

19. *Official Journal, The EU Joint Action of 29 June 1998* (OJ L 191, July 7, 1998), 8.

20. There is still more work to be done, however. There is discussion about entrusting the border guards with new police-like competencies. This would allow them to operate over a larger set of aspects of the borders, not simply to work at the linear border. The staffing of the border guards and the local police needs to be increased.

21. Article 6 of the "Protocol Integrating the Schengen *acquis* into the Framework of the European Union" states: "The Republic of Iceland and the Kingdom of Norway shall be associated with the implementation of the Schengen *acquis* and its further development," Amsterdam Treaty, TA/P/en 9.

Annex 1: EU-15   Current Borders between EU Members and Ten Eastern Candidates

Member	with candidate	Length of border
Austria	with Czech Republic	369 kilometers
	with Hungary	366 kilometers
	with Slovakia	91 kilometers
	with Slovenia	330 kilometers
	(subtotal	1,156 kilometers)
Germany	with Czech Republic	646 kilometers
	with Poland	456 kilometers
	(subtotal	1,102 kilometers)
Greece	with Bulgaria	494 kilometers
Italy	with Slovenia	232 kilometers
All members	with all ten candidates	2,977 kilometers

Only four of fifteen EU member states share borders with present eastern candidates. The borders between these member states and these candidates total 2,977 km in length. Although the Russian Federation is not a candidate, it is worth recalling that its border with Finland is 1,313 kilometers. Turkey is not included in this or the following annexes. Source: *CIA World Factbook*, 1998, op. cit.

Annex 2: EU-21   New EU Eastern Borders after Enlargement to Luxembourg Group ("First Wave" of Czech Republic, Estonia, Hungary, Poland, and Slovenia)

Member	with neighbor	Length of new EU border
Czech Republic	with Slovakia	215 kilometers
Estonia	with Latvia	339 kilometers
	with Russia	249 kilometers
	(subtotal	633 kilometers)
Hungary	with Croatia	329 kilometers
	with Romani	443 kilometers
	with Slovakia	515 kilometers
	with Ukraine	103 kilometers
	with Yugoslavia	151 kilometers
	(subtotal	1,541 kilometers)
Poland	with Belarus	605 kilometers
	with Lithuania	91 kilometers
	with Russia	206 kilometers
	with Slovakia	444 kilometers
	with Ukraine	428 kilometers
	(subtotal	1,774 kilometers)
Slovenia	with Croatia	91 kilometers
New members	with eastern states	4,254 kilometers

An enlargement to these five eastern candidates would create 4,254 kilometers of new EU eastern borders. The "Luxembourg Group" also includes Cyprus, so this is an EU-21 variant. Source: ibid.

Annex 3: EU-27   New EU Eastern Borders after Enlargement to All Eastern Candidates ("Second Wave" of Bulgaria, Latvia, Lithuania, Romania, and Slovakia)

Member	with neighbor	Length of new EU border
Bulgaria	with F.Y.R.O.M.	149 kilometers
	with Yugoslavia	318 kilometers
	(subtotal	467 kilometers)
Estonia	with Russia	294 kilometers
Hungary	with Croatia	329 kilometers
	with Ukraine	103 kilometers
	with Yugoslavia	151 kilometers
	(subtotal	538 kilometers)
Latvia	with Belarus	141 kilometers
	with Russia	217 kilometers
	(subtotal	358 kilometers)
Lithuania	with Belarus	502 kilometers
	with Russia	217 kilometers
	(subtotal	729 kilometers)
Poland	with Belarus	605 kilometers
	with Russia	206 kilometers
	with Ukraine	428 kilometers
	(subtotal	1,239 kilometers)
Romania	with Modova	450 kilometers
	with Ukraine	531 kilometers
	(subtotal	981 kilometers)
Slovakia	with Ukraine	90 kilometers
Slovenia	with Croatia	91 kilometers
New members	with eastern states	4,787 kilometers

An enlargement to these all eastern candidates would create 4,787 kilometers of new EU eastern borders. The "second wave" is presumed to include Malta, so this is an EU-27 variant. Source: ibid.

12

The Mobility Money Can Buy: Human Smuggling and Border Control in the European Union

Rey Koslowski[1]

The 1986 Single European Act's mandate for the free movement of persons within the European Union (EU) prompted member states to develop common policies on visas, border controls, asylum application, and illegal migration. In the early 1990s, EU member states intensified their cooperative efforts in response to increasing numbers of refugees and fears that the collapse of communism would unleash mass east-west migration. A subset of EU member states entered the 1990 Schengen Convention, which harmonized asylum application procedures and called for a common visa policy, harmonization of policies to deter illegal migration, and an automated information system to coordinate actions toward individuals denied entry. The 1990 Dublin Convention provided rules for determining which member state had jurisdiction in asylum applications in order to eliminate abuse of member state asylum application processes through multiple application (so-called "asylum shopping"). Title VI of the 1992 Maastricht Treaty formalized the process of member state cooperation in Justice and Home Affairs (JHA) and marked the emergence of an international regime governing migration to the EU. Even though the objective of the intra-EU migration regime has been free movement across borders, member state cooperation on migration from without has focused on restriction. EU member states are restricting migration through cooperation to reduce asylum applications and they have erected a common external border with tougher controls than member states pursued individually.

Human smuggling adds another dimension to the debate on border control by changing the circumstances of international cooperation on immigration policy, border control, and asylum. Although states may be enhancing their capacity to control "unwanted" migration, whether on an individual basis or through cooperation with other states, so has the marketization of illegal migration by organized traffickers increased the capacities of the "unwanted" to migrate. Yes, state power has been demonstrated with migration controls, such as tougher EU asylum policies, which have decreased the numbers of asylum seekers. However, many of those who would have applied for asylum are crossing borders clandestinely with the help of smugglers. Yes, state power is being redeployed on the EU common external frontier in the form of more police at border crossings and deputized carrier personnel at airport checkpoints. However, smugglers are countering these redeployments by taking advantage of humanitarian crises, shifting routes, and using counterfeit documents. The countervailing tactics of migrants and their smugglers may mean that EU member state actions to collectively control their borders may not amount to a net increase in effective state capacity to control migration flows. As Peter Andreas has pointed out (in the introduction to this volume) beefed-up EU border controls may be a show of force that is more symbolic than substantive.

The argument in this chapter proceeds in three steps. The first section examines the debate over state control of borders and the changing dynamics of control in the EU introduced by the increased use of human smugglers by those migrants who are "unwanted" by states. The second section reviews the impact of the Kosovo refugee crisis on human smuggling and EU efforts to limit clandestine and illegal entry. The third section examines the increasing use of counterfeit documents by illegal migrants and the role of smugglers in document fraud. I conclude with a discussion of the meaning of EU cooperation to control borders for member state sovereignty.

STATE CONTROL OF BORDERS AND
THE CHALLENGE OF HUMAN SMUGGLING

The debate about whether or not states could control their borders with respect to unwanted economic migration and asylum seeking has largely been framed in terms of the state as a strong but reluctant border enforcer confronted by individuals who are trying to defy state controls.[2] Responding to the push factors of unemployment and poverty in sending countries and the pull factors of relatively high wages and social benefits in receiving countries, the cost/benefit-calculating individual migrant is the primary unit of economic and certain demographic and sociological analyses of migration.[3] The individual migrant in possession of human rights under international law becomes the protagonist in certain sociological discussions of the decline of state sovereignty and the ascendance of postnational membership.[4] Some political scientists have countered with the primacy of the state in determining migration flows by focusing on increasing state capacities to control borders.[5] Regardless of disciplinary perspective, the contest is framed in terms of the state against the migrant.

The problem with such state-centric approaches to framing this debate is that they tend to miss the role of nonstate actors, which may in fact be used by the state in efforts to extend and increase migration controls.[6] The problem with focusing on migrants as individual economic actors or rights bearers is that it tends toward atomistic depictions of migrants as objects to be controlled by the state or objects of legal contests between the state and international (and supranational) legal authorities that enforce human rights regimes. Depictions of migrants as economic or legal entrepreneurs who manage to take advantage of liberal economic systems or liberal constitutional orders shed the imagery of migrant passivity. However, the field of battle remains the same: the state against the individual migrant.

Moreover, many scholars tend to depict European cooperation to increase external border controls in terms of increasing the effectiveness of member state border controls as measured in decreases in migration—for example, fewer asylum seekers.[7] EU states banded together to stop "asylum shopping" by the individual who had been able to take advantage of member states' lack of communication and divergent policies. In the EU, the battle becomes one of a group of states against the individual migrant.

The problem with these common depictions is that the unwanted migrant is not simply an object of state control and his or her crossing of an international border is not necessarily the product solely of his or her own efforts. Just as states cooperate to control unwanted migration of illegal workers and asylum seekers to the EU, unwanted migrants can cooperate as well to form social networks that facilitate international migration.[8] Just as states deputize private sector actors, such as airlines, to enforce tougher migration controls and thereby change "the gatekeepers" that confront the prospective migrant, migrants are employing nonstate actors, smugglers, to foil restrictions imposed by states,[9] and thereby transform the "gatecrashers" from hapless peasants who may have never traveled abroad to teams of border crossers led by professionals, often using the latest technologies money can buy.

It is very difficult to even begin estimating the extent of contemporary human smuggling worldwide because of its clandestine nature. Nevertheless, cases gathered by researchers associated with the International Organization for Migration (IOM) and regional estimates paint a picture of a recent increase in smuggling.[10] The IOM has estimated that as many as four million people are smuggled across borders on an annual basis with total global 1997 revenues reaching up to $7 billion,[11] up from a 1994 United Nations (UN) estimate of $3.5 billion.[12]

There is very little in the way of official estimates of illegal migration to the EU, let alone estimates of the number of illegal migrants who have been smuggled into the EU. The International Centre for Migration and Policy Development (ICMPD) estimated that in 1993 between 15 and 30 percent of illegal migrant workers and between 20 and 40 percent of non-bona-fide asylum seekers who entered western Europe used smugglers.[13] The ICMPD estimated that in 1998 some 300,000 people entered the EU illegally and that 50 percent (150,000) used smugglers.[14]

There have been increasing numbers of cases of smugglers ferrying migrants from North Africa to Spain, from Albania to Italy, and from Turkey to Greece; of Chinese flown into the EU via Moscow; of individuals from Yugoslavia and Romania entering through the Czech Republic to Germany; and of Russian and east European women trafficked throughout western Europe to work as prostitutes.[15] Recently, increasing numbers of cases have been noted in Germany,[16] the UK, and France,[17] as well as transit countries like Poland and Hungary.[18] It is estimated that tens of thousands of women from Russia and eastern Europe have been smuggled into the EU under false pretenses of finding work as hostesses or dancers only to have their passports taken upon arrival, to be forced into prostitution to work off their smuggler's fee and, ultimately, to find themselves in debt bondage situations.[19]

Perhaps the largest flows have been those of Kurds and Kosovo Albanians fleeing conflicts within their countries. Between July 1997 and January 1998, some 3,000 people, mostly Kurds from northern Iraq and southwestern Turkey, paid smugglers $2,000 to $8,000 for passage to Italy by boat.[20] As the conflict between the Kosovo Liberation Army and the Yugoslav police intensified during 1998, increasing numbers of Kosovo Albanians were apprehended while trying to enter the EU illegally. Having accepted the bulk of those fleeing the Bosnian civil war, Germany, as well as Austria, refused to provide temporary protection to the Kosovo Albanians up until after the March 1999 NATO bombing of Yugoslavia and the accompanying refugee crisis.[21] Faced with a low probability of finding a safe haven within the EU by seeking temporary protection or asylum, increasing numbers of Kosovo Albanians turned to smugglers to get them into the EU, particularly to Germany,[22] which, together with Switzerland, already hosted most of the EU's population of Kosovo Albanians. Of the 12,000 persons apprehended while being smuggled into Germany in 1998, the largest group (between 4,000 and 5,000) was Kosovo Albanians.[23] Of the 4,918 persons apprehended while attempting to enter Switzerland in the first half of 1998 (including asylum seekers), 1,594 were Kosovars. In the first half of 1999, 7,851 foreigners were intercepted at the border, of which 6,350 were identified as Kosovars.[24]

The sophistication and scale of smuggling operations is exemplified by the "Pilsener Group," a Kosovo Albanian gang operating in the Czech Republic. Markus Leitl, chief investigator of the German border guard at Waldmuenchen, notes that "They have cellular phones with network cards, they routinely replace personnel, they have fast cars, night vision equipment and excellent maps."[25] Such smugglers based in the Czech Republic guarantee a successful crossing, and if customers are intercepted at the German border and turned back, they repeatedly receive the smugglers' service without additional cost until they are successful. It is estimated that the Pilsener group reaped millions of marks in profits by smuggling some 40,000 of their refugee compatriots through the Czech Republic into Germany.[26]

Despite the fact that many of these smuggled Kurds and Kosovo Albanians were genuine refugees fleeing for their lives, the reception of these asylum seekers had not been positive largely because of perceptions based on high-profile cases that associated them with criminal activity and terrorism. The Kurds have been associated with the revolutionary Kurdish Workers' Party (PKK), which several EU member states categorize as a "terrorist organization." This is partly due to increasing evidence that the PKK itself is involved in human smuggling and uses the proceeds to support its activities. For example, Italian prosecutors collected evidence pointing to a PKK smuggling operation that over the course of several years moved approximately 2,000 migrants per month into Italy and then into its fellow EU member states to the north.[27] In the media, Kosovo Albanian refugees and migrants have been associated with the Albanian criminal organizations that have become prominent in Europe's drug trade and forged alliances with Italian criminal organizations, such as Sacra Corona Unita,[28] as well as the Kosovo Liberation Army (KLA), which was reported to have funded its operations with contributions from and involuntary taxation of the Albanian diaspora as well as drug trafficking.[29] Such widespread negative public perceptions of Kurds and Albanians supported efforts by policymakers to treat their cases in terms of security threats.

Although human smuggling prompted EU action as early as 1993 when the EU's JHA Council agreed to a set of recommendations for member states to combat trafficking,[30] JHA ministers have recently refocused their attention on human smuggling, particularly on the transportation of Turkish and Iraqi Kurds to Italian shores by Turkish and Italian criminal organizations and the trafficking in women and children by Russian Mafiyas. In November 1996, JHA ministers adopted a joint action initiated by the Commission to establish an information exchange between officials responsible for combating trade in human beings and the sexual exploitation of children.[31] The objectives of this joint action were partially realized in an October 1997 Conference of Ministers on the Prevention of Illegal Migration. EU and other ministers involved in the so-called "Budapest Process" dealing with illegal migration as well as representatives from relevant international organizations adopted recommendations in areas including "harmonization of legislation to combat trafficking in aliens" and "linkage in trafficking in aliens and other forms of organized crime."[32] On January 26, 1998, EU foreign ministers adopted a forty-six-point plan directed at reducing the numbers of Kurds arriving illegally in the EU.[33] JHA ministers took up the action plan at their January 29–30 informal summit meeting in Birmingham where Germany pressed for implementation of the plan and expressed fears that Kurds arriving in Italy would easily move on to Germany.[34]

The January Action Plan aims to reduce the entrance of Turkish and Iraqi Kurds described as "illegal refugees" as well as "illegal immigrants." The Council stated that these migrants "almost always make use of traffickers, of whom the majority appear to be part of organized crime networks, with contacts in the EU."[35] Only three of the forty-six points were devoted to "ensuring that humanitarian aid makes an effective difference," while most points were focused on more restrictive measures—six on "effective application of asylum procedures"; six on "preventing abuse of asylum procedures"; and twenty on "combating illegal immigration" most of which were devoted to enhanced border control and effective removal.[36]

Such cooperation to tighten controls may potentially exacerbate the problem they were designed to combat. Very simply: as more restrictive policies increase the obstacles to crossing borders, migrants increasingly turn to smugglers rather than pay the growing costs of unaided attempts that prove unsuccessful. For example, Czech officials noticed an increase in human smuggling that was correlated to stricter visa policies implemented in 1994.[37] The more applicant states try to raise their border controls to meet EU standards, the greater the incentives for increased human smuggling. The vicious circle continues as increased cases of smuggling lead to pressure from the EU on applicant states to toughen their border controls.[38]

Illegal migrant workers are not the only clienteles of human smugglers. As EU member states have adopted more stringent asylum policies and increased their cooperation to restrict multiple applications and abuses, the number of "asylum seekers" has decreased.[39] On the other hand, the number of cases in which people fleeing civil wars who use the services of human smugglers appears to have increased. For example, Kurds fleeing civil war in Iraq often find themselves unable to get official passports from Baghdad; they give up on going through regular asylum application channels; they purchase false documents that are readily available in northern Iraq; and they pay thousands of dollars to the growing numbers of Turkish smugglers for the short, but dangerous, trip to Greece or Italy.[40] Similarly, the same substitution effect has become increasingly pronounced in the case of Kosovo Albanians.

Whether or not stepped-up border controls and stricter visa polices will reduce human smuggling, however, is very unclear because of the inherent dilemma of control. If tougher border controls increase smugglers' fees beyond that which their customers are willing to pay, controls may decrease smuggling. However, if potential migrants are willing to pay the additional costs while at the same time stiffer border controls prompt more migrants to enter into the market, border controls will most likely increase the profits of human smuggling and entice new entrants into the business. Moreover, if illegal economic migrants are willing to pay higher prices and incur debts to pay smugglers, "illegal refugees" who are in fact fleeing for their lives may be even more willing to do so.

THE KOSOVO CRISIS AND NATO INTERVENTION

With the NATO air strikes against Yugoslavia and the Kosovo refugee crisis, human smuggling to the EU entered a new phase that highlights the difficulties encountered by EU member states as they attempt to restrict migration and tighten border controls. As mentioned above, large numbers of Kosovo Albanians used smugglers to get into the EU and the number of cases grew during 1998 and early 1999 in conjunction with increasing Serb operations directed at villages suspected of harboring members of the Kosovo Liberation Army and sporadic massacres of civilians. Without temporary protection status, smuggled refugees who were apprehended were often held in detention or returned to transit countries.[41]

Determined to avoid opening the door to large-scale migration via temporary protection, most EU member states refused to extend temporary protection to

Kosovo Albanians even after highly publicized massacres of civilians. When NATO began bombing, Serb militias and police began systematic large-scale ethnic cleansing, and Macedonia threatened to close its borders to refugees if they did not have a second country of asylum to go to, several EU member states relented and announced that they would provide temporary protection. Germany agreed to take in 40,000; Greece 5,000; Italy, the Netherlands, and Ireland several thousand each. An April 7, 1999, JHA Council meeting reaffirmed that displaced persons who were in need of protection should receive it within the region. It argued that long-term accommodation outside of area would only consolidate displacement and help Serbian leaders achieve their objectives of cleansing Kosovo of Albanians. Finally, the council cited stress on receiving states in the region, such as Macedonia, as a justification for individual member states to offer temporary protection. By the end of April, European states allocated a total of 85,000 slots for the entry of Kosovo refugees.[42] When combined with pledges made by the United States (20,000) and Turkey (20,000), the total number of slots for refugees exceeded 125,000. Still, this was a small fraction of the 800,000 Kosovars who had already been driven from Kosovo and remained in the region, primarily in Albania and Macedonia.

The circumstances of smuggling Kosovo Albanians were transformed by the NATO military action in several ways. First, as the refugee crisis quickly melted resistance among EU member states to extend temporary protection, Kosovo Albanians could have entered the EU through regular asylum channels and should therefore not have needed the smugglers. Second, the European media image of smuggled Kosovo Albanians changed. Smuggled "illegal refugees" associated with criminal organizations suddenly were depicted as genuine refugees fleeing ethnic cleansing compared to the Holocaust. The KLA became viewed as "freedom fighters" who were legitimate representatives of the Kosovars.

Although one might think that the extension of temporary protection and the outpouring of public sympathy for Kosovo refugees should have eliminated the need for Kosovo Albanians to turn to smugglers in order to get into the EU, this was not the case. To begin with, the airlift evacuation was focused on relieving the pressure placed on Macedonia. Albania steadfastly kept its borders open and argued against removal of refugees from its territory. Hence, the option to be evacuated to the EU (or other countries) was not necessarily given to the bulk of the Kosovars who were in Albania. Moreover, although tens of thousands of refugees were flown out of Macedonia, receiving governments chose which refugees could go, and the bureaucratic red tape contributed to a situation in which some evacuation flights departed with a fifth of their seats left empty.[43]

Rather than being put out of business by the NATO intervention and the changing status of their Kosovar customers, Albanian smugglers expanded their operations. Many Kosovo refugees in Albania, who decided to leave without having to endure the application for evacuation to the EU from the camps, made their way to Vlore, the primary embarkation point for the speedboats that cross the Adriatic to Italy. Smugglers plied their services in Albanian cities and even in the refugee camps. Indeed, Albanian gangsters even posed as aid workers, approached young girls and women with fake documents, and offered to get them into "teacher training programs" in Italy. Some young women disappeared from the camps.[44] An Albanian smuggler depicted the smuggling market:

> Kosovars pay 1,000 German marks [DM] each from the border at Kukes to Italy, all inclusive. The Albanians pay DM 1,200. From here, from Vlore, the Kosovars pay DM 500 and the Albanians pay DM 700. . . . The Kosovars are already here, and there are stacks of them. Once they cross over, they get dumped wherever it is convenient to dump them, even in the sea before reaching the shore. There is no need to fix a rendezvous with the Italian taxi drivers. There is more work involved in ferrying the Albanians, and then there is the cost of the taxis.[45]

Extensions of temporary protection to Kosovo Albanians meant that smugglers could cut back on the services provided and take fewer risks on the Italian side of the Adriatic. At the same time, the number of customers grew partly because temporary protection eliminated refugees' fears of deportations in the event of capture. Once in Italy, many Kosovars make their way, with or without the assistance of smugglers, to join relatives further north in Germany and Switzerland. Even if they were stopped at or near the Italian border, they were not returned to Kosovo as had previously often been the case. For example, in the beginning of April, France granted residency permits to twenty-seven Kosovars who sneaked across the Italian-French border and President Chirac declared that France would grant asylum to Kosovars who were driven out by ethnic cleansing.[46] Finally, since Serb militia routinely seized identity documents from fleeing Kosovo Albanians, it is difficult for EU authorities who are not fluent in Albanian dialects to differentiate Kosovo Albanians from Albanian nationals, thereby enabling smugglers to take advantage of the loosening of controls prompted by the humanitarian crisis to move Albanians as well as Kosovars.

Although it is not clear how many refugees have been smuggled to Italy since the bombing began, an Organization for Security and Cooperation in Europe (OSCE) observer estimated that as many as ten boatloads of forty or more left Vlore each night.[47] Aid workers in the Puglia region of Italy across the Adriatic from Albania estimated that some 1,000 per day made it to the Italian coast in the last week of April 1999.[48] It has been estimated that Albanian smugglers made DM 10 million by smuggling Kosovo refugees in the first few weeks after NATO bombing began.

These changing circumstances of the smuggling of Kosovo Albanians make it increasingly difficult for EU member states to combat human smuggling, at least of Kosovars, despite the resolve demonstrated by EU action plans and stepped-up border controls. In 1998, Kosovo Albanians were already the largest group to be smuggled into Germany, the primary target country for migrant trafficking into the EU. Hence, it is likely that in 1999 Kosovo Albanians will constitute an even greater share of the customers of those who smuggle migrants into the EU.

With Serbian withdrawal from Kosovo, it would appear that Kosovo Albanians would no longer need the services of the smugglers. Despite the massive and rapid return of the refugees from Albania and Macedonia to Kosovo, the widespread destruction of homes and uncertain security future of Kosovo may lead a significant portion of the refugees, especially those in the EU, to think twice about returning.[49] Moreover, the EU quickly announced a reconstruction fund for Kosovo to the tune of $500 million per year for three years. However, much of the money for rebuilding Kosovar homes will most likely come from where it has in the recent past—Kosovo Albanians working abroad. According to a 1998 International Monetary Fund (IMF) estimate, Albanian migrant workers—many of whom are in the EU illegally—sent home remittances to the tune of $1 million per day.[50] Moreover, given that Britain and other EU member states stated their refusal to provide funds to rebuild Serbia as long as Milosevic is in power, it is anticipated that "hundreds of thousands" of Serbs will go abroad in search of work.[51] Displaced Kosovo Serbs have joined displaced Kosovo Albanians among the destitute and desperate to whom the smugglers' market their services. For example, in July 1999 the number of asylum seekers in Germany from Yugoslavia who were not ethnic Albanians was nearly twice as much as that of July 1998.[52] If EU member states do not provide rapid and sufficient financial assistance to Kosovo and Serbia, there will be pressure for Kosovo Albanian and Serb families to institute their own foreign aid programs by sending one or more family member abroad. EU member states may choose to tolerate such illegal migration for the sake of lowering the need for official foreign aid (as the United States did for Central Americans in the aftermath of Hurricane Mitch). If not, one can be sure that smugglers will be waiting for the migrants.

EU cooperation to toughen asylum policies led asylum seekers into the arms of smugglers and prompted the EU to step up efforts to combat the smuggling of "illegal refugees." Although the EU has increased cooperation to combat smuggling of such "illegal refugees," refugee crises that trigger humanitarian intervention can quickly neutralize such efforts by reclassifying certain unwanted "illegal refugees" into bona fide refugees who are greeted at the EU's external border with offers of shelter and assistance. Moreover, once temporary protection is offered to those refugees who use smugglers to get to the EU, it reduces the number of services provided by smugglers necessary for successful entry. By offering refugees a greater probability of entry at a discounted price, smugglers can take advantage of refugee crises to expand their operations at the expense of EU efforts to control clandestine migration.

STATE POWER AND DUELING NONSTATE ACTORS: HIRED SMUGGLERS VERSUS THE STATE'S DEPUTIES

While increasingly effective EU cooperation to restrict unwanted migration prompts human smuggling, and refugee crises become opportunities for smugglers to poke holes in increasingly restrictive asylum policies, the expansion of the human smuggling business may counter European states' outsourcing of migration control functions to private-sector actors such as airlines. By means of imposing fines on airlines that transport people without proper documentation, states have compelled airlines to essentially extend border controls to the check-in counters and gates of airports in sending and transit countries.[53] Document checks by airline employees may have stopped many would-be migrants from ever getting close to an airplane, but human smugglers are changing the equation by shifting routes and providing fraudulent documents to the migrants that states are trying to keep out.

As Salt and Stein point out, as the trafficking business expands, the smugglers, rather than the migrants and asylum seekers, make more decisions regarding where their customers actually go.[54] Part of the smugglers' success in getting migrants across borders is the smugglers' ability to change routes and destinations in order to overcome obstacles that states have placed in their way. In a sense, the traffickers gather and process information about the weak links in terms of transportation systems, border controls, and liberal visa and asylum policies, and then they provide it to their customers. Therefore, shifts in the flows of illegal migration via air travel have accelerated and those flows move to where it is easiest to gain entry using false documents.

Smugglers may actually provide false documents to clandestine migrants as part of a "package deal," much like a tour operator. For example, Kurds pay $6,000 in Istanbul for passage and a fraudulent passport that will get them to Italy via Albania. There are similar packages available from Albania offered by a smuggler known as Shaqir. While the poor pay $600 for a speedboat to Italy, those who can pay $4,000 can purchase a "luxury" package that includes airfare (to Paris even), a passport with a valid visa, and bribes for officials at the airport. With the $2,000 "standard" package to Italy, the passport must be returned upon arrival to one of the smugglers who ride along. Shaqir uses a passport with a valid visa three to four times by replacing the photo until the damage becomes noticeable.[55]

Smugglers may also simply inform the would-be clandestine migrant as to where he or she may purchase false documents, much as a travel agent may provide information to tourists about where and how to get visas. The smuggler is an intermediary who has both the information that the migrant needs as well as the access to the counterfeiters' target market. In this way, counterfeiters can more effectively (and perhaps more quietly) market their products than if they attempted to reach the pool of would-be clandestine migrants directly by themselves. The division of labor enables expert counterfeiters to devote more resources and time to making better false documents. Smugglers, therefore, help to increase demand for counterfeit documents among clandestine migrants who might not otherwise have used them. They also provide expert counterfeiters easier (and potentially safer) access to the illegal migrant market, thereby encouraging production of more fraudulent travel documents.

The EU is developing a new European passport, which will include state-of-the-art features such as an optical reading zone, holograms, and special textured topographical printing. Nevertheless, "The most secure document in the world can be counterfeited or altered. The true test of the security of a document is how difficult it is for a forger to simulate successfully the genuine to the point that it can fool those tasked with inspecting it."[56] Document security is a function of the quality of the document, whether or not that document is attached to a database and the quality of inspection. While the growing smuggling business has prompted the development of higher quality counterfeits, increasing reliance on nonstate personnel to inspect travel documents has increased the opportunity for successful evasion of border controls.

Countering document fraud with high technology has its limits. Counterfeiters need only acquire the same computer technology as the state.

> (D)ocuments are effectively counterfeited using many of the same techniques that are used to create the corresponding genuine documents. . . . A scanned image of a genuine security document can be then endlessly manipulated using software, e.g. Corel or Adobe Photoshop. The computer savvy manipulator can also duplicate bar codes, magnetic stripes, background printings, and special fonts. These images can then be printed or sent around the world as email attachments.[57]

Ironically, documents produced using new computer technologies are often easier to counterfeit than less sophisticated documents produced with handcrafted plates. Moreover, known defects in authentic documents produced by lower tech means are often signifiers of authenticity—in other words, defect-free counterfeits may be "too good" in some cases. Finally, it is unlikely that high technology will substitute for the inspection of documents by humans, especially in all places that the documents might be used.[58]

Application of new technologies often only increases the price of reproducing a document rather than making it foolproof. In the face of such increasing costs of counterfeiting, the growing market and influx of cash from human smuggling has subsidized the research and development of the counterfeit document business and increased its sophistication. It is also important to remember that even though it might cost a great deal to produce the first high-quality counterfeit of a new more secure document and discourage its production, the next copy costs much less and the profits on subsequent copies help amortize the initial investment to produce the first.[59] In this way, counterfeiters, working in conjunction with smugglers, counter one technological advance in document production after the other.

As the expansion of the human smuggling business promotes migrant use of ever better fraudulent documents, it calls into question the effectiveness of states' extension of migration controls through document checks by airline personnel. In general, the more that document inspection and verification is devolved to nonexpert personnel, the greater the chances that fraudulent documents will not be detected and the greater the likelihood that migrants using them will be successful in evading migration controls. It is important to remember that fraudulent documents often only need to be good enough to board aircraft. Migrants may destroy fraudulent documents and flush them down the toilet and then apply for asylum once they arrive in the target country. Indeed, migrants have even boarded planes using identity and travel documents with the names of countries such as British Honduras, Burma, Rhodesia, South Vietnam, and Zanzibar. The production and purchase of such documents is perfectly legal since the purported issuing authorities no longer exist as states.

Receiving countries may require airlines to take such migrants back to the country of embarkation. However, the airline may find itself in a catch-22 situation because that country may not accept a returnee without an established identity and travel documents. Since it is well known that when confronted with such situations, many receiving countries with liberal asylum procedures have, in the end, allowed asylum seekers to remain until their cases are adjudicated, the false document that got the migrant past an airline employee often also gets the migrant into the target country. Although the stay may only be as long as the asylum application, appeals, and deportation processes last, these processes can take up to several years in many countries. Moreover, if the smuggled asylum seeker is not detained until deportation, he or she may simply vanish into the underground economy.

Given that virtually any document can be reproduced for the right price, the only secure document is one that is linked to a database and that document is only as secure as the database to which it is linked. Document fraud could be virtually eliminated by identity document systems in which a biometic identifier (e.g., hand geometry or facial recognition) that is stored in a database can be called up by a border guard and compared to a scan of the bearer of a document. A future EU passport with biometric identifiers has been envisioned. The problem, of course, is that however much continental Europeans may accept registration with state authorities and use of national identity cards, European norms regarding personal data protection militate against building such a database of biometric identifiers, let alone establishing a requirement that travel documents include fingerprints. Moreover, for the delegation of document inspection to carriers to be effective in using such secure document systems, the biometric databases maintained by the government would have to be opened to private corporations—an unimaginable proposal given existing norms and laws governing personal data protection.

CONCLUSIONS

EU member states have taken cooperation on migration beyond that of any other group of states in the world. This cooperation and the integration of member state migration policymaking into supranational institutional frameworks can be viewed as one more issue area in which member state sovereignty is being transformed in the context of policy formation at the European level. EU cooperation can also be a means through which member states more effectively control their territorial borders and thereby reassert sovereignty with respect to "unwanted" migration. Hence, a member state may actually sacrifice its sovereignty vis-à-vis the states with which it is cooperating in order to exercise sovereignty over its borders.[60]

The collective exertion of state power by EU member states to restrict illegal migration and non-bona-fide asylum seeking has further implications for member state sovereignty. On the one hand, if the recent EU activity to combat human smuggling is any indication, the policy discourse in the EU linking integration of migration policy to public concerns with personal security facilitates the formation of a political dynamic that may make major future transfers of sovereignty to the EU increasingly possible.[61] On the other hand, human smuggling, particularly of asylum seekers and in the context of humanitarian intervention, calls into question the effectiveness of the redeployment of state power to the EU and nonstate actors.

Gallya Lahav argues that the transfer of policymaking to the EU by member states does not indicate that "states are 'losing control' or abdicating sovereignty. European states are increasingly delegating policy elaboration and implementation to third party actors—especially the European Union itself—as a means to increase policy effectiveness."[62] Lahav is correct: the delegation of border control functions to the EU and nonstate actors is not necessarily a sign of the decline of state capacity, and enlisting nonstate personnel to assist in border control may simply be thought of as a redeployment of state power. This argument depends, however, on whether the lifting of internal border controls while fortifying common external borders is truly effective when smugglers are able to shift flows of illegal migrants to the most permeable points along that external border. It also depends on whether nonstate actors such as deputized carriers are actually effective. If such redeployment of state power amounts to increasing reliance on non-expert document examiners to detect increasingly sophisticated document fraud, it may be more a matter of dereliction of duty on the part of the state rather than an efficacious redeployment of power that increases state capacity.

Although the practice of human smuggling is age-old, the study of its policy implications is in its infancy. The EU systematically gathers and reports asylum-seeker statistics, but EU-wide statistics on illegal migration or apprehensions of the smuggled and smugglers along the common external border have yet to appear. Declining numbers of asylum applications demonstrate the effectiveness of EU cooperation on asylum policy to reduce one form of "unwanted" migration. Until better evidence can be generated, we can only point to the redeployment of state power to combat illegal migration. Whether or not this redeployment is effective or merely symbolic is not clear. Whether or not cooperation within the EU enables member states to more effectively control their borders and thereby reassert one dimension of their sovereignty through such cooperation also remains an open question.

NOTES

1. For supporting the revision of this chapter, I thank the Center of International Studies at Princeton University.

2. Wayne A. Cornelius, Philip L. Martin, and James F. Hollifield, *Controlling Immigration: A Global Perspective* (Stanford: Stanford University Press, 1994).

3. Brinley Thomas, *Migration and Economic Growth* (Cambridge: Cambridge University Press, 1973); Sidney Weintraub and Chandler Stolp, "The Implications of Growing Economic Interdependence," in *The Future of Migration* (Paris: OECD, 1987); Richard Layard, Oliver Blanchard, Rudiger Dornbusch, and Paul Krugman, *East–West Migration: The Alternatives* (Cambridge, Mass.: The MIT Press, 1992); Douglas Massey et al., *Worlds in Motion* (Oxford: Clarendon, 1998).

4. Yasemin Nuhoglu Soysal, *Limits of Citizenship: Migrants and Postnational Membership in Europe* (Chicago: University of Chicago Press, 1994); David Jacobson, *Rights Across Borders: Immigration and the Decline of Citizenship* (Baltimore: Johns Hopkins University Press, 1996).

5. Gary P. Freeman, "Can Liberal States Control Unwanted Migration?" in Mark J. Miller, ed., *Strategies for Immigration Control, Annals of the American Academy of Political and Social Science*, vol. 534 (May 1994): 17–30.

6. Gallya Lahav and Virginie Guiraudon, "The Devolution of Immigration Regimes in Europe," presented at the European Community Studies Association Meeting, Seattle, Washington, May 29–June 1, 1997; Gallya Lahav, "Immigration and the State: The Devolution and Privatization of Immigration Control in the EU," *Journal of Ethnic and Migration Studies*, vol. 24, no. 1 (1998): 675–694.

7. Myself included: Rey Koslowski, "EU Migration Regimes: Established and Emergent," in Christian Joppke, ed. *Challenge to the Nation-State: Immigration in Western Europe and the United States* (Oxford: Oxford University Press, 1998).

8. See, for example, Douglas Massey et al., "Theories of International Migration," *Population and Development Review*, vol. 19, no. 3 (1993): 431–466.

9. Lahav, "Immigration and the State," 680.

10. John Salt and Jeremy Stein, "Migration as a Business: The Case of Trafficking," *International Migration*, vol. 35, no. 4, (1997): 467–494; Bimal Ghosh, *Huddled Masses and Uncertain Shores: Insights into Irregular Migration* (Doredrecht: Kluwer Law International, 1998).

11. IOM, "Trafficking in Migrants: IOM Policy and Activities," at: www.iom.ch/IOM/Trafficking/IOM_Policy.html.

12. IOM, "Organized Crime Moves into Migrant Trafficking," *Trafficking in Migrants, Quarterly Bulletin*, no. 11 (June 1996).

13. Jonas Widgren, "Multilateral Co-Operation to Combat Trafficking in Migrants and the Role of International Organizations" (Vienna: International Centre for Migration and Policy Development, 1994).

14. Mario Kaiser, "Spediteure des Elends," *Die Zeit*, September 9, 1999.

15. IOM, "Organized Crime Moves into Migrant Trafficking," *Trafficking in Migrants, Quarterly Bulletin*, no.11 (June 1996); IOM, *Trafficking in Migrants, Quarterly Bulletin*, no. 17 (January 1998); Global Survival Network, *Crime and Servitude: An Expose of the Traffic in Women for Prostitution from the Newly Independent States* (Washington, D.C., 1997).

16. "More Human Smuggling Across the Eastern Border," *Migration News Sheet*, no. 186/98–09 (September 1998): 5; Karin Dalka, "Smuggling of Human Beings Experiencing Upswing," *Frankfurter Rundschau*, March 12, 1999.

17. IOM, "Organized Crime Moves into Migrant Trafficking," *Trafficking in Migrants, Quarterly Bulletin*, no. 11 (June 1996).

18. "Interior Minister Reports Crime Rise in 1997," *PAP Polish Press Agency*, February 18, 1998; "Conference on Border Control," MTI Hungarian News Agency, April 22, 1998.

19. IOM, *Trafficking and Prostitution: The Growing Exploitation of Migrant Women from Central and Eastern Europe* (Geneva: IOM, 1995); Global Survival Network, *Crime and Servitude*.

20. IOM, *Trafficking in Migrants, Quarterly Bulletin*, no. 17 (January 1998).

21. "Germany Cannot Receive Kosovo Albanians," *Migration News Sheet*, no. 186/98–09 (September 1998): 12; "No Temporary Protection for Kosovo Albanians," *Migration News Sheet*, No.186/98–09 (September 1998): 10.

22. "More Human Smuggling Across the Eastern Border," *Migration News Sheet*, no. 186/98–09 (September 1998): 5; "Large Smuggling Ring Broken Up," *Migration News Sheet*, no. 186/98–09 (September 1998): 6.

23. Dalka, "Smuggling of Human Beings Experiencing Upswing."

24. "Increasing Number of Persons Arrested for Clandestine Entry," *Migration News Sheet*, no. 197/99–08 (August 1999): 6.

25. Kaiser, "Spediteure des Elends," author's translation.

26. Kaiser, "Spediteure des Elends."

27. Diego Pistacchi, "PKK Leaders Sentenced for Smuggling Illegal Immigrants," *Il Giornale* (Milan), January 4, 1999.

28. Frederika Randall, "Italy and Its Immigrants: Refugees from the Balkan Peninsula," *The Nation*, May 31, 1999.

29. Roger Boyes and Eske Wright, "Drugs Money Linked to the Kosovo Rebels," *The Times* (London), March 24, 1999.

30. Justice and Home Affairs, Council of the European Union, "Recommendation on Trafficking in Human Beings," Council Press Release 10550/93 of November 9 and 30, 1993.

31. Justice and Home Affairs, Joint Action 96/700/JHA at: europa.eu.int/comm/sg/scadplus/leg/

32. "Conference of Ministers on the Prevention of Illegal Migration," *Migration News Sheet*, no. 177/97–12 (December 1997): 3–6.

33. "Influx of Kurds Prompts Adoption of a 46-Point Action Plan," *Migration News Sheet*, no. 179/98–2 (February 1998): 4–6.

34. "Justice and Home Affairs: EU Struggles to Define CEEC Strategy," *European Report*, no. 2288, February 4, 1998.

35. Quoted in "Influx of Kurds Prompts Adoption of a 46-Point Action Plan," *Migration News Sheet*, no. 179/98–02 (February 1998): 4.

36. "Influx of Kurds Prompts Adoption of a 46-Point Action Plan," 4–6.

37. Paul J. Smith, "Smuggling People into Rich Countries is a Growth Industry," *International Herald Tribune*, June 28, 1996.

38. David Rocks, "Europe's Would-Be Elite Struggle with Porous Borders," *The Chicago Tribune*, September 10, 1998.

39. Eurostat, "Asylum-Seekers in Europe 1985–1995," *Statistics in Focus, Population and Social Conditions*, no. 1, 1996.

40. Jon Hemming, "Alien Smuggling in Turkey," Reuters, November 21, 1997.

41. "Germany Deports 75 Kosovo Albanian Refugees," Reuters, October 18, 1998.

42. "UNHCR Urges Non-European Countries to Take Kosovo Refugees as the Refugee

Crisis in the FRY of Macedonia Worsens," Press Release, United Nations High Commissioner for Refugees, Geneva, April 30, 1999.

43. Daniel McGory, "Scandal of the Empty Seats on Mercy Flights," *The Times* (London), May 26, 1999.

44. Janine di Giovanni, "Refugees Face a New Terror," *The Times* (London), May 4, 1999.

45. Quoted in Fabrizio Ravelli, "Albanian Crime Chief Views Refugee Smuggling Methods," *La Republica* (Rome), May 1, 1999.

46. "France Takes in Border-Crossing Kosovo Refugees," Reuters, April 7, 1999.

47. Carol J. Williams, "Traders in People Prey on Refugees Stuck in Albania," *Los Angeles Times*, May 24, 1999.

48. Randall, "Italy and Its Immigrants."

49. See, for example, "France: Very Few Kosovars Have Volunteered to Return to Their Home Region" *Migration News Sheet*, no. 198/99–09 (September 1999): 9.

50. "Italy: New Law, Albania," *Migration News*, vol. 5, no. 3 (March 1998).

51. "Rebuilding the Balkans," *Economist*, June 19, 1999.

52. "Number of Serb Asylum-Seekers Has Doubled," *Migration News Sheet*, no. 198/99–09 (September 1999): 10.

53. Lahav, "Immigration and the State," 684–686.

54. Salt and Stein, "Migration as a Business."

55. Kaiser, "Spediteure des Elends."

56. James Hesse, "Testimony of James Hesse, Chief Intelligence Office, Forensic Document Laboratory, Immigration and Naturalization Service," House Judiciary Committee Subcommittee on Immigration and Claims Hearings, July 22, 1999, at: www.house.gov/judiciary/hess0722.htm

57. Larry F. Stewart, "Statement of Larry F. Stewart, Assist. Laboratory Director, U.S. Secret Service," House Judiciary Committee Subcommittee on Immigration and Claims Hearings, July 22, 1999, at: www.house.gov/judiciary/stew0722.htm.

58. These points were made by staff members of the Immigration and Naturalization Service (INS) Forensic Document Laboratory, March 29, 1999.

59. Staff members, INS Forensic Document Laboratory, 1999.

60. See Koslowski, "EU Migration Regimes."

61. Rey Koslowski, "Personal Security, State Sovereignty and the Deepening and Widening of European Cooperation in Justice and Home Affairs," in Virginie Guiraudon and Christian Joppke, eds., *Controlling a New Migration World* (forthcoming).

62. Lahav, "Immigration and the State," 675–676.

13

Conclusion: The Wall around the West

Timothy Snyder

As the twenty-first century begins, as the Cold War recedes into memory, as economic integration and the process of "globalization" advances, what is the significance of borders dividing rich states from poor? The authors in this volume have addressed this question not by speculating about the implications of these trends, but by attending to state policies in Europe and North America that seek to control the movement of people across borders. Taken together, their findings provide an unambiguous conclusion. As the military and economic functions of borders lose some of their significance, the traditional police function of borders has been reasserted in both Europe and North America. As the instant transmission of images across borders becomes a cliché, and the free trade of goods becomes more of a reality, human beings who have not the good fortune to be citizens of rich states are confronted with more barriers in their attempts to cross borders. As rich states seek to control the movement of such people, they confirm and reinforce traditional state territorial functions. This final chapter will first summarize these findings with regard to Europe and North America, and then suggest what the wall around the West means for the future of state power and the idea of globalization.

THE WALL WITHIN NORTH AMERICA

Although not everyone will find at the U.S.–Mexico border, as do Gustavo Mohar and María-Elena Alcaraz, an "image of a region at war," the evidence of mounting U.S. state power is unmistakable. Mohar and Alcaraz, diplomats themselves, note that immigration is now the subject of "formal conversations" between the Mexican and U.S. governments, which is to say that it has increasingly become a subject of traditional diplomacy. Foreign policy is a traditional prerogative of the state, and

219

the categorization of immigration as a matter of foreign policy is a clear signal of its perceived importance. Meanwhile, the evidence of heightened policing of the U.S.–Mexico border is overwhelming. Joseph Nevins's finding of "historically unparalleled levels of law enforcement" is justified by the facts. As he points out, both the budget of the Immigration and Naturalization Service (INS) and the number of its agents working at the U.S.–Mexico border more than doubled during the 1990s. The INS is now the most heavily armed law-enforcement organ of the U.S. government. In his careful study, David Spener notes that INS agents and others charged with border control "appear to be diligently attempting to reach their objective of preventing the unauthorized entry into sovereign territory." As he notes, the number of individuals sentenced for immigration crimes increased by more than a factor of six during the 1990s. The absurd result is that the border town of Del Rio, Texas (population 30,705) sees more felony indictments yearly than does Houston (population 1,630,553).

Opinions are divided as to the ultimate effectiveness of heightened controls along the southwest U.S. border. Along the southeast border there is less room for disagreement. As Christopher Mitchell demonstrates in his study of the Caribbean, U.S. efforts since 1980 have "dramatically curtailed illegal migration from two major migrant-source nations, Cuba and Haiti." In Mitchell's closely reasoned account, enhancing the traditional police function of the border (in the form of increased Coast Guard patrols), along with the categorization of immigration as an issue of state security (prompting sustained diplomatic efforts and the deployment of U.S. military forces in 1994), proved very effective in reducing migration. Mitchell's concludes that the success of such efforts is a function of the cooperation of source countries. As a general proposition, this is confirmed by the European cases discussed in the second half of the volume.

Yet one must not confuse the effectiveness of border control efforts with the reassertion of state power that such policies entail. The nature of border control is such that failure to achieve a given goal does not necessarily indicate the weakness of state power. Take, for example, the case of a Mexican who seeks to cross the border, is apprehended, and is returned to Mexico, but then succeeds the next day in reaching the United States. If U.S. policy is to prevent his crossing, then it has failed. At the same time, his apprehension required the exercise of power: the employment of agents, the appeal to the law, the use or threatened use of force, the coerced return to Mexico. Indeed, in regions and conditions where border control is popular, policy failure is consistent with a stronger state. Peter Andreas shows that the state can create an image of control at certain politically important segments of the border, even when the overall flow of migrants is not appreciably altered.[1] Rey Koslowski's account captures the inherent problems of escalation and spillover as states and immigrant smugglers use ever more sophisticated methods.

The increasing complexity of the border control task suggests that we must know where to look for state power. This is a central message of Gallya Lahav and Virginie

Guiraudon, who maintain that border control efforts often take place "away from the border and outside the state." Rich states mobilize private actors, local governments, and indeed other states to do their dirty work for them. This, of course, is a sign not of the weakness of rich states, but of their flexibility. The delegation of border control by richer states to poorer states is most evident in Europe. After the end of the Cold War, the rich states of western Europe effectively deputized their poorer east central European neighbors in an attempt to keep immigrants and asylum seekers from entering the territory of the European Union (EU). As in North America, this involved the use of traditional diplomacy in the service of migration control (a "web of readmission agreements," in Milada Vachudová's phrase), as well as the concentration of police power at the border (of the EU, and increasingly at the borders of plausible future members of the EU, such as Poland).

Whereas the consequence of border control policy in the United States is a shift of the resources of an existing national territorial state to its periphery, the consequence of European border control efforts is the creation of police resources at the new common external border of the EU. In North America, the irony is that economic integration has coincided with stronger measures to prevent Mexicans from entering the United States. In Europe, the irony is that the success of a far more ambitious project of regional integration has required the creation of a hard external border dividing rich EU members from their poorer neighbors. The EU has built a wall around its periphery precisely because it has succeeded in removing border controls among its members.

THE WALL AROUND "EUROPE"

"Schengen" is the name given to the common external border of the continental members of the EU, and to the absence of border controls among them. The former was a logical consequence of the latter. The intention of the French, German, Belgian, Luxembourgois, and Dutch governments who signed the original Schengen treaty in 1985 was not to create an external border, but to remove border controls among themselves. As Malcolm Anderson notes, they meant to set a good example for other European Community (EC) members by fulfilling one of the main aspirations of European integration, the free movement of people. Although they rightly anticipated that west European citizens would favor easy movement for themselves, they also understood that state borders play an enormously important psychological function in west European societies. These governments understood that west Europeans deprived of the sense of security arising from national borders would have to be "compensated" by the creation of an external frontier comprising all participating states.[2] As the Schengen zone grew to include all of the continental members of the EU, and was incorporated into the EU's institutions, the coupling of the removal of internal borders with a strengthened common external border was unquestioned by all participants.[3]

For two major reasons, allowing the unhindered movement of people within the EU has unintended consequences quite distinct from allowing the free movement of goods. First, although Schengen (like European integration in general) began as an elite project, it is one of the few EU initiatives that harmonizes with public opinion. Once in place, both internal freedom of movement and the hard external frontier became untouchable at the level of the domestic politics of participating states. Second, more than other projects of European integration, the creation of an external frontier directly requires the EU to take on state-like functions, assume state-like roles, and acquire state-like capacities. The theories of European integration held by most European elites contend that the creation of European political structures will emerge from governmental cooperation, social interaction, or economic integration. Border control is the unplanned but irresistible shortcut: it is the policy that demands that the EU behave like a territorial state.

Within Malcolm Anderson's analysis (and that of other European contributors) it is impossible to miss developments that suggest that the EU, as a state-like entity, is in the process of being born at its borders. The main point bears repeating. The EU, like a modern territorial state, now has an external border. Anyone seeking to enter a continental EU member state now confronts a common border regime, regardless of point of entry. Moreover, from the moment that the Treaty of Amsterdam entered into force in May 1999, the provision of freedom of movement within the EU and the control of its external frontier is the job of the EU. Even in areas where the EC is not formally responsible for border policy, the venue of the EU allows national governments to coordinate policies. As Vachudová notes, throughout the 1990s "more and more decisions on how to fight the influx of illegal immigrants were made at the EU level by agreements among national governments in the European Council." As a result of the common external border, national governments have harmonized their asylum policies.

Important consequences include increased police cooperation, new initiatives in information gathering, and emphasis on state secrecy. First, cooperation among national police forces was not initiated by the Schengen regime, but has been noticeably accelerated by it. The same can be said for the official European police organization, EUROPOL. Second, in order to control its new border, the EU has undertaken for the first time to collect and coordinate personal information on a massive scale. The Schengen Informational System, an index of at least ten million entries of "undesirables" and suspected criminals, is physically located in Strasbourg. But its computerized database is available to police officers and border control agents of all participating states. In other words, agents of national states are enforcing a European border with the help of European resources. (Resources that, in this case, are already more imposing than their U.S. counterparts.) Third, and perhaps most telling, the common external border is the first major EU policy whose outlines have been shrouded in secrecy. It has been difficult, even for national governments, to establish just what the Schengen system is. This is partly because the incorporation of Schengen into the EU was enormously complicated, but also partly a result of the logic of ambitious projects of state control of borders.

In his masterful treatment of the history of state immigration controls, John Torpey provides a neo-Weberian definition of the state as an entity that monopolizes the legitimate control of the movement of human beings across borders. In this sense, the EU is taking on state-like attributes. Torpey also exploits the Arendtian notion of the state as a membership organization. In this sense as well, the Schengen regime is rendering the EU more like a state. Those who are citizens of EU member states enjoy the benefits of easy travel. In a part of the world where vacation is a central pleasure of life, this appeals to societies at large as well as business elites. For the average EU citizen, freedom of movement is perhaps the most easily perceived benefit of the European project. On the other hand, Europeans who are not citizens of EU member states are no longer simply excluded from a set of nation–states: they are excluded from a unit which goes by the name of "Europe."[4] When the Schengen wall was raised in 1995, Hungarians and Slovenes who were used to easy access to the EU were suddenly required to obtain visas. Although their countries, like most other plausible future EU members, now enjoy visa-free regimes with Schengenland, elites and businesspeople from most Balkan states and most of the former Soviet Union find it extremely difficult to enter "Europe." This sense of exclusion is problematic, since these elites are expected to spread Western ideas of integration and globalization. A prominent Bulgarian intellectual speaks of "a Schengen majority, people who cannot travel freely, who have thus ceased to believe the promises of the West."[5] The expression "Schengenized," meaning excluded from Europe, is heard more and more often. However exaggerated such rhetoric might be, one should not underestimate the effect that physical exclusion has upon the identities of the excluded.

True, at the moment, some countries are neither included nor excluded from the EU. But it should not be imagined that states negotiating to join the EU are a chink in the Schengen armor, nor that their negotiators enjoy any leverage on the question of border control. Membership in the EU is so attractive that serious candidates will not hesitate to implement the elements of the European project that they are instructed to apply. EU directions on this point are unambiguous: candidates unable to implement Schengen will not be admitted.[6] Since enlargement is a difficult and contested process, and since immigration is the aspect of it that raises the greatest concern in west European publics, east central European candidates can afford no false steps. Leszek Jesien makes this point in terms of the trust that Polish negotiators (such as himself) and Polish society must earn in the eyes of their EU counterparts. To convince the EU that they "belong," Poland must (among other things) show that it understands that other states, such as Belarus and Ukraine, do not.[7]

When the EU enlarges, its hard external frontier will enlarge along with it. New member states will have been obliged to drop visa-free regimes with their eastern and southern neighbors, and will have demonstrated that they are capable of Schengen-style border enforcement. A more easterly border of Schengenland will bring the same regime to the frontiers of the former Soviet Union. Roland Freudenstein provocatively contends that the new eastern border of an enlarged EU will also correspond to a "Huntington border": a division of civilizations.[8] Freudenstein is a German liberal, and there is nothing inherently illiberal in the notion that civilizations exist and are home to incommensurate values. Perhaps the twentieth century's leading liberal thinker, Isaiah Berlin, believed that "What is clear is that values can clash—that is why civilizations are incompatible."[9] Berlin's solution was what he called pluralism: the intellectual recognition that differences in value judgments cannot always be reconciled, the political implication that attempts to implement perfect solutions are bound to fail, and the practical recommendation of humility. In our context, the concern is that the construction of the wall around the West—the overlap of economic, political, and cultural divides—transforms disagreements about ideas such as "European integration" and "globalization" into certainties about what is right and wrong.

THE SIREN SONG OF STATE POWER

In a final attempt to grasp the link between border controls and disagreements about globalization, let us follow the trespasses and transgressions of a globalized symbol. The wanderings of the image of a "siren," linked to travel, and associated with both the irresistible and the forbidden, will perhaps lead us to identify what barriers to movement have to do with perceptions of world order. In Greek myth, the lovely music of the sirens calls sailors to their doom. The image of Odysseus lashed to the mainmast as his sailors, ears plugged, row past Sirens' Island was a favorite of antiquity.[10] Medieval sculptors favored the image of the siren herself, with scaly legs spread. An updated version of this latter image is the "Starbucks Siren," the corporate logo of the Seattle-based coffee importer and globalization poster child.[11] (Neither its friends nor its foes usually notice that the Starbucks logo suggests impulses stronger than the caffeine habit.) As it happens, the "syrena" is also the coat of arms of the Polish capital of Warsaw.[12] Polish mermaids adorn the trains that bring petty traders from Ukraine or Belarus to the Polish capital, as well as the buses you might take to buy (for example) pirated music from Ukrainians or Belarusians at Warsaw's suburban bazaars. (These Warsaw sirens, as dignified as their Seattle cousins are inviting, bear swords and crowns.)

In these examples of images and commerce, our wandering sirens retain, if faintly, the association of allure or attraction. In other cases, from the realm of state power over human movement, the "siren" takes on something like the opposite meaning. For U.S. citizens, a "siren" is the noisemaker atop a police car. To an illegal immigrant near the southern border of the United States, a "sirena" is a warning of an encounter with U.S. law enforcement. Far from an invitation to approach, such sirens are a warning that the time has come to flee. In the EU, the word "siren" has taken on a meaning even strikingly more at odds with the original. The national offices of the Schengen Informational System are known in EU jargon as SIRENE (Supplément d'Information Requis à l'Entrée Nationale). This "siren" goes beyond sounding the alarm: it is the business end of a system designed to prevent "undesirable" human beings from entering EU territory. If, for example, an asylum seeker files multiple applications with different European states, this "siren" will blare. Here the "sirène" has attained a significance precisely opposite to that of the *Odyssey*'s original: far from issuing an irresistible invitation to weary travelers, it categorically rejects the undesired. As if to complete the irony, "Odysseus" is the name of an EU program that trains national officers to recognize false passports.

In a globalized world, images (such as siren, sirène, sirena, and syrena) travel light and adapt well. In the right conditions, goods (such as Mexican coffee in a mermaid cup, or pirated music enjoyed while riding home in a mermaid-emblazoned bus) will also travel, and usually be easily assimilated by their consumers. People who transport goods (importers of coffee, traders in computer disks) generally fare well, depending upon the trade regime in force. The coffee importer has a bright future in North America; the trader in illegal compact disks will be banished from Warsaw the moment Poland joins the EU. People who wish to sell their labor (the migrant caught at the California or Texas border, or off the Florida coast) or wishing to leave their home and settle anew (the double asylum applicant exposed by SIRENE) are in the most difficult position.

The United States and the EU can and do seek to decide what elements of "globalization" named in our siren stories—images, goods, traders, laborers, refugees—cross into their territory. In the effort to allow most images and most goods, but to categorize and discriminate among human beings, the United States and the EU are in effect building a wall around the West. In the North American case, we observe the assertion of police power at a national border *within* a larger zone of free trade. In the European case, we see that the zone of free trade *matches* the zone of the free movement of people—tariffs and policed borders coincide at a common external border. The price of thin, NAFTA-type integration between rich and poor states is stricter border controls between them. The price of creating an EU-style zone of free movement among rich states is the construction of a wall around that zone. While the U.S. government reasserts police power at its southern border, European governments have created common state-like attributes at a new European border. In both cases, each step forward toward integration brings with it state efforts to control the movement of human beings across borders.[13]

This reaction to projects of integration, and this contradiction within the idea of globalization, have to do with basic differences between ideas, goods, and human beings.[14] For reasons that we have set aside in this volume, but which in broad outline should be fairly obvious, human beings are not portable in the way that ideas and goods are. People within rich societies react to the influx of human beings according to impulses that are not generally aroused by adaptable ideas or consumable goods. The same holds for poorer people who wish to cross into richer countries. Their adaptations to new languages and new situations, however able on a human scale, are incomparably slower than the transmission of images or the consumption of goods.

Most fundamentally, immigrants do not regard *themselves* as images or as goods. They can have ambitious projects that can be frustrated, can embark upon ambivalent odysseys that end in failure. In this sense, the very contradiction within the idea of a "siren" describes the ambiguous experience of people confronting increasing state power as they seek to enter rich parts of the world. After all, people can be at once repelled and attracted, disdainful and desirous. (Odysseus himself wished to respond to the sirens' call, but had himself physically constrained from doing as he wished.) People can, for example, believe that their dignity is injured by the treatment that they receive as they attempt to cross borders: in being told what they are not, they may come to new ideas about what they are. At the same time, people can contemplate the power of states that prevent them from doing as they wish: and then regard this as a model if they return home. In both of these ways, as attraction and as repulsion, "globalization" at the center breeds nationalization at the periphery.

This suggests that the sense of "globalization" is dependent upon perspective and experience. Whether globalization is meaningful to people in the twenty-first century will depend less upon whether their ideas or their exports can cross borders, and more upon whether they themselves can cross borders. In general, people who can physically move will find the idea comprehensible, and those who cannot will not. Whether globalization is an accurate description of the international political order will depend upon whether it accounts for one of this book's main conclusions: that attempts to control the movement of people across borders continue to consolidate states as territorial and as membership organizations. On the analysis of this book, globalization along rich–poor divides is less the swan song of state power than its siren song—to immigrants who wish to cross into "El Norte" or "Schengenland," to rich societies longing for security, and to state agents capable of providing its semblance.

NOTES

1. See Peter Andreas, *Border Games: Policing the U.S.–Mexico Divide* (Ithaca, N.Y.: Cornell University Press), 2000.

2. I am describing here the anticipation of problems, and do not mean to suggest that the anticipated feeling of insecurity was not justified. The Schengen system does indeed simplify matters for drug dealers and organized criminals inside the zone.

3. As of this writing, Great Britain and Ireland (which themselves comprise a zone of free movement) have opted out of the Schengen regime. Norway, which is not a member of the

EU, is a member of the Schengen regime.

4. This is true of Turks and North Africans as well, although we have not treated these cases in this volume.

. 5. Ivan Krastev, as quoted in "Wojny balkanskie 1991–1999," *Unia-Polska*, August 2-16, 1999, 20–21. This point has been made by at least one participant in every relevant east European conference I have attended since 1995.

6. See Article 8, "Protocol Integrating the Schengen *acquis* into the Framework of the European Union," Treaty of Amsterdam, Conference of the Representatives of the Governments of the Member States, September 23, 1997. See also Anthony Georgioff, "EU: Leaders Agree to Fight Illegal Immigration, Organized Crime," Radio Free Europe/Radio Liberty (RFE/RL) Report, October 18, 1999.

7. Poland has taken some steps to preserve its links with its eastern neighbors. The EU would no doubt prefer that Poland immediately rescind its visa-free regime with Ukraine, but the Polish position is that it will be maintained until Poland actually joins the EU. Timothy Snyder, *The Reconstruction of Nations* (New Haven: Yale University Press, forthcoming), chapter 12.

8. The reference is to Samuel Huntington, *The Clash of Civilizations and the Remaking of World Order* (New York: Simon and Schuster, 1996).

9. "The Pursuit of the Ideal," in *The Crooked Timber of Humanity*, Isaiah Berlin, ed. (Princeton, N.J.: Princeton University Press, 1990), 12.

10. See, for example, "Ulysse passant près de l'ile des Sirènes," Plaque Campana, Second Century C.E., Département des Antiquités Grecques et Romaines, Musée du Louvre, Paris.

11. Sirens have also featured in advertisements for McDonald's and IBM.

12. Warsaw was (according to myth) founded at the invitation of a "syrena." The Czechs also have quasi-urban mermaids: see for example "O vodní panne z Tuní," in Václav Cibula and Cyril Bouda, *Prazské povesti* (Prague: Orbis, 1970), 459–461.

13. There are other instances of enduring state structures shifting resources to their peripheries in the inherently ambiguous search for security. The "barbarian at the border," not the "barbarian at the gate," is the key figure in the long decline of the Western Roman Empire. See Brent D. Shaw, "War and Violence," and Patrick T. Geary, "Barbarians and Ethnicity," in G. W. Bowersock, Peter Brown, and Oleg Grabar, eds., *Late Antiquity* (Cambridge, Mass.: Harvard University Press, 1999), 130–169 and 107–129.

14. Some might find this a suitable place for a Foucaultian analysis. It would have to account for important differences between border controls and incarceration (as described in *Surveiller et punir*): that in the case of illegal immigration, bodies commit crimes primarily by virtue of where they are rather than what they have done; that in controlling borders states aim not to incorporate but to separate human beings; that people are usually simply expelled rather than punished for illegally crossing a border; that states aim not to render border violations visible but to render them invisible. Perhaps the deeper difference is that the state is attempting to affect the "souls" of its members by moving the bodies of the aliens, rather than affecting the "soul" of the prisoner by enclosing and observing his body.

Index

About the Contributors

María-Elena Alcaraz, a career member of the Mexican Foreign Service, represents the secretariat of external affairs at the Office of Migration Affairs at the Embassy of Mexico in Washington, D.C. She studied international relations at the National Autonomous University of Mexico, and political science at the University of Houston. She was the first Mexican director of the Secretariat of the North American Commission for Labor Cooperation. At the Secretariat of External Affairs she has been an advisor on North American affairs to the undersecretary for bilateral affairs, and has worked in Mexico's consulates in Vancouver, Canada, and Houston, Texas.

Malcolm Anderson (M.A., D. Phil, D. Litt, University of Oxford) was formerly professor of politics and director of the International Social Sciences Institute of the University of Edinburgh. His books include *The Irish Border: History, Politics, and Culture* (ed., with E. Bort, Liverpool University Press, 1999); *Frontiers: Territory and State Formation in the Contemporary World* (Polity Press, 1996); *Policing the European Union* (with others, Clarendon Press, 1995); *Policing across National Boundaries* (edited with Monica de Boer, Pinter, 1994); *Policing the World: Interpol and the Politics of International Police Cooperation* (Oxford University Press, 1989); *Frontier Regions in Western Europe* (ed., Frank Cass, 1983). Forthcoming publications include *States and Nationalism* (Routledge, 2000), and *The Frontiers of the European Union* (Macmillan, 2000).

Peter Andreas (B.A., Swarthmore College; Ph.D., Cornell University) is assistant professor of political science at Reed College. He has recently held fellowships from the Harvard Academy for International and Area Studies, the SSRC–MacArthur Foundation Program on Peace and Security, and the Foreign Policy Studies Program at the Brookings Institution. Recent publications include *Border Games: Policing the*

239

U.S.–Mexico Divide (Cornell University Press), *Drug War Politics: The Price of Denial* (coauthor, University of California Press), and *The Illicit Global Economy and State Power* (coeditor, Rowman & Littlefield).

Roland Freudenstein (M.A., University of Bonn; special student at the University of Southern California) is the director of the Warsaw Office of the Konrad Adenauer Foundation, where he works on civic and political development assistance. He has been a research fellow at the German Society for Foreign Affairs (Bonn), and a member of the foreign policy planning staff of the European Commission in Brussels (focusing on central Europe). He has published numerous articles on central Europe, German–Polish relations, and European integration.

Virginie Guiraudon is chargée de recherche at the National Center for Scientific Research (CNRS) in France. She holds a Ph.D. in government from Harvard University (1997) where she focused on comparative immigrant policies in Europe. Her publications include "Citizenship Rights for Non-Citizens: France, Germany, the Netherlands" in Christian Joppke, ed., *Challenge to the Nation-State* (Oxford: Oxford University Press, 1998); "Third Country Nationals and European Law: Obstacles to Rights Expansion" in *Journal of Ethnic and Migration Studies* (November 1998); "European Integration and Migration Policy: Vertical Policy-making as Venue Shopping" in *Journal of Common Market Studies* (June 2000); and *Les politiques d'immigration en Europe* (Paris: L'Harmattan, 2000). As a Jean Monnet Fellow at the European University Institute in 1997–1998 and a visiting fellow at Princeton the following year, she initiated a project on the denationalization of migration control policy in Europe and North America.

Leszek Jesien (M.A., Ph.D., Warsaw University) is an advisor to both the prime minister of Poland and the chief negotiator of Poland's accession to the European Union. He previously served as an expert within the Polish government's Office of the Committee for European Integration. He has been a senior associate member of St. Antony's College, Oxford, a Research Fellow at the College of Europe–Natolin, and the west European editor for the Polish daily *Gazeta Wyborcza*. His recent publications include *Europe in the Mirror of Euroscepticism: The British Conservative Party and European Integration* (Nowy Sacz, 1999); *After Amsterdam, Before Enlargement: A Political Panorama of the European Union* (Warsaw, 1998); and *Roads to Europe* (coauthor, Warsaw, 1998); all in Polish.

Rey Koslowski (Ph.D., University of Pennsylvania), an assistant professor of political science at Rutgers University–Newark, contributed his chapter while a visiting fellow of the Center of International Studies at Princeton University (1999–2000). He was a research associate of the Center for German and European Studies at Georgetown University's School of Foreign Service (1996–1997). He is the author of *Migrants and Citizens: Demographic Change in the European States System* (Cornell

University Press, 2000) and coeditor (with David Kyle) of *Global Human Smuggling in Comparative Perspective* (Johns Hopkins University Press, forthcoming).

Gallya Lahav is assistant professor of political science at the State University of New York at Stony Brook. She holds graduate degrees from the London School of Economics and the Graduate Center, City University of New York, and has been the recipient of the Mellon/SSRC Post-Doctoral Fellowship Award in International Migration. She was formerly on the faculties of Wesleyan University and Wellesley College, and a research affiliate at the Center for European Studies at Harvard University. Lahav has served as a consultant to the Population Division of the United Nations. Her articles have appeared in *Comparative Political Studies,* the *Journal of Common Market Studies, Global Governance,* and the *Journal of Ethnic and Migration Studies.* She is currently completing a manuscript on "The Politics of Immigration and the Construction of the European Union."

Christopher Mitchell (B.A., Ph.D., Harvard University) is professor of politics and director of the Center for Latin American and Caribbean Studies at New York University. His current research focuses on politics in Caribbean nations and on Latin American migration to the United States. His publications include *Changing Perspectives in Latin American Studies* (ed., Stanford University Press, 1988), *Western Hemisphere Immigration and United States Foreign Policy* (ed. and contributor, Penn State Press, 1992), and "The Future of Migration as an Issue in Inter-American Relations." in Jorge I. Domínguez, ed., *The Future of Inter-American Relations* (New York: Routledge, 2000).

Gustavo Mohar is currently minister for political and congressional affairs at the Embassy of Mexico in Washington, D.C. He studied law at the Universidad Iberoamericana and public finance at the National Autonomous University of Mexico. At the Ministry of Finance he was involved in international economic affairs. He has served as head of European operations for Petróleos Mexicanos, and as minister for migration affairs as representative of the Ministry of the Interior at the Mexican Embassy in Washington. He has published articles on economic integration in Latin America and on migration between Mexico and the United States.

Joseph Nevins (Ph.D., University of California–Los Angeles), a geographer, is a Rockefeller Foundation Residential "Community in Contention" postdoctoral fellow at the University of California, Berkeley (2000–2001). He is researching the process of reconstruction and reconciliation in East Timor, and finishing a book on the U.S. Immigration and Naturalization Service's Operation Gatekeeper.

Timothy Snyder (B.A., Brown University; D. Phil., University of Oxford), a historian, is presently an academy scholar at Harvard University, and will shortly take up an assistant professorship at the University of Virginia. Among his publications are *Nationalism, Marxism, and Modern Central Europe: A Biography of Kazimierz Kelles-Krauz (1872–1905)* (Harvard University Press, 1997); and *The Reconstruction of Nations: Poles and Their Eastern Neighbors, 1569–1999* (Yale University Press, 2001).

David Spener (Ph.D., University of Texas–Austin) is assistant professor of sociology at Trinity University in San Antonio, Texas. He is a coauthor (with Frank D. Bean and others) of *Illegal Mexican Migration and the United States/Mexico Border: The Effects of Operation Hold-the-Line on El Paso/Juárez* (1994, United States Commission on Immigration Reform), and coeditor (with Kathleen Staudt) of *The U.S.–Mexico Border: Transcending Divisions, Contesting Identities* (1998, Lynne Rienner Publishers). He is currently conducting research on the smuggling of Mexican migrants into Texas.

John Torpey (Ph.D., University of California, Berkeley) currently teaches in the departments of sociology and history and the Institute for European Studies at the University of British Columbia in Vancouver. He is the author of *The Invention of the Passport: Surveillance, Citizenship, and the State* (Cambridge University Press, 1999), and coeditor (with Jane Caplan) of *Documenting Individual Identity: The Development of State Practices in the Modern World* (Princeton University Press, forthcoming).

Milada Anna Vachudová (B.A., Stanford University; M. Phil., D. Phil., University of Oxford), a political scientist, is a Jean Monnet Fellow at the European University Institute in Florence, Italy. She has taught at the Central European University and at Charles University in Prague, and at Columbia University. She has also been a fellow at the Center for European Studies at Harvard University, the European Union Center of New York City, and the Center of International Studies at Princeton University. Presently, she is completing "Revolution, Democracy and Integration, East Central Europe Since 1989" for Oxford University Press, and has published on questions of comparative East European politics, ethnic conflict, regional cooperation, and European security.